ROMAN
RULERS
AND
REBELS

ROMAN RULERS

AND

REBELS

P. GORDON B. STILLMAN

Riverdale Country School
New York

Illustrated by
JOHN B. SEVERANCE

Independent School Press

Wellesley Hills   Massachusetts

8182

789

PRINTED IN THE UNITED STATES OF AMERICA.

0-88334-048-8

CONTENTS

PREFACE

I. HANNIBAL AND THE CRISIS OF SURVIVAL 3
   1. Rivalry and development of Carthage and Rome 3
   2. First Punic War and its aftermath 7
   3. Across the Alps! 10
   4. Early battles of the Second Punic War 13
   5. Cannae 15
   6. The war turns against Hannibal and ends at Zama 17
   7. Disappointments of Hannibal's later years 22
   8. Estimate of Hannibal and his career 24

II. THE GRACCHI—AN ATTEMPT AT RADICAL
    REFORM 29
   1. Tiberius Gracchus 29
   2. The problems of expansion 30
   3. Problems at home—economic, social, and political 33
   4. The new tribune's plan for land redistribution 36
   5. A constitutional crisis—and how it was temporarily
      resolved 40
   6. The "problem" of Tiberius 42
   7. Caius Gracchus: a new reform program 44
   8. The problem of colonies and the downfall of Caius 47
   9. Critical appraisal of the Gracchi 50
   10. Aftermath: an unhappy century 53

III. JULIUS CAESAR—FROM REPUBLIC TO
     DICTATORSHIP 59
   1. Rome flourishes under Caesar's rule 59
   2. Caesar's early career 61
   3. The problem of government 64
   4. Developing ambitions: The First Triumvirate 68
   5. "All Gaul is divided into three parts . ." 71
   6. Tension mounts in Rome 73
   7. Caesar vs Pompey 75
   8. Civil war 77
   9. Political revolution and the reaction to it 81
   10. Character of Julius Caesar 85

IV. AUGUSTUS CAESAR—FROM DICTATORSHIP
    TO EMPIRE 91
   1. The succession? 91
   2. Octavius and Cicero 92
   3. The Second Triumvirate 95
   4. Rivalry of Octavius and Antony and the outcome of it 98

V

    5. Character and policies of Octavius 101
    6. The Principate: Augustus Caesar 107
    7. Accomplishments of the Principate 110
    8. A look to the future 115

V. DIOCLETIAN REGENERATES THE ROMAN
    EMPIRE 123
    1. The Empire to 284 A.D.: decline in power and wealth 123
    2. Diocletian gains the throne 128
    3. Reorganization of the political and economic systems 129
    4. Success and failure of Diocletian's reforms 133
    5. Diocletian abdicates and confusion ensues 138
    6. Emergence of Constantine, as sole emperor 141

VI. CONSTANTINE LEADS THE EMPIRE INTO A
    NEW ERA 147
    1. Continuation of Diocletian's policy 148
    2. Errors of Constantine's later years 151
    3. The beginnings of Christianity; its rivals 153
    4. Further history of Christianity; persecution, then
       toleration 158
    5. Constantine accepts and favors Christianity and
       seeks cooperation of Church and State 161
    6. Church unity is maintained in the face of challenges 165
    7. Constantinople 168
    8. The accomplishment of Diocletian and Constantine
       seen in perspective 171
    9. The Roman Empire moves into the Middle Ages 176

    BIBLIOGRAPHY AND NOTES 179

    EXERCISES 192

    INDEX 204

PORTRAITS

Hannibal 1
Scipio Africanus 19
Tiberius and Caius Gracchus 27
Julius Caesar 57
Cicero 65
Augustus 89
Virgil 113
Diocletian 121
Constantine 145

MAPS

Carthage against Rome 2
Italy—Heart of the Republic 58
The Roman Empire 122

PREFACE

During the first five hundred years of her existence, Rome grew from a rural hamlet into a thriving city-state. Then, for more than five hundred years, she dominated the world, and the history of western civilization centers in Rome. For a thousand years after that, her offspring, Constantinople, ruled and defended the Near East, and Rome's image survived in the minds of European men. Clearly we should know something about Rome.

The struggles of past epochs come most alive for many readers when they are recounted in personal terms. Biography provides the local setting and the human detail that make the story concrete and comprehensible. The individual man existed. We can understand his plans, ambitious or unselfish, and sympathize with his agonies of uncertainty or frustration. He had friends to mobilize, enemies to defeat, obstacles to overcome, compromises to accept, hopes to defer but to continue to strive for. We can participate vicariously in his strivings, as though we ourselves faced the problems and had the chance and the obligation to make the decisions.

Today's world sometimes seems too big for the people who occupy it. History can only be made in the late 20th century, it seems, by the confrontation of titanic abstract forces—revolution against racism, youth culture against establishment, mammoth corporation against government, market economy against welfare state. In this kind of environment the individual often feels helpless and tends to withdraw from the fray rather than involve himself in it.

Even such a powerful leader as President Kennedy complained that, when he and his executive advisers had made a decision concerning the nation, his real problem was to get the government to go along with it. He could not command, in other words; he had to struggle to induce support among Congress, bureaucracy, and ultimately press, public, and pressure groups, so that his decision could be put into operation. Occasionally, Roger Hilsman reports in *To Move A Nation*, Kennedy boasted of his own individual influence, as when he said, "Today I actually made a little policy."

History in ancient times, apparently, did not produce such deep ideological conflicts, although nation competed against nation and class against class for survival and power. Leadership, now so often a matter of persuasion, involving concessions and compromises, seems then to have been more personal, direct, decisive, and absolute. Emperors were not frustrated by their lack of authority.

These chapters, the outgrowth of experience in the classroom, are not intended to incorporate every detail of the story of Rome's development. Rather they introduce us to the leaders who shaped political, economic, and social trends and were responsible for the turning points of Roman history. Traditionally, the "hero" theory states that history is produced by the words and deeds of outstanding individuals who dominate, indeed create, their worlds. Nowadays, however, we realize the great man is molded by the conditions of his time and locale. He rises in response to the needs and opportunities of his particular society and environment. He develops abilities and characteristics which set him apart from his contemporaries but are not quite unique enough to consign him to exile. He makes plans—some carefully conceived, others hastily contrived. He attracts support or arouses opposition.

The "heroes" of history are men distinguished for their skills of ability, understanding, and imaginative insight and for their personal qualities of courage, perseverance, and leadership. But the great man is not necessarily a success. Of the seven protagonists of this book, one killed himself and three met violent deaths, to say nothing of a host of their chief supporters or opponents whose lives ended in murder or suicide. Even among those whose deaths were natural, one was disappointed in his dynastic hopes, another failed to accomplish several important aspects of his program, and a third had children who undid much that he had done.

Failures may have diminished the achievements of the great men of Rome but they did not annihilate their importance. Each "hero" was aware of the pressing problems of his era. In attempting to solve these problems, each proposed original ideas and made critical decisions. Each, then, was the creator of a part of the story of Rome.

The success or failure of the policies of these great men often hung in the balance for years, affected both by chance and circumstance and by underlying currents of opinion and personal prejudices. The eventual outcome was the progress of human history. As we look back on it, how inexorable and inevitable it seems. But how problematical and unpredictable—and how crucial—it was to those who lived through it.

I would like to acknowledge my special debt, in the preparation of this volume, to Mr. John B. Severance for the novelty and grace of his illustrations; to the Choate School teachers of Ancient History for their willingness to experiment with this material; and to Mrs. Betty Curtis for her painstaking labor and invaluable help in putting the entire text into presentable form.

GORDON STILLMAN

Wilmington, North Carolina
December, 1971

ROMAN
RULERS
AND
REBELS

Chapter I

HANNIBAL

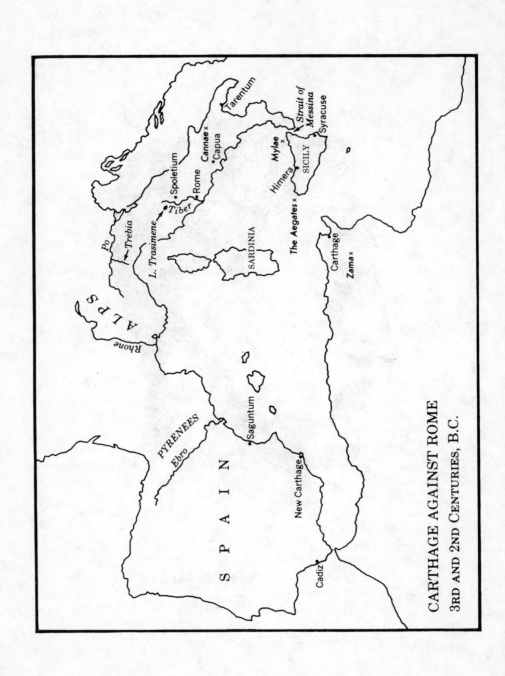

CARTHAGE AGAINST ROME
3RD AND 2ND CENTURIES, B.C.

HANNIBAL AND THE CRISIS OF SURVIVAL

Go climb the rugged Alps, ambitious fool,
To please the boys, and be a theme at school.

It was about Hannibal, the Carthaginian general, that the Roman satirical poet Juvenal wrote these lines.[1] In them he refers to the most romantic and remarkable of Hannibal's exploits—leading an army across the towering Alps. Had Hannibal done nothing else but cross the Alps, however, he would not now be a theme at school. The story of Hannibal is the story of one of the great crises, the turning points, in world history.

1. Rivalry and development of Carthage and Rome

Hannibal was born in 247 B.C. on the island of Sicily, the stepping stone between Italy and North Africa, where the central Mediterranean reaches its narrowest point. He was born in the midst of a war which had been going on since 264 B.C., known in the history books as the First Punic War. The antagonists in this war, which the Greek historian Polybius called the longest, most continuous, and most severely contested war in ancient times, were Rome, the chief city in Italy, and Carthage, the leading seaport of the Mediterranean, situated on what is now the Gulf of Tunis. Hannibal's father was Hamilcar Barca, who had recently been appointed to the supreme command of the Carthaginian forces in Sicily. Hamilcar was engaged in the task of organizing and training a field army—disciplined, efficient, responsive to the will of its commander, and devoted to his cause. With this army Hamilcar was to be able for six years to repulse all Roman attacks and to use guerrilla tactics to be a constant thorn in the side of Rome until the end of the war.

The reasons for the First Punic War were almost exclusively economic. The aim of each side was the control of Sicily, and particularly its main city, Syracuse. The importance of Sicily was its location, commanding the narrow waters that connected the eastern and western halves of the Mediterranean. The nation which dominated Sicily would automatically be able to dominate the trade of

3

the Mediterranean. It would be able to impose taxes on the ships of other nations or even to restrict their voyages to certain specified ports. The goal of the war, then, was the commercial supremacy of the Mediterranean. Should it be Rome or Carthage which would regulate the trade for the luxuries of the eastern world?

The rivalry of Rome and Carthage was a comparatively recent development. For more than two centuries, Sicily's trade and wealth and political importance had centered in Syracuse. Syracuse had been originally a Greek colony. Indeed, in 480 B.C., when the Greeks were defeating the Persian fleet at Salamis, the Syracusan Greeks at Himera defeated the Carthaginians who fought as subjects of the Great King. And the Greeks had spread their colonies northward to Cumae and Tarentum, city-states in "Great Greece", the mainland of Italy itself. But in the 4th century Alexander the Great, and with him the whole Hellenistic world, had turned his back on the West as poor and crude and uncivilized and had marched to establish his empire to the East.

Taking advantage of their isolation from the main stream of history, Rome and Carthage had both been growing in wealth and importance, as Syracuse found it increasingly difficult to summon the manpower and the political stability she needed to maintain her preeminence. Rome conquered her Etruscan and Gallic neighbors to the north, subdued the Samnites and other tribes in central Italy, and advanced southward against the Greek colonies. Meanwhile, Carthage resisted the invasion of the Syracusan dictator Agathocles and wrested more and more strongholds on Sicily itself from a weakened Syracuse. In their concurrent struggles against the Greek influence, Rome and Carthage had been at least loosely allied. When Tarentum in desperation appealed for aid to King Pyrrhus of Epirus, a Carthaginian fleet hung off the Italian coast, ready to give aid to the Roman forces. The aid was not needed. Rome was strong enough to defeat Pyrrhus and his elephants, and to annex Tarentum. The international situation changed almost overnight. Rome had extended her power to the very tip of Italy. Carthage had gained control of most of Sicily. These two rising and vigorous powers faced each other across the narrow Straits of Messina. No matter what their protestations of friendship in the past had been, a conflict between the two soon became inevitable.

Of the two cities Carthage was the older, the larger, and the richer. Founded originally as a trading station by the Phoenicians, Carthage had so prospered as a seaport as to rival even Tyre. The first interests of the Carthaginians were always the sea and the opportunities it presented as a cheap and rapid highway of commerce. Carthage established her own trading stations around the shores of the Mediterranean and on its islands. At such stations Carthage overawed the natives with armed garrisons and traded with them on her own terms. She did not colonize; she exploited. Carthaginian ships passed through the Pillars of Hercules and were based at Cadiz, to carry on trade up the coast of Europe to Brittany and England and down the western coast of Africa. When Syracuse declined and Tyre fell to Alexander's siege, Carthage gained the commercial monopoly of the Mediterranean and became the first sea-power of the day—a supremacy she had no desire to share. Although trade was the chief source of Carthaginian wealth, it alone could not have supported the city's population of nearly a million. An abundant source of food was vital, and so Carthage won control over the fertile plains which stretched eastward and westward along the North African coast, subjugating the populations and putting their fields under intensive cultivation.

Gradually, therefore, Carthage had become the ruler of an empire. She was the center of a veritable spider's web. Enmeshed in it like flies were her conquered dependencies, which supplied her with raw materials, with manpower for her armies, with ready capital in the form of tribute money. The empire was a one-way proposition. Carthage, as the trading center, was the sole beneficiary. Between the capital city and her dependencies there was no love, no unifying feeling of joint achievement and mutual benefit. Carthage considered herself the ruler of inferior races and allowed them no political freedom; in turn, the subject peoples abhorred their oppressed condition. Their loyalty was never spontaneous but was forced by the weight of Carthaginian arms and by restrictive trade arrangements. Carthage used her empire to multiply her own wealth; her subject races, consequently, were always ready to revolt.

As the empire existed solely for the benefit of Carthage, so Carthage might be said to exist for the benefit of one segment of her population—the rich. The great Carthaginian merchants—businessmen, we must admit, with expanding vision and enterprising initiative—grew enormously wealthy. For prestige and for security they usually put their profits into land. They bought up vast estates and farmed them with slave labor, sometimes as many as 20,000 slaves working for one landlord. The richest merchants were thus the greatest landlords. Wealth accumulated in the hands of a small, select group.

Originally the Carthaginian constitution had contained some element of democracy. A Popular Assembly could cast the deciding vote in cases of disagreement between the executive authority—two suffetes chosen to serve for one year—and the normal legislative body, the Senate. But the real power had long since

passed to a permanent council, known as the Hundred, which had
the authority to review all the actions of the government. Since
there was no appeal from its decisions and its punishments were
usually severe, it is easy to see that Carthaginian suffetes, senators,
and generals hesitated to do anything of which the Hundred might
disapprove. This government by a few is known as oligarchy. In
Carthage it was based on wealth. A strict caste system was enforced
so that it was difficult to become a member of the rich ruling class.
This class looked at problems from the standpoint of its own interest
rather than of the welfare of the city or the empire. It invariably
resisted innovations, since they might weaken the authority of the
Hundred. The habits of thought of the ruling class were rigidly
fixed. Within their own group the oligarchy were selfish, jealous,
and narrow-minded. The innovator, the reformer, the champion of
any new idea, would inevitably be suspect. The Carthaginian state
would not take easily to change.

Rome, on the other hand, was a state that had been constantly changing since its foundation as a village at a convenient
ford of the Tiber River. Located inland, Rome had looked for its
wealth not to the sea but to the land around it. The Romans, to
begin with, were a race of independent farmers, working their own
small holdings of land, coming into the city on occasion to vote on
the political questions of the day, and serving when needed in the
citizen' army. These Roman farmers were strong enough to expel
Tarquin, their Etruscan king, in 509 B.C. Then they won the leadership of the Latin League and gradually conquered all of Italy
from the Po River to the Straits of Messina.

Commerce had developed of course, because Rome's position at the ford was favorable for trade, but the merchant interest
had grown up alongside the farming interest. No one class had
gained a dangerous domination over the state. The two consuls,
who shared the executive and military authority, were elected annually. The chief governing body, the Senate, was to be sure composed largely of the members of old and rich families, known as
the patricians. But this senatorial class was not a closed caste. Common people, known as plebeians, could marry into the aristocracy.
The holding of certain offices—notably the consulate (one consul
was legally required to be a plebeian)—automatically raised a Roman to senatorial rank.

Nor were the plebeians deprived of a voice in the governing of their city. They made their views known in their periodic
meetings, voting by tribes or by centuries (a division in the army).
Although this system had never proved satisfactory in giving the
plebeians their legitimate share in Roman government, they held
effective checks over senatorial decrees. First they had used the

weapon of the strike, refusing to serve in the army and threatening to form a new city of their own. Later they were granted the privilege of electing tribunes, officials devoted to the interests of the plebeians and authorized to veto any decision of the Senate. It is not to be supposed that the Roman state functioned always smoothly or that there were no real differences between patricians and plebeians. But, in general, farmer, trader, craftsman, banker had found that they did best when they co-operated with one another. The different classes worked out a practical way of living together harmoniously. In Rome, not the authoritarian decree of a selfish coterie, but the will of men associated in a political unit, ruled the state.

It was a state in which every Roman took pride. Patriotism, obedience to the laws, and the sense of duty to the state were of a high order. To be a citizen of Rome brought one both distinction and obligation. Polybius said that the Roman people thought nothing was impossible once they had determined upon it. In this spirit, the Romans spread their authority over Italy, as though such an advance had been willed by the gods. And this domination the Romans made a blessing not only for themselves but for Italy. Most of the tribes and the cities Rome conquered were confirmed in their local self-government. They were allied to Rome, rather than subjected to it. Trade among them was made freer and safer. The Romans constructed straight and durable highways to serve as its arteries. A standard coinage, a universal language, were introduced. Rome took over the protection of her allies, denying them only the right to make treaties without Roman authorization. From the allies, Rome demanded army service when needed and certain moderate taxes. To the more distinguished men in the allied cities she opened the privilege of Roman citizenship, with its freedom from taxation and its grant of the security of Roman law. By tolerance and wise policy, Rome thus made her power that of a confederacy rather than of an empire.

2. First Punic War and its aftermath

When Rome took over the Greek colonies in southern Italy, she was taking over prosperous commercial centers. It no longer seemed so reasonable that Roman ships should be prohibited from trading in most of the Mediterranean ports or prevented by Carthaginian power from sailing freely around the toe of Italy. For the power that had extended itself throughout Italy, Sicily seemed to be the logical next step. War with Carthage came when Rome decided to give aid to a band of brigands who had taken over the city of Messina in defiance of both Carthage and Syracuse.

It was Carthage, supreme on the sea, against Rome, irresistible on land. In Sicily the legions of Roman citizens proved superior to the conglomerate masses of native troops hired by the Carthaginians for the occasion and commanded by unenterprising generals fearful of the wrath of the Hundred. But the reasonable and determined Romans realized that to hold Sicily, to beat off the Carthaginian raids on the Italian coast, above all to gain the commercial privileges their expansion demanded, they must be able to face the Carthaginians in naval warfare. They set to work building warships, copying a Carthaginian quinquireme which had been shipwrecked. They trained their oarsmen on land. They gave the command to one of the consuls, although he knew nothing of naval warfare. The miracle of the First Punic War is that the Roman effort to take to the sea was crowned with success.

The first naval test was the battle of Mylae, 260 B.C. Here the Carthaginians, who were accustomed to outmaneuvering and ramming enemy vessels, were astonished by the new tactics of their clumsy opponents. On their ships the Romans had mounted on swivels hinged grappling hooks. When a Roman ship came close to a Carthaginian, the hook was dropped and the ships remained locked together. The fight then became hand to hand, as on land, and the Romans, who had many more soldiers on board each of their ships, were overwhelmingly victorious. The victory was repeated in 256 B.C. at Ecnomus.

A Roman army then landed in Africa but in the ensuing battle was surrounded and destroyed. Its captured commander, the consul Regulus, persuaded the Carthaginians to delay executing him so that he could return to Rome to negotiate a peace. Instead, he exhorted the Senate to renew their courage and their military efforts. Then, as he had promised his captors, he sailed back to Carthage to face certain death. Regulus exhibited the fortitude and selfless loyalty that epitomize the character of ancient Rome at its best. The task of overcoming such a foe might prove too difficult for the Carthaginians.

For a while, fate was unfriendly to the Romans. Two new fleets were almost entirely destroyed by storms, and the assumption by Hamilcar Barca of the Carthaginian command in Sicily gave Rome an enemy she could not defeat. Facing bankruptcy and failure, the Roman people by voluntary contributions built one last fleet. At the battle of the Aegates in 241 B.C., this fleet utterly defeated the Carthaginian. Hamilcar Barca was cut off in Sicily, and Carthage sued for peace. Sicily and a few small islands were ceded to Rome, and a war indemnity of about $3,000,000 was to be paid. But the Carthaginian power was far from obliterated, and the undefeated Hamilcar had visions of revenge.

About the childhood of Hamilcar's most famous son the historian knows virtually nothing. One vivid scene is preserved to us. In 237 Hamilcar was preparing to depart for Spain as commander of the Carthaginian forces there. The traditional religious ceremonies were held, and Hamilcar killed the sacrificial animal. Then he called Hannibal to his side and learned that the boy was anxious to go with him to Spain. Hamilcar placed Hannibal's hand upon the altar and made him swear an oath—never to be a friend of the Romans. This vow Hannibal was to make the keystone of his life's work. It was not a crude swearing of blood-vengeance. It was an act of devotion to a cause greater than personalities. For Hamilcar saw, and Hannibal was to see after him, that unless the Roman power was halted, Carthage was ultimately doomed.

Hamilcar did not go to Spain as an exile, although many of the Hundred no doubt feared his personal influence over his troops. Rather, with the support of a group of capitalists, he went to Spain with the firm policy of creating there a new center of power—both financial and military—from which he could one day be again strong enough to challenge the might of Rome.

Why Spain? To us modern observers the selection of Spain as a base of operations would seem strange, but there were several good reasons for Hamilcar's choice. The Carthaginian stations in Spain were among the oldest and most secure in the empire. The Spanish tribesmen had proved their courage and ability as infantrymen in the mercenary army, as the occupants of the nearby Balaeric Islands had earned their status as light-armed troops with their famous slingshots. Spain was far from Rome and in the direction opposite to that in which the Greek influence was urging the Romans to look. Carthaginian activity in Spain might go unobserved, or at least unopposed. No less important, Spain was far from Carthage, and Hamilcar might complete his plans there free from the curious, shortsighted, and avaricious interference of the rich oligarchs at home.

More compelling than all these considerations were the riches of Spain. At this period in history, Spain was Eldorado, the distant golden land whose wealth was inexhaustible. Not only was Spain rich in mineral resources, especially silver, but she exported grain, olive oil, wine, honey, and dyestuffs. Spain was the ideal field for the Carthaginian merchant. The capitalists behind Hamilcar, headed by Hasdrubal who became his son-in-law, made their fortunes from his enterprise. Hamilcar paid his soldiers, bought the alliance of native chieftains, and kept his war chest always full with the proceeds of Spanish produce. Spain provided such a large share of the mercantile wealth of Carthage that she was indispensable to the mother country. Consequently, the Hundred, albeit unwilling, found it advisable to let Hamilcar act as he chose. He became virtually a king, ruling Spain as his private province.

It is important to remember a fact which was always present in Hamilcar's mind. There was an overland route from Spain to Italy. From Spain a Carthaginian army could march to Rome without the assistance of the Carthaginian fleet. The initiative for future action had passed from the Hundred at Carthage to the dictator in Spain.

Hamilcar was drowned while campaigning against rebellious natives in 229 B.C. As Hannibal was still a youth, the governing power passed, apparently without complaint from Carthage, to Hasdrubal. With an eye to profits, Hasdrubal continued Hamilcar's policy of pacifying the various Spanish tribes and enlisting their support. At last, Rome showed some interest in affairs in Spain. She was urged on probably by the inhabitants of Massilia (now Marseilles) who feared for their monopoly of the tin trade from Britain. Hasdrubal made a pact with Rome which established the Ebro River as the boundary, south of which the Carthaginian influence was acknowledged to be paramount. Then, in 221, Hasdrubal was assassinated.

3. Across the Alps!

Hannibal was now twenty-six. From his first arrival in Spain he had captured the attention and admiration of the whole army. According to Livy, the earliest of Rome's notable historians, the soldiers saw in him his father's vigor and determination. Hannibal shared in all the hardships of their life and learned the arts of war and of command by experience. He was fearless and self-possessed in the midst of danger. No physical exertion, no loss of sleep, no extreme of climate, seemed to affect his mind or body. No leader was more courageous or resolute; so there was none "in whom the men placed more confidence or under whom they showed more daring."[2] He was the obvious successor to Hasdrubal as supreme commander. The soldiers supported him, and what authority at Carthage dared challenge Hannibal with his army at his back?

Hannibal had seized the initiative, and his actions in the opening months of his command were marked by swiftness and sureness. Like a wise general he consolidated his base, pushing back the unfriendly natives to the north and west. Then he sent spies and ambassadors across the Pyrenees to search out the easiest routes across southern Gaul. For we must remember that Hannibal had inherited from his father the desire to bring Rome to her knees and also the outline of a scheme by which to do so. In 219 B.C., Hannibal judged that the time to attack Rome was at hand. He looked around for a pretext.

The pretext was Saguntum, a town *south* of the Ebro, established as a free city and anxious to avoid Carthaginian domination. Saguntum appealed to Rome for support and the Senate voted to send it. Strictly speaking, Rome's action was in defiance of her agreement with Hasdrubal. Hannibal saw that an attack on Saguntum would be an attack on Rome. Without hesitation he sat his army down before Saguntum and took the city. Then Hannibal rewarded and rested his soldiers. But a large share of "booty" was sent to Carthage. So, when a Roman delegation reached Carthage with the impossible demand that Hannibal be surrendered, the Carthaginian ruling class was happy to make the choice of war.

So began the Second Punic War, which many prefer to call the Hannibalic War, because it was truly Hannibal's war against Rome—the war of an individual's genius against a nation's will and power. This war, wrote Livy, was "the most memorable of any that have ever been waged. . . . No nations ever met in arms greater in strength or richer in resources, . . . in so high a state of efficiency. . . . And yet, great as was their strength, the hatred they felt towards each other was almost greater."[3]

Hannibal, as we should expect, acted first. Leading a mixed force of perhaps 70,000, comprising all arms—heavy Carthaginian horse, light Numidian horse, Spanish and Libyan infantry, Balaeric slingshooters, and war elephants, he crossed the Pyrenees. By diplomacy, occasionally by fighting, he reached the Rhone River. Here the Romans had designed to join their loyal Gallic allies to halt Hannibal's advance. But when the Roman general landed at the mouth of the river, he learned that Hannibal had already turned the Gallic flank and was crossing the river to the north. Hannibal's purpose suddenly became clear. His drive was on Rome itself. He was making for the Alps! The Roman general could do nothing but re-embark, hoping to get back in time to meet Hannibal as he debouched from the mountains. Because there were plenty of Roman troops in Italy, the army at the Rhone was ordered to Spain, to operate against the Carthaginian bases.

Hannibal pressed on towards the Alps. When he sensed some doubts and hesitation among his soldiers, he rallied their spirits by reminding them of their past achievements—their victories in Spain, the crossing of the Pyrenees, the passage of the mighty Rhone—and by scorning their unaccustomed fears. What were the Alps, he asked, but mountains, which many others had crossed in times past? As the Carthaginians started to climb the steep mountain passes, however, their real difficulties had just begun. Unfriendly tribesmen stood on the heights, ready to roll huge stones down on Hannibal's men where the path was narrowest. Others, promising to show them the easiest way, led them into an ambush. Only the eternal vigilance and cool leadership of the general prevented the demoralization and rout of the army.

Ultimately, the natural obstacles proved more formidable than the human. The army reached the summit in nine days; then two days were spent in rest and rehabilitation. Despite Hannibal's promise that the remainder of the journey would be smooth and down hill, the descent proved more precipitous and difficult than the ascent. At one point a recent landslide had carried away the narrow path and left the army blocked by a huge rock. "Impassable" was the report, as the army waited for the general. Here was a test for Hannibal. Surveying the scene, he ordered the soldiers to find a way around, through the trackless snow. A fresh fall covered a frozen layer below. As the men cut through the snow, they lost their foothold on the bare ice and disappeared down the slope. The hoofs of pack animals pierced the ice and became imbedded.

Finally, exhaustion dictated that the ground be cleared of snow and camp be pitched again. But, above the line of vegetation, the elephants could find no forage and would grow steadily weaker. There was nothing to do but hack a passage through the rock.[4] After four days of ceaseless effort, the descent continued. At last a tired army of "bearded desperadoes" looked down over the valley of the Po.

This leading of an organized army including elephants across the Alps ranks as one of the great feats of arms of all times. Hannibal had come from New Carthage to northern Italy in five months; the actual crossing of the Alps took only fifteen days. Was it worth it? From the strictly military point of view, perhaps not. Hannibal's casualties in both men and elephants were stupendous, probably more than half of his effective force. He might have reached Italy more quickly and easily by sea. But the moral effect of the crossing was overwhelming, and this was what Hannibal had been counting on. He and his army had accomplished something which men had thought impossible. Moreover, they had moved so fast that the crossing was done almost before the Romans even suspected their plans. Northern Italy trembled at the sudden appearance of Hannibal's men. His was a miracle army.

It was a tested and confident army, too. Hannibal played on the pride and ambition of his men. Poised as they were at the very gates of their mortal enemies, turning back was unthinkable. No one of them would willingly try again the passage of the fearsome Alps. Fortune had imposed on them the necessity of fighting. But they need not despair. Fortune also held out the bounteous rewards of victory. In front of them lay Italy with its sunlit fields and comfortable towns. They could and would defeat the Romans: in what regard could the Roman army be considered the equal of the Carthaginian? They would advance to the banks of the Tiber. After one or two battles, the vast riches of Rome, the capital of the world, would fall into their hands. Everything that the Romans possessed, all that they had amassed through many triumphs, would be theirs. Above all, the soldiers must remember, they had no safe haven; they could not retreat. For them there was no choice other than victory or death. "You are compelled," said Hannibal, "either to conquer or to die in battle. . . . There is no keener weapon in men's hands than a contempt for death."5

So Hannibal inspired his men with the prospect of quick victory. He had never failed them before; he had looked after their needs with a fatherly care; he had outwitted all their enemies. Their loyalty was to him, not to Carthage; they followed Hannibal with one heart.

4. Early battles of the Second Punic War

Like all the Carthaginian ruling class, Hannibal surveyed any situation with the practical eye of a businessman. He was not one to be carried away by the emotional effect even of his own oratory. He studied the resources available to him and to the enemy and sought to use what he had to best advantage. What was his proper course of action? Should he attempt a rapid onslaught on the capital? With his small army an outright defeat of Rome was impossible. A daring raid, no matter how successful, would be inconclusive. The Carthaginians, cut off from any support, would lose whatever they had gained and would, in the long run, be annihilated. Hannibal discarded at once the idea of a speedy and easy victory such as he had outlined to his troops.

What was the alternative? Hannibal laid plans for a grand strategy of warfare. Rome's control of parts of Italy was recent and not firmly established. The Celts in northern Italy, some of the tribes in the far south, and some of the old Greek city-states were lukewarm in their attachment to Rome. Their status as Roman allies was of doubtful security. Hannibal would march throughout Italy, persuading them to renounce their alliance. He would fight the Roman army, of course, and would defeat it, but such victories would be of value only insofar as they influenced the political situation in Italy. He must show the allies that Rome was an idol with feet of clay. He must prove that Rome's promised protection was worthless. One by one he would detach the allies from their allegiance to Rome, until the capital, deprived of their support in men and money, found itself unable to fight any longer. Such a slow but total conquest, such a humiliation of Rome, would break her power forever and end her threat to Carthaginian supremacy.

The success of Hannibal's plan depended on his prestige with the allies; prestige, in turn, depended on his ability to win victories. His first major victory was not long denied him. In December, 218, he faced a Roman army near the Trebia River. Enticed by the Carthaginian light horse, the Romans pressed on through the cold water. The Roman army had been marched hastily north from Sicily (where it had been preparing an invasion of Africa), and this morning had not even had time for breakfast. The Carthaginians, however, had slept comfortably, had eaten a hot breakfast, and had anointed their bodies with oil. Unmindful of the cold, they waited until the Roman army was over the river. Then they attacked, and the 2000 Carthaginians whom the wily Hannibal had concealed under the river bank fell on the Romans from the rear. Over two-thirds of the Roman army were killed or captured. The frightful defeat confirmed the revolt from Rome of the Celtic tribes in the north. Hannibal restored all his allied prisoners to freedom, saying that he had come not to subjugate them but to liberate them from the cruel hand of Rome. Early in the next spring, he devastated the rich fields of the province of Etruria, to prove that Rome was not able to provide her allies with adequate protection.

A fever contracted in the marshes cost Hannibal the sight of one eye, but his depredations stung the pride of the Romans. A bold but inexperienced general named Flaminius, resolving to destroy Hannibal, followed him in June, 217, as he marched his army eastward along the shore of Lake Trasimene. On the heights surrounding a little valley running up from the shore, Hannibal stationed his men and concealed a force near the single road that entered the valley. In the heavy mists of early morning Flaminius, impatient to overtake Hannibal, hastened blindly into the trap. The Carthaginians charged suddenly down on the marching columns. As the mists cleared, the ruin of the Roman army was disclosed. Only a few thousand Romans escaped.

Rumors of the disaster at Trasimene dismayed and terrified the inhabitants of Rome. Men and women gathered in the Forum or wandered the streets, waiting for definite news. Mothers died of grief as they learned of the death of their sons; others died of joy when their sons appeared, unexpected survivors.[6] But the battles of Trebia and Trasimene did not have the full effect on Rome's allies which Hannibal had hoped for. He continued south eastward, failed to capture the fortified town of Spoletium, crossed the Apennines, and rested by the sea. His soldiers needed reequipment. Hannibal boldly solved the problem by issuing captured Roman weapons to them.

Meanwhile the Roman Senate, awake at last to their danger, took the constitutional action reserved for times of crisis and appointed a dictator. This emergency magistrate superceded the consuls, wielding all executive power, but he could serve for only six months. The man chosen was Fabius, a patrician senator well-versed in the art of politics and a man respected for his uprightness and strength of will.

Fabius found the situation critical but not hopeless. If he could not protect Italy, he could strengthen walls and demolish bridges in preparation for the defense of the capital. The Romans could mobilize fresh armies, but apparently they could not meet Hannibal successfully in open battle. To win the war, on the other hand, Hannibal had to gain decisive victories. Without more support from the allies than he had yet received, he could not maintain himself indefinitely in Italy. A war of attrition would wear down Hannibal's forces. Supplies would be denied him, his stragglers cut off, his raiding parties ambushed. Hannibal wanted a battle; so Fabius would not give him one. He was, said Hannibal, a thundercloud always hovering on the horizon; some day the storm would break. Time was on the side of the Romans; so Fabius would delay. Indeed, Fabius gained the title of Delayer, and his plan of avoiding battle while harassing the enemy at every opportunity has ever since been known as a Fabian Policy.

5. Cannae

But attrition works on both sides. The Romans were ashamed of the apparent cowardliness of Fabius and urged him to fight. The maintenance of their citizen army was expensive. And Hannibal was ravaging some of the best lands in Italy. Once, indeed, it looked as though Hannibal were caught. A guide misled him in Campania and Fabius' army encamped on the hills surrounding him. Hannibal's inventiveness saved him. At night he drove some oxen with fire brands on their horns high into the hills. The Roman sentries, fearful lest the Carthaginians get above them, followed the lights. Hannibal marched his army safely out on the main highway while the cautious Fabius, suspecting a trick, remained inactive.

No great victory was won to increase the fame of Hannibal among Rome's allies. But the period of Fabius' dictatorship passed, and Rome elected two new consuls. One of these was Varro—the favorite of the plebeian or popular party, which had been suffering especially severely from the warfare of destruction and exhaustion. Varro was a blusterer, with little real ability, who felt the people had given him a mandate to fight. He and Paulus, the other consul, took turns commanding the army a day at a time. Varro did everything possible to precipitate a battle; his colleague was more prudent. Hannibal, it goes without saying, wanted nothing so much as another major battle. The meeting occurred, in 216, on a plain near Cannae, a supply base in east central Italy which Hannibal had occupied.

For the battle of Cannae the Romans had collected an unusually large army, upwards of 80,000 men. Hannibal, outnumbered about 8 to 5, called forth all his military sagacity and made a most unusual disposition of his forces. His cavalry he posted, traditionally enough, on his flanks. His infantry he stretched out in a long thin line, the center of which bulged outward toward the enemy, in the shape of a crescent. On his wings, at the tips of the crescent, he posted Libyan footmen. Their lines bent so sharply backward as to be almost perpendicular to the main front.

The impatient Varro was the aggressor. The cavalry on the Roman right was unable to stand up to Hannibal and fled the field in disorder. The cavalry on the left could make no real progress against the elusive Numidian horse. But the Roman legions in the center were surprisingly successful. First they pushed in the Carthaginian bulge. Then they bent the central Carthaginian line backwards. Anxious to pursue their advantage, more and more Romans pressed into the battle. Hannibal's tactical innovation was working to perfection. The Romans, crowding more and more closely together, were advancing into a pocket. The Spaniards opposed them in front. Now the Libyans faced inward and took them on both flanks. The Roman army, fighting fiercely and apparently winning, had succeeded almost in surrounding itself. At this critical moment the cavalry commanded by Hannibal's brother Hasdrubal, who had ridden over to aid the Numidians sweep the left wing of Roman cavalry from the field, reappeared directly in the rear of the Roman infantry. The only escape route was cut. It was slaughter. The Roman army simply ceased to exist. Paulus was killed; Varro and a few companions made good their escape.

Cannae was a brilliant victory. The triumphant Hannibal sent his brother Majo to Carthage with news of his successes. Majo carried with him a bushel or so of gold rings stripped from the fingers of dead Roman nobles, and begged the Hundred to send Hannibal the aid he needed to end the war. The road to Rome lay open, he said; the citizens were struck almost dumb with grief and panic.

Meanwhile the Roman Senate remained steadfast and resourceful. Led by Fabius, it established order in the city and prepared to carry on the struggle. 177 new senators were nominated to replace those killed already in the course of the war. Varro was welcomed because "he had not despaired of the state." Not a Roman spoke of surrender. Hannibal's offer to ransom his prisoners was scornfully refused.

The aftermath of Cannae has puzzled nearly everyone for 2000 years. Hannibal did not lead his victorious army down the open road to Rome. Maharbal, his cavalry chieftain, pleaded for a prompt advance; then said to him in disgust, "Hannibal, you know how to win a victory but not how to make use of it."[7] Perhaps he was right. Perhaps Hannibal, accustomed to the dogged pertinacity of the Romans, underestimated the collapse of morale which immediately followed Cannae. Perhaps he overestimated the power of the city to resist an attack by his exhausted field army, which was, to be sure, lacking in siege machinery. Perhaps he was momentarily appalled by the massive slaughter. More probably, Hannibal judged that the time was not yet ripe for the decisive thrust against Rome itself. Such a thrust might serve as a rallying cry for his enemies. He should first continue his strategical plan of exposing Rome's weakness and breaking her authority throughout the rest of Italy. Mommsen, the famous 19th century authority on Roman history, praises Hannibal for knowing "Rome better than the foolish people who in ancient and modern times have fancied that he might have ended the war by a march on the capital," for not "sacrificing practicable and important successes for the sake of empty demonstrations."[8] In any case, Hannibal chose to move on Capua instead of on Rome, and the citizens breathed a sigh of relief.

6. *The war turns against Hannibal and ends at Zama*

The news of Cannae spread rapidly over the world, resulting in the development of a situation highly favorable to the Carthaginian cause. The Carthaginian rulers, enthusiastic about Hannibal at last, sent him small reinforcements and directed Majo to raise a new army in Spain for his support. The annihilation of the Roman army had a compelling effect on the wavering Roman allies. All the south Italian tribes joined the Carthaginians, and Capua, the second city in Italy, declared for Hannibal. Ambassadors came to him from King Philip of Macedon (who ruled over the original nucleus of Alexander's Empire) proposing a broad alliance against Rome. Hiero, the aged ruler of Syracuse who had favored the Roman side, died, and Carthaginian officials gained control of the city after the assassination of his youthful successor Hieronymus. It looked as though the direct sea route from Carthage to Hannibal could be re-opened. In addition, the Roman financial system was near collapse.

Hannibal was encouraged by each one of these factors, but his hopes in each case were disappointed. The two Scipio brothers

who commanded the Roman forces in Spain were so successful there
that the new Carthaginian army was kept fully occupied until 212
and could not come to Italy. Another Carthaginian force, which
might have proved decisive under Hannibal's command, was di-
verted to a foolish campaign to seize Sardinia, where it was destroyed. So Hannibal was deprived of reinforcements. The Italian
provinces which had revolted to Carthage proved almost as much
a liability as an asset. They demanded protection against Roman
vengeance, and Hannibal hurried back and forth trying to supply
it. Finally the Romans besieged Capua in overwhelming force.

Not properly equipped to attack the siege works, Hannibal
tried to entice his enemy into raising the siege by marching toward
Rome. This rapid but desperate thrust proved abortive. "Hannibal
was at the gates!" as countless Roman children of later generations
would be warned. But he turned away from Rome after defiantly
hurling a javelin over the walls. Once again he missed what now
looks like a chance to achieve conclusive victory. Was he deterred,
as some have suggested, by superstitious fear of the gods, who produced a sudden hail storm to show him that the time was not yet
ripe for the fall of Rome? Was Hannibal's character flawed by a
puzzling strain of irresoluteness? Livy records a remark attributed to
Hannibal at this juncture, "that sometimes he lacked the will to
capture Rome, at other times the opportunity."9 Perhaps it is more
logical to surmise that there was in him a certain unwillingness to
bring to an end the military phase of his conflict with Rome. War
was a game he played well, despite all its danger and discomfort. It
was a game that had monopolized his life and that he enjoyed. It
was a game he now prolonged in order to postpone the moment of
facing the political problems of final victory and of the peace that
neither Carthage nor Hannibal knew how to exploit.

In any case the Romans did not rise to his lure, and Capua
in 211 fell back into their hands. They made an example of Capua
to discourage further disloyalty to Rome: the inhabitants were sold
into slavery. Roman secret service activity delayed the signing of the
treaty with Philip. Then the Macedonian showed himself a careless
general and, after his camp was surprised at Apollonia in Illyria,
was of no active assistance in the war. Although the average Roman
citizen was impoverished and so normal taxation was unproductive,
a group of bankers subscribed to what we today would call a war
loan and provided the money to ward off Roman bankruptcy.

Syracuse provided the saddest blow of all for Hannibal. This
city, in earlier days, had resisted siege after siege. Its fortifications
had been further improved by the mathematician and scientist
Archimedes, who had invented extraordinary machines for his patron Hiero without a thought as to how they would be used. After

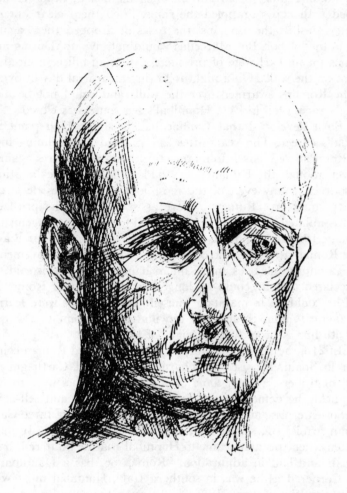

SCIPIO AFRICANVS

the Carthaginians gained control of Syracuse, the enterprising Roman general Marcellus laid siege to it. When his ships sailed up to the walls, great cranes invented by Archimedes dropped huge weights to sink them or to kill the men on board; other cranes equipped with claws grappled the ships, lifted them clear out of the water, dashed them against the rocks or dropped them again to sink in the harbor. But Marcellus would not give up. During negotiations for an exchange of prisoners, a Roman officer noticed a low spot on the walls. On a night following a carnival day in Syracuse, the Romans swarmed over the walls and could not be dislodged. Syracuse fell in 211; Hannibal's sea route was closed.

So it developed that Cannae had been the high point in Hannibal's career. The years after 211 marked his declining fortunes. Rome stirred herself to more active military measures against him, even though the Fabian policy had come near to exhausting her resources. Many even of the most loyal Latin allies declared that they could give Rome no more assistance, and the price of grain was inflated to three times its normal level. But arrangements were made for vast shipments of grain from Egypt, and three aggressive Roman armies restricted Hannibal's freedom of movement. When Tarentum fell back into Roman hands, Hannibal is said to have declared that he could no longer hope to conquer Rome. It was all he could do to maintain himself. The Romans were learning his tactical methods, but their unwillingness to come to a showdown with him is proof of the weight of his prestige.

In 210, the youthful Publius Scipio was named Roman commander in Spain. He used his charm, and the old Carthaginian method of bribery, to win some of the Spanish tribes over to his side. Quickly he demonstrated qualities of fortitude and self-confidence, of enterprise and imagination. Under the eyes of three Carthaginian armies, he seized their capital, New Carthage. It may have been when this news came to Hannibal that he muttered, half in despair and half in admiration, "Rome, too, has a Hannibal."

Cornered as he was in southern Italy, Hannibal must win one more decisive victory. To do it, he must have reinforcements, and they must come from Spain. In 208 his brother Hasdrubal slipped away from Scipio and crossed the Alps into Italy. Hannibal, far to the south, awaited news of his coming so that he could march to join him. Claudius Nero, watching Hannibal, secretly and rapidly moved north with part of his army and joined Livius. Together they forced Hasdrubal to fight at the Metaurus River and defeated him. One night, Hasdrubal's head was tossed into Hannibal's camp.

Meanwhile, in Spain, Scipio completed the defeat of the remaining Carthaginian forces and brought the whole country over to the Roman side. His success in Spain captured the imagination of the Roman people, and on his return to Rome popular acclaim elected him consul. Scipio now made the revolutionary proposal that the war should be carried into Africa. With Hannibal still in Italy, the Senate was horrified at Scipio's bold suggestion but found it impolitic to refuse. Although every official obstacle was put in Scipio's way, he collected an enthusiastic army by voluntary recruiting, and it is said that his fleet was provided and fitted out in forty days. Landed in Africa, based on the port of Utica, and supported by the Numidian chieftain Massinissa, Scipio's expedition was speedily and devastatingly successful. By a ruse the Carthaginian camp was set afire and destroyed, and the Carthaginian army was annihilated at the pitched battle of the Great Plains which followed. Carthage, defenseless, asked for peace terms.

Scipio's first requirement, obviously, was the withdrawal of the Carthaginian troops from Italy. Orders to this effect were sent to Hannibal, who obeyed them without interference from the Romans. Disappointed though he must have been to abandon his attempt to conquer Rome, Hannibal came home with new plans. The appearance of his undefeated army inspired his countrymen with fresh hope. Hannibal was given virtually dictatorial powers. The seizure of a Roman supply fleet signalized the breaking of the peace terms. Once again the Carthaginians trusted in Hannibal's genius to baffle the Romans. Hannibal first made a wholly unexpected request: that the two generals should meet in parley. Reminding his opponent of his military prowess, attested by his unending victories in Italy, and arguing the folly of risking in one contest all that the younger general had recently gained, Hannibal urged Scipio to accept a peace settlement which would leave Sicily and Sardinia and Spain in Roman hands. Sensing his material and psychological advantages, however, Scipio refused to negotiate.

So, the final battle of the war, between Hannibal and Scipio, was fought at Zama in October, 202. Scipio had grown to manhood during the years of Hannibal's greatest successes. It might be said that in the art of war he had "gone to school" to Hannibal. He now had on his side Hannibal's former ally Massinissa. The most vital point of all was that in cavalry he was decisively superior to Hannibal, who had been forced to leave his horses in Italy.

The battle opened with the charge of Hannibal's "heavy tanks"—his eighty war elephants. This charge was dispersed by the Romans who opened lanes for the elephants and terrified them by the noise of trumpets. The Roman cavalry drove off the Carthaginian cavalry on both flanks and pursued them from the field. The Roman legions scattered the first two lines of Carthaginian light infantry and advanced in long thin ranks against the close-packed

veterans of Hannibal's Italian army. This was the crucial moment
of the battle, for which Hannibal had prepared. His veterans, fresh
from having been held in reserve, must have won over the extended
and battle weary Romans. But at this juncture the Roman cavalry
reappeared on the field and took the Carthaginians in the flanks and
rear. Hannibal's own brilliant tactics were used against him. Scipio
and the Romans had their revenge for Cannae. Of the surrounded
Carthaginians, 20,000 were killed, 20,000 were made prisoners.

7. *Disappointments of Hannibal's later years*

Carthage was prostrate. Polybius later commented that it
was quite as much the duty of a leader to see when it is time to give
in as when it is time to win a victory. Hannibal exhibited this practical good sense, faced the inevitable, and counseled surrender.
Against the hot-headed ranting of the Carthaginian senators, Hannibal argued the reasonableness of the peace terms which Scipio
offered, anxious to avoid the delay and trouble of reducing the
city. Carthage gave up Spain and Sicily for good. She surrendered
her naval vessels and war elephants. She agreed to pay a large war
indemnity in fifty annual installments.

Hannibal accepted this defeat. But he did not abandon all
his hopes. Carthage had not suffered irremediable harm. The city
was intact. Her manufacturing and her commerce could continue
to flourish. Rome had broken Carthage's trading monopoly, but
was herself seriously weakened by the long struggle. Carthage retained the ability to prosper. She was so rich that she could manage
to pay her war debt from her income, without imposing any new
taxation. She might again grow strong in military force and political
influence. She might even renew her contest with Rome. No one
defeat, not even a Zama, could destroy her.

All these factors Hannibal understood. In the existing situation he saw reason to economize and reform, no reason to despair.
He realized that of all the rivals Carthage had faced Rome was the
most tenacious, most capable, most dangerous. Rome was to be
feared. The keynote of Carthaginian policy should be to plan a
new opposition to Rome. To effect such a policy, the first essential
was to break the stranglehold of the commercial oligarchy on the
Carthaginian government. Hannibal's failure to conquer Rome
could be laid largely to the inability of the rich to govern Carthage
wisely. In their jealousy they had begrudged power to the one
among them who might have been able to humble Rome. In their
selfishness they had refused to give Hannibal the supplies and reinforcements he so vitally needed and had frittered them away on
secondary schemes. In their narrow-mindedness they had failed to

understand Hannibal's intentions and had believed that their own lives and prosperity could remain unaffected by the struggle Hannibal was waging for them.

The rulers of Carthage had lost one war because they were unwilling to allow any interference with "business as usual". Apparently they had learned no lessons from their loss. They now seemed totally unaware that Rome, set upon the path of Mediterranean supremacy, would inevitably achieve it unless forcibly halted. Again they wanted "business as usual", blind to the fact that with the political downfall of Carthage would come her commercial decline as well. Against the influence of these hidebound reactionaries, whose control stultified all Carthaginian initiative, Hannibal set himself. The years following Zama show him engaged in politics in the effort to reform the Carthaginian government.

For a while, with his great fame and forthright manner, Hannibal carried all before him. He exposed the corruption of the ruling class, which had attempted to give short weight of about 25% in the first payment of tribute to Rome. He proved that the tribute could be paid in full out of profits (much to the disappointment of the Romans who had considered the amount staggering). He lessened the authority of the Hundred and made it more responsive to the popular will by forcing passage of a law which said its members should be elected each year rather than hold office for life.

But Hannibal, although devoted to Carthage and anxious to see it well-governed, was not a good politician. His experiences as dictator in Spain and general-in-chief in Italy had given him no mastery of the arts of compromise and conciliation. He could command the instant and affectionate obedience of his soldiers, but he could not reason with his equals. Accustomed to giving orders, he was too impatient to cajole or convince those whom he wished to move. He had placed himself in direct conflict with what we today call a "vested interest". The ruling class desired to keep things as they were—to maintain the status quo. Any exposure of its graft, any proposal to weaken its position or broaden its membership, aroused its united opposition. And the man who suggested the changes, especially because he was a Hannibal, became the object of its fear and hatred.

To the Romans, of course, Hannibal was a source of universal dread. They suspected him of planning to consolidate all the anti-Roman powers of the Mediterranean in a league strong enough to defeat Rome. Hannibal almost certainly was pursuing such a policy. He had relied first on Philip of Macedon to impede Roman expansion. After Philip's defeat at Cynoscephalae in 197 left Greece in Roman hands, Hannibal turned next to Antiochus of Syria. Then the Carthaginian ruling class reached its nadir of selfish stupidity. Considering the temporary ease and prosperity and political dominance of their own class more important than the entire future welfare of Carthage, they appealed to Rome to imprison Hannibal, accusing him of treasonable efforts to subvert the terms of peace.

This was the final betrayal. The recovery of national power and pride was subordinated to class interests. When they repudiated Hannibal, the Carthaginian oligarchy doomed their city to destruction by Rome. But Hannibal refused to give up his efforts to check the spread of Roman power. To avoid arrest, he fled from Carthage, taking refuge eventually with Antiochus. This ruler had grandiose schemes but lacked the good sense to make use of Hannibal's talents in proposed joint operations against Rome. The defeat of Antiochus at Magnesia in 190 sent him back across the Taurus Mountains and left the Romans in charge of all of Asia Minor.

Hannibal was forced again to flee, first to the island of Crete which was inhabited mostly by pirates, and then to Bithynia, where he served as general for King Prusias in local wars. The Romans, still fearful of the aging Hannibal, sent a mission to Prusias demanding the surrender of the Carthaginian. Prusias implied that if they wanted Hannibal they should get him themselves. Consequently, one night in 183 B.C., bands of Romans surrounded Hannibal's house. When he discovered that even his secret roads of escape were blocked, Hannibal took poison, remarking that he was "releasing the Romans from their long anxiety." So died in obscurity one of the world's outstanding military geniuses.

8. *Estimate of Hannibal and his career*

The policy of restricting the growth of Rome to which Hannibal had devoted his life had ended in complete collapse, caused as much perhaps by the errors and weaknesses of the Carthaginians as by the exertions of the Romans. After his death Roman power expanded inexorably. At the end of the Third Punic War in 146, the city of Carthage was destroyed and the Carthaginian commercial power disappeared. In the same year, with the sack of Corinth, Rome reduced Greece to the status of a minor province. In the years following, Rhodes and Syria and Egypt came under the control of Rome, until the entire Mediterranean was a Roman lake. This was the course of events that Hannibal had tried to avert.

Hannibal failed in his attempt to win mastery of the Mediterranean world for Carthage instead of Rome. But he and his war had still a great effect on history. Rome emerged from her conflict with Hannibal a far different state from what she had been in 219

B.C. Her defeat of Carthage gave her a taste of imperial expansion. Her new provinces, especially Spain, gave her new problems of government outside of Italy. Her assumption of some of the Carthaginian trade drew her attention to the East, and her new interests there demanded that she became first the policeman, and then the ruler, of that unsettled world. From Syracuse and from the East were brought back to Rome the statues, the literature, and the well-educated slaves that were to establish the dominant Greek influence in Roman culture. New luxury was introduced into the hardy, simple Roman life.

Within Rome itself the struggle with Hannibal caused significant changes. The hardships of the war had disrupted the Roman economy, destroyed the class of small landowners, and reduced the importance of the large landowners. Bankers and merchants rose to new prominence, became the leaders in the popular assembly, and forced Rome to assume the commercial leadership lost by Carthage. Although the old Roman republican government had survived the test of the war, one element in it might be seen to have acquired particular significance. It was a constitutional dictator, Fabius, who had first held Hannibal off. It was the consul Scipio, without the support of the government but with the enthusiastic support of the people—especially his Spanish veterans, who defeated Hannibal. Scipio might be said to have risen in Hannibal's own image. Here was the element of personal authority, based ultimately on armed support, able to resist the normal forces of the government and, in the end, to direct its policy. Here was the seed of the breakdown of the Roman Republic.

Hannibal failed to achieve his goal. Repudiated by his country, he was "on the run" in his final years, and he died—ignominiously—as a hunted exile. But there were elements of unusual strength in his character. He was a man of courage and of stern self-control, indifferent to hardship or defeat. His clear vision of practical affairs and his devotion to his cause gave him singleness of purpose. Yet his inventive imagination enabled him to respond with flexibility to new challenges, whether of military tactics or of national policy.

Hannibal's heroïc career, however noble, ended in futility. Despite his failure, we think of Hannibal as a great force in history. First, for his military accomplishments. He crossed the Alps, won astounding victories, maintained his mixed army undefeated in a hostile land for fifteen years, and virtually single-handed held the forces of Rome at bay. Second, for the strength of his personality. Mommsen has written:

> The Romans charged him with cruelty; the Carthaginians
> with covetousness. . . . Though anger and envy and mean-

ness have written his history, they have not availed to mar
the pure and noble image which it presents. . . . He combined in rare perfection, discretion and enthusiasm, cau-
tion and energy. . . . Every page of the history of the
period attests his genius as a general. . . . The power
which he wielded over men is shown by his incomparable
control over an army of various nations and many tongues
—an army which never in the worst times mutinied
against him. He was a great man; wherever he went, he
riveted the eyes of all.[10]

Third, for his effect on the development of Rome. After the Punic
Wars, Rome rose to be for five hundred years the leading nation
of the western world. Never again until the barbarian invasions
did a foreigner threaten Rome as Hannibal had threatened her.
The irony of his life is that his efforts to establish Carthaginian supremacy hastened materially the growth of Roman power and influence. Rivalry with a Carthage driven by Hannibal's determination pushed Rome—to some extent unwillingly and unwittingly—
toward achieving hegemony in our ancient world.

Chapter II

TIBERIVS & CAIVS GRACCHVS

THE GRACCHI—AN ATTEMPT AT RADICAL REFORM

1. Tiberius Gracchus

One day in 138 B.C. a young Roman citizen was traveling north from the capital across the broad fields of Etruria. He was astonished to observe that in what had formerly been one of the richest farming districts in Italy scarcely any land was now under cultivation. Instead of a host of sturdy peasants tilling the soil, he saw only an occasional nearly-naked slave tending a herd of cattle. The spectacle of the decline of agriculture in the heart of the Roman dominion impressed itself on the mind of the young traveler.

His name was Tiberius Gracchus and he was already well-known in Roman society. He came of distinguished lineage. His mother's father was that Scipio who had broken Hannibal's veterans at Zama and won himself the title Africanus. Cornelia his mother was intensely proud of her two "jewels", Tiberius and his brother, and intensely ambitious for their future as leaders in the state. "How long," she asked expectantly, "am I to be called the daughter of Africanus and not the mother of the Gracchi?" The repetition of this question dinned into the ears of her dutiful elder son. She gave him the benefit of the most complete education available. Tiberius was so apt at his lessons, so assured in his mastery of facts, that his Stoic tutor Blossius dared not contradict him: "If Tiberius said anything was right, right of course it must be."[1]

As a mere youth, Tiberius had gone to the Third Punic War under his brother-in-law, the younger Scipio, and had won a decoration for valor. It was reported he was the first to mount the walls of Carthage. Such a paragon was Tiberius—so brave and noble, so well-mannered, so talented—that all the mothers of the patrician class wished him as a husband for their daughters. The wife of Appius the senator was infuriated to be told one night when he returned from a dinner party that he had arranged a marriage for their daughter. When she heard that the future son-in-law was Tiberius, however, her fury changed into the keenest delight. And this even though Tiberius, taking his rank from his father, was officially a plebeian.

Tiberius could not be unaware of his reputation. Great things were expected of him. As he rode northward, he was starting on a journey to Spain. He was going on his first service as a public official. Appointed a quaestor, he was charged with the administration of financial affairs. Spain was the province which his grandfather had wrested from the Carthaginians. Spain was the province in which his father had made himself highly respected as an upright and efficient magistrate before he returned to Rome to serve as consul. The fates were smiling on Tiberius.

2. *The problems of expansion*

The fates, as we know, had recently been kind to Rome as well. Since the great victory of Zama, Rome's armies had been everywhere triumphant, and broad territories had been brought under her sway. Philip V and Antiochus had been defeated. Macedonia and part of Asia Minor had been reduced from independent kingdoms to Roman provinces. The interior of Spain had been subdued. With the fall of Corinth, the history of Greece as a free country had come to an end. With the extinction of Carthage, Rome was ready to dominate North Africa. By 138, no other nation was strong enough to dispute the supremacy of the mistress of the Mediterranean.

A period of unexampled peace and prosperity should have ensued from these successes. But they proved not to be an unmixed blessing for Rome. If the commerce she had acquired from Carthage was to prosper, it was clearly necessary for Rome to keep order in the Mediterranean, preventing costly wars and suppressing piracy. But Rome had no conscious intention of changing her role from that of a policeman who keeps order from outside to that of a governor who directs all internal activities. A governor has too many responsibilities toward those he governs. First of all, he must provide them with protection. On the borders of Rome's new provinces lived half-civilized peoples, who gazed into the Roman territory with envious eyes and who could be held in check only by substantial military forces. Then the governor must furnish firm administration and honest justice, preserving his subjects from exploitation by their conquerors. Tax-collection must be fair: the returns ample enough so that it is worthwhile for Rome to control the provinces but not so ample as to destroy the bases of local prosperity. Finally, it is the duty of the governing country to keep open the sea-lanes between herself and her provinces so that international trade will not stagnate.

Here were large new responsibilities for Rome—responsibilities which her people had neither the training nor the desire to shoulder. The Roman was extremely proud of his citizenship, which set him apart from all other people and which he was not willing to share. The Roman citizen was an important individual in a comparatively restricted community; he did not want to lose his individuality in a larger, more cosmopolitan world. He disliked and despised foreigners. Travel abroad did not appeal to him. Above all, he shied away from the prospect of long residence as a military or civil official in any province. He did not want to leave the familiar scenes of the Roman farm and the Latin countryside, where he could live serenely confident of his rights as a Roman citizen.

Therefore, Rome had harbored no ambition and had laid no serious plans for the acquisition or control of a Mediterranean empire. No one can really be said to have plotted the expansion of Rome's power. The excuse of self-defense had tempted her to an ever-widening range of self-assertion. Almost unaware of the succession of events by which extensive territory had fallen into her possession, she was totally unprepared to manage it. Her small republic had had no experience with the control of distant or overseas lands. Could Rome preserve and consolidate her new empire?

To meet this unfamiliar problem Rome was equipped only with the time-honored machinery of her republican government. This machinery had sufficed to bring glory and riches to the comparatively compact and exclusive groups which can be called the SPQR, the Senate and the People of Rome. The practical and economical Romans intended, therefore, to put it to use in the government of their newly-extended dominions.

We have already seen that even in Italy this machinery was based on a compromise between the conflicting aims of the patricians and the plebeians. It was inevitable that, with new sources of wealth and honor to enjoy and exploit, the quarrel between the classes should be re-opened. In theory, the final authority or ultimate sovereignty in Rome resided in the people, who voted in the public assembly by tribes. But this assembly had fallen far from its earlier status as the meeting of proud and independent Roman countrymen. In the 2nd century B.C., its meetings were regularly attended only by the impoverished mob of shiftless city-dwellers, who had little idea of where Greece was, let alone of how it should be governed. The popular assembly had come more and more to serve as a rubber stamp for the decrees of the Senate which had assumed, in practice, the real governing power.

It should not be surprising that in the early years of the Republic the Roman people had customarily chosen the men of intelligence and property among them for positions of responsibility and leadership. If these elected officials filled their posts with success and satisfaction, they might well encourage their children and grandchildren to seek election to the same posts, and even give them special training for public service. The ruling authority tended quite naturally, therefore, to be centered—in actuality, although not according to any law—in a comparatively few families, who were called noble.

It grew customary, also, for the political leaders at the conclusion of their terms of elected office to be nominated for membership in the Senate, where they would serve for the rest of their lives. The Senate, then, represented the accumulated wisdom and experience of the governing class of Roman citizens. In the planning of policies and in the choice of practical means of administration, the Senate should provide guidance far superior to anything that could be expected from the popular assembly.

Originally, the Senate had been established to give advice to the consuls. Reasonably and naturally, however, it was not long before the executive officers of the government, elected as they were for only a one-year term, came to rely on the Senate for the origination and the direction of major government policy. The maintenance of orderly relations in society, the handling of revenues and finance, the determining of foreign relations, came, especially, under the control of the Senate. The consuls, in many cases, were content merely to carry out senatorial orders.

The life term of the senators had the advantage of ensuring that their deliberations would be thoughtful and thorough, unaffected by sudden shifts of the political winds or by popular enthusiasms. It had the tremendous disadvantage, on the other hand, of rendering it impossible to hold the senators to account for their decisions. The Senate was perfectly capable of ignoring the needs and desires of the vast multitudes of the people. It could depend, forever, on the "good old ways", never seeking to experiment with imaginative solutions to the problems of the new day. It was not responsible to the electorate. By the time of the Gracchi, the Senate represented only a small segment of the population. It was a complacent body of proud, rich nobles, a narrow oligarchy of former magistrates. Its thinking was reactionary.

Indeed, however much local wisdom the Senate might command, it was in actuality no better able than the popular assembly to administer the provinces. They were too far away, often separated from Rome by a dangerous sea voyage, and communication with them was too slow. Orders sent from Rome were out-of-date before they were received. Even the most loyal provincial governors found it necessary to act on their own initiative, sometimes contrary to the senatorial directives. The less conscientious magistrates governed for the benefit neither of Rome nor of the province but for their own convenience and self-enrichment. It was difficult to discover and prove irregularities in provincial administration. It was virtually impossible in a senatorial court to convict an official, often himself of senatorial rank, of misgovernment or embezzlement. It is not surprising that the calibre of the magistrates deteriorated and that the provinces were in a constant state of confusion and unrest. The Senate might compose good laws. It could not direct or compel the execution of any sound, over-all scheme of imperial government.

3. Problems at home—economic, social, and political

Had the Senate been faced only with the new problems of overseas empire, the situation would have been critical enough. But in conquering foreign lands, Rome subjected herself to certain new conditions which resulted in the break-up of the traditional way of life at home. In the normal fashion of ancient times, Rome safeguarded herself by forcing her most desperate defeated enemies into slavery. When tens of thousands of these unfortunates were sold as slaves to the rich landowners in Italy, they served as grievous and unfair competition to free laborers. For a slave was a single person, who could be provided with the barest minimum of food and clothing and abandoned when he could no longer work. Many free laborers, who lost their jobs to slaves, tended to wander toward Rome in their search for new work.

More far-reaching even than the influx of slaves in its effect on Roman farming was the enormous increase in the importation of grain. Large areas of the territory newly subjected to Roman rule, notably Sicily and Egypt, could produce grain far more cheaply than it could be grown on Italian farms. Inexpensive maritime transport brought it to Rome's seaport, Ostia, and in the central market at the capital it could substantially undersell the native crop. Gradually the price of grain came down until the Roman farmers saw their profits disappear.

The Senate had no special competence in handling these problems of the national economy. As a matter of fact, the government found itself the means by which the impoverishment of the farmers was accelerated. Because of the lack of sufficient quantities of coined money, a large part of the tribute paid annually to Rome by the provinces had to be in the form of commodities. Sicily, for instance, paid her taxes in grain. To obtain the funds necessary to run the country, the government had to sell this grain, in bulk and without expensive delay. It sold in a buyers' market; the merchants obtained the grain on their own terms, and the market price came down still further. Alert Roman farmers made the decision to cease large-scale production for profit and to attempt only to supply the needs of their own families. But mortgage payments had to be met, and tracts of uncultivated land were nothing but a drain on a farmer's shrinking resources. First, he sold off his fields. Then, oppressed with debts, he sold his house and garden for whatever they would bring. As a last resort, he joined the march of his ex-laborers to the capital.

So the acquisition of an empire had presented Rome with a practical problem of government which could not be solved by her traditional methods. Prompt, efficient, and economical administration of the provinces could not be provided by either Senate or popular assembly. Nor could the governance of millions of subject peoples be based on the local compromise between the classes of the old Roman state. In addition, by Tiberius' day, the competition of the provinces had virtually ruined Roman agriculture. The independent yeoman had disappeared, along with the small farm which he couldn't afford to operate. The *vox populi* ceased to speak the reasoned opinions of a sturdy middle class and began to shout the heated passions of a rootless multitude. In the future no Roman government would be able to ignore the clamorous demands of the city mob—the jobless laborers, the bankrupt farmers, the boastful freedmen, the sharp-eyed aliens—come to the metropolis to seek their fortunes.

Years earlier, Cato had wondered what would become of Rome when she no longer had an enemy state to fear. Foreign threats had kept her government alert and efficient; patriotism had called forth sacrifices from all ranks of the population. Now that Rome had proved her superiority over her neighbors, would the great city which had conquered all her external foes fall victim to the difficulties of internal organization and administration? The spirit of cooperation seemed to have given way to a ruthless contest for the spoils of victory. All were anxious to make their fortunes. Surely so much new territory and power, so many new slaves and sources of supply, should offer chance for profit to both the state and the individual. At the same time, there seemed less need for self-restraint and self-discipline, for sober gravity and hardy perseverance, for a sense of duty and of obligation to others, and so there was a marked decline of these ancient Roman virtues. Instead, it was every man for himself, and the prevailing motive was avarice. The historian Sallust tells us: "The patricians carried their authority, and the people their liberty, to excess. Every man took, snatched, and seized what he could. There was a complete division into two factions."[2] These factions were separated from each other not by significant differences of political principle but simply by their self-seeking competition for material gain.

The man with abundant capital is prepared to weather a financial storm. For a time, the rich landlords of the patrician class seemed even to profit from the disaster overtaking the small farmers. The rich bought their lands for a song and consolidated them into large estates. The supply of slave labor was limitless and cheap, and the slaves could be worked literally to death. The great land-owner could continue farming or, better yet, he could convert his fields to pasture and raise livestock. Here costs were low and foreign competition at a minimum, for the Roman merchant marine was not equal to the task of carrying herds of cattle across the Mediterranean. Intent on squeezing the last cent of income from his sud-denly-enlarged estate, the great landowner hardened his heart against the fate of those he made homeless and unemployed as he swallowed up their ancestral acreage.

Meanwhile, the homeless invaded the slums of Rome and seethed in inactivity. They might have migrated abroad, to gain a fresh start in life in a likely but uncrowded part of the empire. But the Romans had not yet learned the Greek art of colonization, and the citizen could hardly exercise his right to vote in Africa. They might have earned an honest living as artisans in the city, but such manual labor had for years been performed only by slaves. The city mob was thus without visible means of support, but it had to live. And it had one effective weapon, its control of the public assembly. It is "a difficult task to argue with the belly," the sage Cato had said. A protective tariff against imported grain might have given some measure of relief to the Roman producers, but nothing must be permitted to raise the price of grain. The populace demanded food. The government had storehouses crammed with grain. When it was sold cheap to the Roman mob, more farm laborers lost their jobs and flocked to Rome, to demand more grain at still cheaper prices.

The two factions faced each other across a widening chasm. The Senate spoke for the landowners, unwilling to surrender any of their new gains. The public assembly spoke for the city rabble, unwilling to consider any policy until their bellies had been filled. Small wonder that the business of governing the state was at a stand-still. It began to look as though in gaining an empire Rome had bitten off more than she could chew. In what Polybius called the general demoralization of society, the great modern historian Toynbee describes the Romans as being agreed that the "only conceivable end of man was an unbridled enjoyment of the grossest pleasures a victor's irresistible material power could place within his grasp." Toynbee speaks of the "governing class transmuted by the intoxication of victory into a band of robbers."[3] Actuated by selfish interests only, no one seemed to care about the public welfare. Indeed no one stood forth to say clearly what was for the public welfare. Rome stood in crying need of a public-spirited man with the vision to conceive a policy and with the popular appeal necessary to put his policy into operation.

4. The new tribune's plan for land redistribution

Such was the condition of Rome when Tiberius returned from Spain. But the man had changed. He who had gone out as the pampered darling of the aristocracy came back as a national hero. When Mancinus, the Roman governor in Spain, had permitted himself to be surrounded by rebellious tribesmen, there had been imminent danger that his entire army would be exterminated. At that juncture, relying on his father's fame and on his own record as an honest and able administrator, Tiberius had stepped in and succeeded in negotiating a settlement with the rebels. If Mancinus was abandoned to suffer a sad fate, that was only what a blunderer deserved. For Rome the important thing was that the army was saved. Its savior was Tiberius. So he came back to receive tremendous popular acclaim.

It would not be fair to say that this applause turned Tiberius' head. But he suddenly recognized in his vast popularity a great opportunity for himself. Tiberius was a thoroughly well-meaning young man, who was convinced of his own righteousness and wisdom. He had brooded over the bad conditions he had noticed in Etruria. Here was a chance for him to correct the evils and put an end to the demoralization at Rome. His tour of duty as quaestor being ended, he would stand for the tribunate.

The tribunes were popularly elected officials, chosen we know for the express purpose of representing the common people and protecting their rights. The office of tribune gave one the leadership of the activities of the Assembly and the veto over harmful measures of the Senate. The tribunate presented itself as the perfect position for a man with a mission to perform. The election of someone as popular as Tiberius, the hero from Spain, could hardly be doubtful. Once elected, he would proceed with his self-appointed mission of regenerating Roman society. The task should not be too difficult; it was fairly obvious what needed to be done. The basic necessity was to get the Roman people back on the land. Their labor would restore the prosperity of Italian agriculture. With more free laborers on the land there would be less chance for a repetition of the horrors of the recent slave revolt in Sicily. These yeomen, furthermore, would strengthen the army (for which only citizens were eligible) and prevent a recurrence of the recent embarrassing reverses in Spain. With his duty so clearly in mind, Tiberius confidently put himself forward as a candidate for tribune for the year 133 B.C.

Sir Charles Oman, in an astute sketch of Tiberius at this point in his career, describes him as possessing "enough brains to see that the times were out of joint, enough heart to feel for the misfortunes of his countrymen, enough conscience to refuse to leave things alone, [and] enough self-confidence to think that he was foreordained by the gods to set all to rights."[4] Brains, heart, conscience, and self-confidence are fine attributes for a public servant. To set all to rights, a program of action is needed. As the platform on which he ran for tribune, Tiberius took over a plan which had been considered, and even experimented with, in years gone by. The state was legally the owner of large amounts of land, throughout Italy, which it had acquired in the course of victorious warfare. Title to this public domain had never been given up, although rights of possession and use had been accorded to temporary occupants—literally, squatters. A comparatively small number of them had possessed themselves of most of the available land. These squatters, said Tiberius, should be dispossessed, and the public domain parceled out to the needy farmers who had lost their own lands and were now in the ranks of the unemployed at Rome.

Safely elected tribune for 133, Tiberius proposed a new Agrarian Law to embody his plan. It was legal, but highly unusual, for a measure of such importance to be introduced in the Assembly. By this time the Senate had arrogated to itself virtually all the law-making and administrative functions which it supposedly shared with the Assembly. But Tiberius no doubt realized that the Senate, composed of former magistrates, no longer felt any responsibility to the electorate and would give no hearing to a proposal benefiting the common people. As a matter of fact, his measure did not appear unduly radical. The present occupants of the public domain were to be dispossessed, but they were to be liberally compensated for the improvements they had made on the land, and they were to be allowed to retain—with a clear title of ownership—500 *jugera,* with an additional 250 for each of two sons. The domain was then to be divided into small holdings—30 *jugera*—and distributed to independent farmers on payment of a nominal rent to the state. To prevent speculation and to ensure permanent cultivation, the law made the tracts so distributed inalienable; that is, they could not be resold or re-leased by the new possessors. To administer the law and mediate disputes, a court of three commissioners was to be appointed by the Assembly.

There was nothing illegal about the details of Tiberius' proposal, but it was supremely impractical and bound to raise a storm of protest from all but the most visionary idealists. The financial hardship involved in the loss especially of good grazing land would be felt by the senators and the knights, the two richest and most influential classes in Roman society. The large "squatters" were unwilling to have their holdings restricted in any way. Some of the domain had been in the hands of "squatters" for nearly a hundred years, and they did not wish to abandon the improvements they had made, whether compensated or not. Other sections had changed hands several times, and the present possessors had bought in full confidence of permanent tenure. No one likes to be compelled to give up his "ancestral estate", and everyone of the dispossessed would have nourished a private grievance against the state. All these criticisms of Tiberius' law may be made without even considering the serious question of whether or not enough small farmers could be found anxious to resume hard agricultural labor under the rather restrictive provisions of the law.

Unconcerned with the possible imperfections of his legislation, Tiberius made an eloquent plea for this plan. His speech exposed the hardships faced by the common man and should have touched the hearts of all but his most callous auditors. Tiberius had been schooled in oratory. He said: "The wild beasts of Italy have their holes and dens to retire to, but the brave men who spill their blood in Rome's cause have nothing left, when they come back from the wars, but light and air. Without hearth or home, they wander like beggars from place to place. . . . They fight and die merely to increase the wealth and luxury of the rich; they are called the masters of the world while none of them has a foot of ground to call his own. . . . Is not a soldier more valuable to the state than a man who can not serve in the army, a Roman than a barbarian? [I] call upon the rich men who now hold the public land to take into consideration the dangerous state into which the Republic is drifting and to yield up their holdings of their own accord, as a free gift if need be, to men who could rear children for the future benefit of Rome. They must be patriotic enough to subordinate their own profit to the good of the state."[5] But, as we have seen, patriotism was at a discount in the 2nd century B.C. So long as his present status was comfortable, no one should be expected to worry about the future. It was precisely the rich, who would suffer from the Agrarian Law, who were not willing to place the good of the state above their private profit.

The "squatters" determined to oppose Tiberius' measure with their full strength. But it seemed inevitable that the law would be passed by an Assembly representing the poor, and the opposition would then be powerless. One method, however, was available to them. There were two tribunes. In ancient time, to prevent the patricians from exploiting the plebeians within Rome, these tribunes had been given the right of veto against all legislation. This veto power was wholly out-of-date and inappropriate, now that Rome was faced with the job of governing all Italy and an overseas empire, but it had never been revoked. The tribune's power was absolute. The tribune's person was sacred—an attack on him was treason against the state. Tiberius' colleague in office, M. Octavius, a conservative in politics and himself a squatter, proved a willing agent for the schemes of the self-seeking capitalists. When Tiberius started to read the preamble of his law to the Assembly, Octavius rose and shouted, "Veto!" All proceedings were thus legally halted before the merits of the bill could even be considered. It was unnecessary for Octavius to explain his action; he could not be challenged.

Obviously the opposition to the law was selfish and partisan. Obviously, also, it was obdurate. Tiberius was stymied. Raging at his impotence, he let his emotion run away with him. Recklessly he turned on Octavius: "You are a considerable holder of public land. I will pay you the full value of it out of my own pocket if you will withdraw your veto." This public suggestion that the veto was motivated solely by personal considerations was an insult Octavius could not forgive. He was honor-bound now to continue his opposition; any withdrawal would indicate that he had succumbed to a bribe.

By nature Tiberius was not prepared for the give and take of politics. His was a one-track mind. Intense and stubborn, he saw things in terms of black and white, right and wrong. He was not adept at blandishment, and, to tell the truth, there was little hope that his opponents would accept any compromise. Tiberius only knew how to meet obstinacy with still greater obstinacy of his own. If his present law could not gain a hearing, he would propose a new one, under which the dispossessed squatters would receive no compensation. And he would prevent the consideration of all other legislation until his law was acted upon! Accordingly, Tiberius interposed a blanket veto on all state business. The Roman Republic was left without any legal or effective government. Tiberius' rash action showed him to be unreliable as a political leader and cost him the support of many moderate reformers. When he brought forward his new bill, there was rioting in the streets. Tiberius was persuaded to try an appeal to the Senate, but that august body was happy to stay out of the dispute by doing nothing.

5. *A constitutional crisis—and how it was temporarily resolved*

Octavius was the hard nut that had to be cracked. The present state of affairs is intolerable, said Tiberius. "When two colleagues of equal power differ on a vital matter and cannot work together, it would be better that one should be removed." Reasonable enough? So let's submit to a vote to decide which one of us shall resign. Unfortunately, Octavius was of course not willing to agree to the "voluntary" retirement which the Assembly would have voted him. Persuasion failing, compulsion remains. But even Tiberius realized that compulsion must always be made to appear legal and logical. A tribune is elected as the representative of the people; his job is to do their will. If a tribune acts contrary to the "will of the people", he is, *ipso facto,* no longer their representative. On this reasoning, the people can, and indeed must, depose the man who fails to perceive, or to act on, their will. So Tiberius urged the Assembly to vote to remove the misguided Octavius from the office which he was so clearly incompetent to fill.

This was not constitutional, for an attack on a tribune was a sacrilege. Nor was it as logical as it sounded. The Assembly was being asked to pull down from its pedestal the chief symbol of the majesty of the people. But it was popular. When the vote went against him, Octavius clung stubbornly to the rostrum until, had he not been dragged away by brute force, he would surely have been killed. This expulsion of Octavius was not an edifying example of Roman *pietas,* that capacity for restrained, serious-minded, and clear-headed conduct which was supposed to distinguish the sober, loyal, and large-hearted citizen. Nor did it help to ensure the success of the Agrarian Law, which the Assembly hastened to pass by overwhelming vote. Tiberius then secured the selection of himself, his brother, and his father-in-law as the three members of the land commission. Who would now be brave enough to say that Tiberius was a disinterested public servant? What could prevent the wrath of all the squatters, evicted without compensation, from falling on the head of Tiberius? This monopolizing of the job of agrarian reform was a "crowning folly", of which no neophyte politician would dream of being guilty. For the self-ordained savior of Rome, it was political suicide.

Tiberius became a marked man. Fortunately, funds to finance the resettlement project were found painlessly when the King of Pergamum (in Asia) died and bequeathed his kingdom to Rome. But the Assembly added another insult to the aristocracy when it specified that this new province was to be administered by the people, not by the Senate. And the eviction of squatters created an increasing feeling of bitterness which sharpened the opposition to the Agrarian Law and to its author. Tiberius, therefore, took a new resolve. He may have been actuated somewhat by fears for his personal safety. A magistrate could be impeached for improper conduct after his term expired, and a tribune stayed in office only one year. Even though Tiberius tried to explain away his actions against Octavius by saying that "a tribune who injures the sovereign people can no longer be sacred and inviolable," he must have understood that his conduct had been unconstitutional to the point of treason. But we may safely grant that Tiberius was more strongly actuated by his passionate conviction that the Agrarian Law was the only means by which the strength and virtue of the Roman state could be maintained. The Agrarian Law must continue in effect. Tiberius was responsible for the execution of the law. Tiberius must, therefore, continue in office. So he resolved to run again for the tribunate.

This was a momentous resolution. It disregarded custom, for which all Romans had deep respect. It openly violated the constitution, which said that the wide powers of a tribune could be entrusted to a single person for only one year. It also marked the recognition by Tiberius of his new position. He could no longer pose as a noble savior of society who appeared as though from nowhere, did his world-redeeming good deed, and then retired to enjoy his fame. By assuming the "duty" of continuing the Agrarian Law in force, Tiberius accepted the job of leader of a political party, as yet ill-organized but potentially powerful. Tiberius ran for a second term as the "friend of the people". In active direction and execution of government policy, he would be the permanent champion of the poor and the weak and the homeless against the rapacious senators and knights.

Tiberius had violated the constitution for the sake of expediency, to achieve a purpose which seemed to him at the moment to be of enormous importance. But he was neither a skilled politician nor a thorough-going reformer. He had no plans for revising the constitution. He had no statesmanlike vision of a future happier Rome under the reign of wiser, more equitable laws. He had devised no means for restoring the spirit of cooperation between Senate and people, for bringing prosperity to all groups in the population, for governing the empire efficiently and economically. Indeed, Tiberius presented no real "platform" at all. He offered a few suggestions: it might be a good idea to ease the terms of service in the army, to end the custom of forming juries exclusively of senators, to permit appeals from all law courts to the Assembly. Beyond these, Tiberius would wait to see what happened.

Tiberius' unparalleled popularity rendered his re-election almost certain. His opponents in the Assembly broached the question of the constitutionality of a second term, but were shouted down.

The atmosphere of riot spread from the meeting to the streets of the capital. His friends surrounded Tiberius with an armed body guard when he appeared in the Forum, but this was an opportunity for his enemies to hoot at him as a would-be tyrant. Both friends and enemies planned to "stuff the ballot boxes" when the election was held; both sides concealed arms under their togas and prepared to use force to achieve their ends.

On the day of the election, Plutarch tells us, the omens were bad for Tiberius. As he came from his house, he stumbled and cut his foot. As he was passing another building, a loose tile fell from the roof, barely missing his head. But Tiberius went on to the Forum. There his friend Flaccus brought him the news that the Senate was voting to declare him a public enemy, so that he could be arrested and executed. The rumor was spreading that Tiberius wished to be king—a title hateful to the Romans ever since the days of the Tarquins. Fearful that Tiberius' cause was lost, his supporters gave out that he had signaled for the use of force, and fighting commenced in the streets. Meanwhile, the consul Scaevola, refusing to be intimidated by the Senate, had scorned to outlaw Tiberius. But the senators were not to be stopped by a legal formality. In the public rioting they saw their good chance to be rid of a radical and dangerously popular opponent. Forming a compact mass under the leadership of one Nasica, they attacked the confused mob on the Capitoline Hill and killed three hundred democrats. Tiberius, it is reported, stumbled over one of the dead and fell. The tribune Publius Satureius was on him in an instant, using a wooden stave to beat out his brains.

Once Tiberius had met this ignominious end, it mattered little that the victorious senators tossed his body into the Tiber. His own brother-in-law, Scipio Aemilianus, said in Spain that it was right for Tiberius to be killed if he was plotting to seize the government. Even so, the Senate found it expedient to dispatch Nasica overseas, so that he could escape the vengeance of the people.

6. The "problem" of Tiberius

Despite his perfect honesty and the very best of intentions, Tiberius had failed to regenerate Rome and had met a rather ridiculous death. Although many people revered him as a martyr, we may perceive that his failure was at least partly caused by his own shortcomings. With the death of Tiberius, his party virtually collapsed, because he had failed to build a program on enduring principles. He was shortsighted, a man who destroyed existing customs and laws without creating others to take their place. He undermined the Senate without reforming the Assembly. He broke down the prestige of the tribunate without erecting any other defense for the rights of the people. He relied too much on his own ability and virtue. Had he triumphed in 133, he would ultimately have presented the Romans with a choice between killing him or making him a tyrant, with a personal veto on all the traditional operations of the state. As Mommsen says, rule by one man who dictates to the lawmakers on the strength of his control over the proletariat is nothing better than absolute monarchy, a form of government no self-respecting Roman would tolerate.[6]

The real danger in the career of a Tiberius—and we have had many "saviors of the state" in the 20th century—is his pretense that his actions are directed by the popular will. Octavius *had* to be removed because he obstructed the desires of the sovereign people. Tiberius *had* to overthrow the constitution in order to carry out the commands of the sovereign people. In reality, whose will was this mysterious and potent "will of the people"? For Tiberius—for any dictator—it is the temporary verdict of a particular group who at a particular moment vote a certain way. For Tiberius, it was the majority of the Assembly, a congregation that included ruffians and beggars from the streets of Rome. The passage of one dubious remedy to the current ills of society was deemed to outweigh the permanent danger of the degradation of the tribunate. Octavius had to go because he opposed the immediate wishes of the rabble. Would their wishes endure? Were their wishes wise and right? Would not such a "will of the people" be highly fluctuating? Tiberius elevated the vote of a local assembly under the influence of a demagogue—albeit a right-minded one—to "the will of the people" and made it the criterion of all governmental action. What becomes then of those who merely vote against the demagogue's proposals? They are traitors to the state. The minority has no rights; the traditional safeguards of life, liberty, and property are swept away. Blinded by his enthusiasm, Tiberius failed to recognize the basic error in the position he assumed. Perhaps his early death precluded his making more harmful mistakes in the future.

The bloody riot at the tribunican election of 133 was an incident in the struggle between Senate and Assembly for the dominant role in the Roman state. With the fall of Tiberius, the Senate began to regain the upper hand. The Agrarian Law was amended to place the judicial power over disputes in the hands of the consuls who, being of senatorial rank, refused to exercise it. Thus the process of dispossession could be halted. Nevertheless, census statistics, quoted by Mommsen, show an increase of some 75,000 landholding citizens in the years 131-125 B.C. But a shiftless member of the urban proletariat could not be changed overnight into a sturdy and prosperous yeoman. The outlook for Roman farming continued bleak. The common people could expect no real improvement in their status until they found a new leader, as intrepid as Tiberius, and more wise.

7. Caius Gracchus: a new reform program

Caius Gracchus had been still very young—only twenty—when his brother was killed. As the years went on, however, it was proper for one of his station to enter the service of the state. In 125 he was made quaestor in Sardinia. His administration was efficient, and he was so scrupulously honest that it was reported he had lost money of his own in handling the state's financial affairs. Naturally some men began to talk of such an unusual public servant as the logical successor to Tiberius.

At first Caius was unreceptive to such suggestions. Then one night, as Plutarch quotes Cicero, the spirit of Tiberius came and urged him to action. "Why do you tarry, Caius? There is no escape. One life and one death is appointed for us both, to spend the one and to meet the other, in the service of the people." Such a promise attracted, rather than repelled, Caius. Two clear-cut motives presented themselves to him. First, he might be able to revenge his brother by undoing the selfish, bigoted perpetrators of his murder. Second, if he could carry on Tiberius' plans and encompass a real improvement in the state of Rome, he would vindicate his brother, gratify his own ambition, and be of service to mankind. The prospect was too pleasing to pass up. To follow in Tiberius' noble footsteps, he ran for tribune for 123. He would be the new democratic leader.

It is not surprising that there were similarities in the character of the two brothers. Caius was impulsive like Tiberius but, Plutarch affirms, far more vehement and passionate. Once his mind was made up, he pursued his course with restless determination, confident of the purity of his aims and of the rightness of his policy. He was aggressive and outspoken, never satisfied with half-way measures, single-minded in his devotion to duty. But the ambition that drove him on was far more sweeping than his brother's. Caius also surpassed Tiberius in intellect and was able to profit from his brother's experience. He made a more thorough investigation into the sources of riot in the Roman state and thought more deeply about possible remedial measures. He would plan with greater foresight.

Caius realized, therefore, that no one measure—the Agrarian Law—could serve as a cure-all, and that Rome could not be regenerated on the strength of favors given to any one element in the population. His program must be well-rounded; it must benefit all groups in society, save only the hated senators, murderers of Tiberius and exploiters of their fellow-men. To carry through his program, Caius recognized the danger of relying on himself alone and the need of creating a political organization strong and cohesive enough to combat the senatorial party. His plans would not be complete with the passage of one or two laws. His reforms must be administered on a continuing basis, so as not to lose their effect. Fortunately, Caius could handle a mass of administrative detail; he had an executive ability the more mercurial Tiberius lacked. Along with all his brother's emotional drive and earnestness of purpose, Caius had a cooler mind. Where Tiberius had been an amateur in politics, Caius would be a professional.

As tribune for 123, Caius planned a real but peaceful revolution. Constitutional changes were to transfer control of the government from the senatorial clique to the people. It had already been made legal for a tribune to remain in office indefinitely, and the tribune was to be the key man in the new scheme of government. In a position perpetually able to over-rule the Senate, he would now also initiate legislation in the Assembly, by which that popular body should exert the guiding influence in all state affairs. The people should once again truly rule Rome. The tribune would be, not a tyrant, but the servant of the people.

The first need was to reduce the specific power of the Senate. Provincial governors, of senatorial rank, were notorious for their shameless misgovernment. They often ruined the economy of their provinces in order to amass fortunes for themselves. At the end of their terms they could be called to account in the Roman courts; but there the juries were composed exclusively of their senatorial colleagues, already predisposed to find the governors innocent in order to preserve the opportunity of doing the same things themselves at a later date. It was impossible for the representatives of the injured province to secure a conviction from a packed jury, and senatorial misgovernment became entrenched. Caius' reform handed the monopoly of jury duty to the equites, or knights, the very class whose wealth would be hardest hit by the extortions of provincial governors. The senators could no longer go their arrogant way unchecked. "I have broken the pride and power of the nobles," boasted Caius. Actually he had introduced jealousy and suspicion into the relations of the two leading classes in society, "casting daggers into the Forum with which the two orders should lacerate each other."[7]

Caius must guard against the ambitious knights being bribed one by one into cooperation with the senators. The knights must be bound together by class-consciousness and by special privilege. Here we see Caius, attentive to detail, aware of the importance of appearances, mastering the art of political management. There were about 10,000 Romans whose wealth qualified them to be knights. To appeal to their vanity, to give them a mark of distinction that would serve also as a badge of party solidarity, Caius arranged for them to wear a special gold ring and to add a crimson border to their togas, in contrast to the senatorial purple. These were trifles, although significant. The monopoly of jury service opened a road to power. But it was wealth that meant most to the knights. Caius revised the method of farming the taxes. A single contract for the collection of the taxes in the rich provinces of Asia was auctioned in Rome. Only the rich knights could provide the capital required to buy this opportunity to extort ever-increasing percentages from the income of the wealthiest section of the empire.

The Land Commission was reinstated in its full powers and the enforcement of the Agrarian Law renewed. It was a sentimental obligation for Caius to carry on Tiberius' favorite policy. It was a measure, of course, to keep the farmers happy, even if it did not succeed in restoring prosperity to Italian agriculture. Farmers might do better in new fields, and so Caius made plans for the establishment of a colony of 6,000 people on the ancient site of Carthage. New settlements within Italy were made at Tarentum and Capua. These should stimulate trade as well as provide opportunities for financial improvement for many "little" men. Some free laborers, as well as a host of slaves, might find employment in the construction of roads. Caius designed a system to cover Italy, complete with accurate milestones, and the whole population would ultimately benefit from such public works. There was also a new opportunity for employment in the building of the giant warehouses to store the state's corn supply. By catering to the soldiers Caius worked for all the citizens. Conscription was regulated on an equitable basis for all; the term of service was shortened; a clothing allowance augmented the legionary's pay.

Caius thus cleverly attempted to meet the needs of the various elements in the population. The government he pictured, under the leadership of the tribunes, was to represent everyone, to advance the welfare of everyone, and thereby to enlist the support of everyone. Caius' Republic was to serve the people as a whole, not to oppress them for the advantage of the few, nor even to benefit one class at the expense of another.

There remained one group which must be mollified if Caius was to retain the office of tribune and if a violent revolution was to be avoided. Land grants and colonies and public works and attractive terms for military service might lure some people from Rome, but shiftless thousands continued to roam the streets of the capital, unwilling or unable to provide their own livelihood. Caius saw the absolute necessity of placating this urban mob which controlled the votes of the Assembly to which he was entrusting the government of Rome. He introduced the dole. Every month the state sold a supply of corn at half the market price to any buyer applying in person. The unemployed rejoiced to find the state undertaking to subsidize them.

8. The problem of colonies and the downfall of Caius

When Caius was re-elected tribune for 122, he was clearly the leading man in Rome, the prime minister of the people. With boundless energy he supervised the execution of all the new measures. He regulated expenditures on roads and dole; he distributed land; he heard appeals. But he never stood on his dignity. Familiar and courteous, he made himself freely available to all, holding a sort of open court. No wonder the people looked upon him as their personal guardian and benefactor. He had the brains to see what needed to be done in the state and the courage and skill to do it. Not the Senate, but Caius Gracchus, ruled Rome.

But there were elements of weakness in Caius' position. He had humbled the conservatives in the Senate but had not converted them to democracy. He had no army on which to rely in case opposition to his program should develop. In the final analysis his leadership of the state depended on nothing but his personal popularity with the mob in the Assembly. Mobs are seldom unselfish or farseeing; they are always fickle, ready to change their allegiance overnight. It was because Caius *was* unselfish and far-seeing that he lost control of the fickle mob.

The traditional constitution by which Rome the city-state had governed itself for centuries was not suitable for the government of Rome the world-empire. The Assembly—nothing but a glorified town meeting—was not competent to assume the responsibility of legislating for the world. The Senate might have had the necessary intelligence but it lacked the necessary breadth of vision, and anyhow Caius had taken the initiative away from it. From the narrowly-limited citizenry of Rome it was impossible to find the trained soldiers and officials needed to keep the peace and control the finances of an empire. With an out-moded constitution and an increasing shortage of honest and capable administrators, Rome was attempting to keep the rest of the Mediterranean world in permanent subjection. It was somewhat as though, in the United States, full rights of citizenship were permitted only to the families of the settlers of the original thirteen states and laws for all the rest of the nation were made by the successors of the Continental Congress.

Caius understood that the situation was unfair, inefficient, and ludicrous. He realized that his program of reforms, concerned mainly with Rome herself and conceived within the framework of an obsolete constitution, was inadequate to solve the broad problems of economic stability and of international leadership which Rome faced.

Caius set out, therefore, to extend his program to cover lands and populations outside of ancient Rome. He proposed not only that Roman citizens should form self-governing overseas colonies but that the rights of Roman citizenship should be extended to thousands of faithful "allies" of Rome throughout Italy. Citizenship involved both privileges and duties—the vote and freedom from certain taxation balanced against the obligation of compulsory military service. Many Italians were agitating for citizenship, both as a recognition of their trustworthiness and of their share in the tasks of world-empire and as a removal of the stigma of inferiority. Caius thought that they deserved it and that the new recruits in the ranks of Roman citizens would supply the strength and vigor Rome needed for survival.

The gradual emancipation of the "subjects" of Rome might ultimately have spread to other parts of the empire besides Italy. Having studied the history of Greek governmental schemes, Caius might have recommended the setting up of a sort of imperial congress with representatives of the various sections making laws for all. He was not to have time for such experiments, but in his second term as tribune he thought the moment propitious for taking the first step. He had already been blamed for inspiring the revolt by which one Latin tribe had protested against the denial of citizenship. Now he asked the Assembly to make a generous extension of citizenship in Italy.

Here Caius over-reached himself; his constituents were unwilling to plan ahead as wisely as he. In the extension of the right to vote to Italians, the jealous inhabitants of Rome saw only a scheme to reduce the value of their votes. To make more citizens was only to increase the list of those whom the government had obligated itself to support and to decrease the share available for the present recipients of the dole. Deaf to the murmurs of provincial discontent, the Assembly was also suspicious of the approbation with which many senators spoke of Caius' proposal. The cry arose that the Roman people were going to be cheated. So Caius' fellow-tribune Drusus, alert to a chance to destroy his colleague's influence, vetoed the extension of citizenship. The people made no protest at this rebuff to their idol.

Unhappy, but unwilling to admit final defeat, Caius departed for Africa to inaugurate the colony of Junonia (Carthage).

This colony Caius hoped would be the model on which many future colonies would be established, and he arranged an elaborate ceremony. A procession toured the location, Roman standards were erected, and stones set to mark the boundaries. But that night in a storm the standards were blown down and howling wolves dug up the boundary-markers. Caius' plans were displeasing to the gods. Meanwhile, in his absence, the complacent enemies of reform saw their chance to ruin Caius by "stealing his thunder". Drusus was to be the demagogue, who by outbidding Caius for popular support, would alienate his following. So Drusus bragged that he had protected the Assembly from being overrun by new citizens. Instead of sending Roman citizens overseas, he would offer them a new start in life by founding twelve colonies within Italy. His Land Commission would distribute farms as Caius had done, but his farms would be rent-free and their new owners could dispose of them whenever and however they wanted. That these proposals were impracticable or in the long run worthless was unimportant. They sounded wonderful to the ignorant Assembly. When Caius returned to Rome he failed to be re-elected tribune.

This election showed that the Roman populace had no understanding of, or appreciation for, Caius' program. The mob had followed him not from conviction but for their own personal advantage. They had voted for Caius because he had offered them material benefits; when Drusus offered them more, they cold-bloodedly abandoned Caius. Roman politics was based on individual popularity—on rabble-rousing, not on principles. Caius' disappointment at his defeat seems almost to have unbalanced his mind. It was not right that he should be checked so decisively in mid-career. He could not believe the people could be so misled. It was criminal that his reform program should be dashed to pieces. Something must be done, immediately, to forestall such disaster.

Caius' loyal adherents were ready for anything. Their excited impatience matched his. The atmosphere was tense and emotions brought to a violent pitch, therefore, when debate was opened on the whole question of overseas colonization. The senatorial party wished to halt it; Caius' friends thought it indispensable. Both sides prepared to fight and hoped for a showdown, although Caius himself was averse to the use of force. The scuffle commenced when the auguries were being taken, and a servant named Antullius was murdered by the democratic crowd as he removed the sacred entrails. A sudden thunderstorm dispersed the gathering, but their dreadful crime left the popular party at a serious moral disadvantage. Not able to agree on their next step, they allowed the reactionaries to gain control of the proceedings. The consul Opimius called out an armed band of retainers to prevent further bloodshed.

Expressing fear of a *coup d'etat,* the Senate declared martial law. This was the momentous decree ordering the consuls "to take care that the republic might receive no harm." The consuls were given *carte blanche,* and a capital offense (by a political opponent) became punishable by death instead of by the usual exile. The popular leaders—the now-morose Caius and the volatile Flaccus—were ordered to court to account for their actions. To go would have been certain death, and so the democrats barricaded themselves on the Aventine Hill, as rumors spread that they were preparing a slave uprising. Flaccus attempted to gain amnesty by negotiations but the Senate demanded unconditional surrender. Opimius denounced Caius and Flaccus as enemies of the state and offered to their slayers the weight of their heads in gold. Caius was apathetic and reluctant to fight, Flaccus was irresolute. Deprived of strong leadership, the democrats scarcely opposed the attack of the senatorial crowd. 3,000 democrats were massacred, Flaccus captured and beheaded.

In the nearby Temple of Diana, Caius brooded over the "ingratitude and treachery" of the city rabble. Instead of brandishing his sword and rallying the popular party, as a would-be tyrant might have done, he prepared to commit suicide. His closest supporters persuaded him to try to escape, and two devoted friends gave up their lives to delay his pursuers. Caius managed to get across the Tiber but sprained his ankle and slowed his flight. Despairing of the future, he halted in the grove of Furina and killed himself. The ruffian who discovered his body cut off his head, weighted it with stones, and was rewarded with 17½ pounds of gold.

9. Critical appraisal of the Gracchi

What estimate can we make of these brother reformers whose mercurial careers were terminated by such sordid deaths? First of all, we must give them credit for high motives and excellent intentions. They were deeply concerned with the plight of Rome, and their plan to restore the citizenry by re-distributing the land was designed solely to serve the best interests of the state. As individuals they stood to profit nothing from it, and we remember that Tiberius was ready to contribute of his own property to procure its success. The Gracchi were never guilty of self-seeking, and we must admire them for devoting their most serious thought and most energetic activity to the service of the state. It was deplorable that in the Rome of their day so few others could be found ready to match their devotion to the welfare of the people. We can only lament the reckless impatience—amounting almost to hysteria—

with which they faced any delay in their plans. As Sallust writes: in "their ardor of victory, there was not sufficient prudence."[8] It was their imprudence—their desire to effect sweeping changes in a hurry—that finally denied them the victory they sought.

James Madison in *The Federalist Papers,* number 45, wrote: "The public good, the real welfare of the great body of the people, is the supreme object to be pursued." This statement might stand as the motto of the Gracchi, and they understood that governments should be judged by their fitness for attaining that object. But the problem is not to be so easily solved. To begin with, what is the public good and how is it to be determined? If the Roman Senate admittedly was incapable of achieving the public good, was the Roman Assembly any better fitted for the job? Were the Gracchi themselves infallible in their opinions?

Accepting the public good as a moral and desirable end, people then ask, how is it to be attained? What must be done to produce "the real welfare of the great body of the people?" What were the means employed by the Gracchi? First, they resorted to demagoguery, an emotional appeal to the masses. They ignored the Senate; they scorned constitutional restraints; they relied on the strength of the mob and overrode the minority. Second, they nourished bad feelings between classes and permitted (if they did not advocate) a recourse to violence to reach their goals. It soon became apparent, for example, that Caius' proteges—the knights— were no better men than the senators whom they were to overthrow, and justice was as shamelessly sold by juries of knights as by juries of senators. It is doubtful if policies adopted only following street-fights are surely the most conducive to the public good. Third, and here we speak of Caius, to relieve the immediate physical need of the populace, he introduced the corn-dole. Buying the votes of the mob by wholesale bribery opened the road to moral degradation. The forced cut in grain prices secured the final ruin of the independent Italian farmers. The reduction to pauperism of the masses in Rome both demoralized them and fatally injured the republic. From this time on, the mob would not beg for bread; it would demand bread as its right, and the state's obligation. No government could survive without heeding this demand.

Not many of the supporters of the Gracchi were notable for wisdom or stability. The youthful idealism of the brothers blinded them to the true character of the city populace, and they totally misjudged the loyalty and the competence of the Assembly. "Those who build on the people build on mud" when the people they choose to rely on are precisely the most selfish, narrow-minded, unsubstantial, and unreasoning element in the population. Could Caius expect such a crowd to be anything but fickle? The Assembly had neither the ability of intellect nor the uprightness of character to be the chief agency in the reform of Rome.

We can acclaim the Gracchi for their sincere interest in people and sympathy for their unhappy plight. But then we must ask, what was really needed for the reform of Roman life and the strengthening of the citizenry? Within the crowded confines of a great city social classes cannot constantly quarrel with each other, seeking selfish advantage. They must live side by side, in mutual support, with some concept of common needs, of unity of purpose, of civic pride. From the constitutional standpoint, the Senate and Assembly must be able to share the responsibility of government, working together, not obstructing each other. There was need for both educated leadership and firm popular support. A sound system must be devised for the administration of the provinces. Ideally the governing body should be representative of the needs of the varying parts of the empire; at the very least, it must be well informed as to local situations and desires and anxious to satisfy them. It must be subject neither to the caprice of a city mob nor to the unchecked avarice of magistrates. The economy should be reorganized so that increased supply of necessities and lower prices for them would raise the standard of living for many people rather than plunge them into abject poverty. Trade should benefit from the expansion of the market and provide opportunities for the development of new occupations like sheep-raising and for the profitable diversification of employment.

In their thinking about the woes of their times and possible remedies for them, did the Gracchi penetrate to the core of the problems facing Rome? Did they seek to accommodate the interests of several groups in a program that would be advantageous to all? Or did they look for scapegoats, who could be blamed for the "whole sorry mess"? Did they seek to obliterate evil-doers—senators with limited vision, capitalists with unlimited greed? With the obliteration of these wicked elements in the population, did they expect to be able to give a plot of land to each unemployed city-dweller and transform him back into an industrious farmer?

Can we then dismiss the Gracchi as naive fools or would-be tyrants? Should we discount the authority of Plutarch? He described them both as valiant and just, industrious and generous, eloquent and large-minded, and wrote "they might have rivaled the best of the Roman commanders if they had not died so young."9 Did they aim more at personal power than at the reconstruction of the state? We have identified the problems Rome was facing as being those of centralized control of an empire and rational reorganization of its economy. Were not these problems of an order and a magnitude not experienced, not even imagined, in previous generations? In trying to cure the ills of their day, the Gracchi were brave and patriotic, and they made an effort when others, more self-centered and cynical, sat idly by. In the Gracchi we can find "right and wrong, fortune and misfortune, inextricably blended."[10]

10. Aftermath: an unhappy century

Shakespeare's words, in *Julius Caesar,*
"The evil that men do lives after them,
The good is oft interred with their bones,"
have been applied to the Gracchi. Their attempts at reform finally accomplished little and were discarded, while the deterioration of the Republic accelerated. The knights proved as dishonest and as avaricious as the senators, and the law courts remained corrupt. The Agrarian Law was gradually abandoned, large estates grew larger, and the number of unemployed multiplied. Overseas colonization was given up and Junonia deserted. The Asian provinces were so devastated by the new method of tax-farming that in 88 B.C. every single Roman citizen within their borders was murdered in retaliation for the tax-collectors' extortions. The Italians were not given the rights of citizens until in 89 B.C. Rome had to accede to their demands in order to halt the disastrous Social War. The Senate never regained absolute control of the state, and the Assembly was equally unable to provide effective government. There remained, from the Gracchan innovations, the corn-dole. No government dared revoke it, even though the expense of it always mounted, because its recipients spoke with an ever-louder voice in Roman politics.

It might have been best if the Gracchi had been set down as failures and forgotten as impractical dreamers. Scoffing at the dangers besetting the Republic, the Romans refused to pursue their high aims. It was tragic that the citizens could not trust and follow these honest and sincere brothers as genuine reformers. Perhaps it was more tragic that they learned the wrong lessons from the careers of the Gracchi. They remembered all too well the wicked means to which the Gracchi had foolishly seen fit to resort—bribery, class warfare, mob violence. Future demagogues, less noble of purpose than the Gracchi, might use these means for less desirable ends.

This danger was realized in later Roman history. The precedents established by the Gracchi were followed, with results fatal to the Republic. Republican theory calls for the people of a state to govern themselves under certain laws and by certain principles on which they agree. Tiberius and Caius were one-man rulers. Their power over the state was based on mob-favor, not on law. Their will became law overnight if they could carry the mob with them.

Under such a regime no property, no person is secure. Men do not govern themselves, they are the pawns of a popular tyrant. Popularity must be sought among the many. The Gracchi assumed that the interests of the rich and the poor were of necessity opposed, that what helped one must automatically harm the other. Their measures were designed to benefit the many poor at the expense of the few rich. To gain the favor of the proletariat they earned the hatred of the capitalists. They introduced a definite economic bias in political thinking. The line they drew so clearly between rich and poor became a deep and lasting cleavage. Never again were the two factions able to agree on a single policy. Popular sovereignty was meaningless when proletariat and aristocracy were bitterly competing for supremacy, which each hoped to use for the destruction of the power of the other class.

We should take note of three "firsts" in Roman history which were occasioned by the Gracchan efforts at reform. The overriding of Octavius' veto by Tiberius, followed by the violent assault on the sacred person of a tribune, was the first direct blow against the republican constitution. It can be called the beginning of the end of the Republic, for when once an act has succeeded in disregard of its constitutionality, there is no logical point at which law-breaking may be stopped. The fighting in the streets that attended Tiberius' effort to be re-elected tribune was the first time in almost 400 years that a party dispute had resulted in bloody conflict between Roman citizens. It foreboded settlement of political issues by the sword rather than by the ballot-box. Putting a price on the life of Caius was the first time that head-money had ever been offered for a political opponent. In the future it might not be safe to lose a political argument; the winner of the most votes might find it convenient to dispose permanently of his temporarily defeated rival. Defiance of the constitution, party battles, political murder—all became common techniques after the Gracchi were dead. The worst of it was that men grew more and more ready to justify such crimes on the pretext that there were committed on behalf of "the public good".

The Gracchi had set out to re-create a healthy, prosperous, and democratic Roman state. Instead, their activities touched off a century of civil conflict, marked by increasing violence and lawlessness, which left Rome hopelessly divided and weak. This perversion of noble intentions is an example of history's irony, which was not lost on Alexander Hamilton. In the first of *The Federalist Papers* he wrote:

> . . . A dangerous ambition more often lurks behind the specious mask of zeal for the rights of the people than under the forbidding appearance of zeal for the firmness

and efficiency of government. History will teach us that the former has been found a much more certain road to the introduction of despotism than the latter, and that of those men who have overturned the liberties of republics, the greatest number have begun their career by paying an obsequious court to the people, commencing demagogues and ending tyrants.

The accusation of courting popularity for the purpose of establishing despotism may not justly be leveled against either of the Gracchi. But many of the ready inheritors of their evil legacy of immoral means were guilty of just this duplicity. For a brief period each of the Gracchi had been the undisputed dictator of Rome. The effect of their careers was to start a trend toward one-man rule—acceptable, even essential, in times of crisis but now to become customary in normal times—which was to destroy the Roman Republic in the 1st century B.C.

Generals of senatorial rank were unable to defeat the ambitious renegade, Jugurtha of Numidia, and utterly failed to repel the barbarians who threatened dangerous inroads in Northern Italy. Jugurtha was brought to Rome in chains under the consulship of Marius, the ill-educated son of a farmer whom the patricians despised as a "new man". Marius then won decisive victories over the Celtic and Germanic tribesmen at Aquae Sextiae and Vercellae. As the price of his success, he reorganized the Roman army, replacing conscripted citizens with professional mercenaries. The soldiers swore loyalty to the commander, not to the state, and they were dependent for their pay on the booty and the land grants the commander could secure for them. The army thus became the tool to work the private will of the commander, and Marius used it to procure his election as consul of Rome no less than seven times.

A competition between Marius and the aristocratic Sulla for the command in a war against Mithridates of Pontus developed into fierce civil war. Its ravages completed the destruction of Italian agriculture and left the whole economy hopelessly unbalanced, with taxes uncollected and expenditures made only for military purposes. Rome, the once-inviolate capital, was degraded into the target of attack by the two generals leading their private armies. When Sulla finally won, he introduced proscription, the wholesale murder of the popular leaders by the hired gangsters of the aristocratic faction and the confiscation of all their property.

What one party had done, another might do. Hatred and fear spread throughout the citizenry of Rome. Two new elements had been introduced into Roman politics—the permanent army, replacing the old citizen levies, and the permanent commander-in-chief, replacing the old annually-chosen consuls. At first these

elements complicated the political scene. Soon they came to dominate it, as the traditional magistracies and the votes of the people
alike were powerless to stand before them. In 70 B.C. two new
victorious generals overthrew the conservative constitution by which
Sulla had hoped to restore senatorial prestige and privilege. Pompey,
the conqueror of the Spanish rebel Sertorius, and Crassus, the
victor over the slave-leader Spartacus, marched their armies to
Rome to overawe the populace and effect their joint election to
the consulate.

In the course of the following decade the regular government proved totally unable to prevent the depredations of Mediterranean pirates on Roman commerce or bring to a favorable
conclusion the war that was dragging on in the East against Pontus.
With wild clamor, the popular faction called for the grant of
supreme command and absolute power to a strong man who
could "do the job". Passed by enormous majorities—despite the
unconstitutionality of their grants of sweeping authority—the
Grabinian Law gave Pompey the *imperium* against the pirates
and the Manilian Law gave Pompey the *imperium* against Mithridates.

Senate and Assembly both had abdicated their responsibilities. The Republic had ceased to function except in name. The
people had cried out for one man to save them, to give them the
leadership they could not and would not give themselves. Marius,
Sulla, Pompey, followed each other as absolute dictators, and
there would be more in the succession. We can look back now and
see that Tiberius and Caius Gracchus were the first names on the
list of these "saviors of the state".

Chapter III

IVLIVS CAESAR

ITALY — HEART OF THE REPUBLIC
1ST CENTURY B.C.

ALPS

Ticino
Mediolanum
Placentia
Po

Rubicon

Lucca

APENNINES

Arretium

Tiber

ADRIATIC

SEA

Rome
Ostia

Beneventum
Capua
Cumae
Pompeii
Brundisium
Tarentum

SICILY

Thapsus x

JULIUS CAESAR—FROM REPUBLIC TO DICTATORSHIP

> ". . . on his choice depends
> The safety and the health of this whole state."
> —*Hamlet*

At the beginning of 45 B.C. Julius Caesar is said to have asked one of his friends: "Who can have any interest in compassing my death? Surely my life is the only guarantee of peace and security."[1] His statement was true. Rome owed a great deal to Julius Caesar. For the first time since the disturbed days of the Gracchi, peace seemed assured both inside and outside Roman territory, and business was expanding on a wave of prosperity.

1. Rome flourishes under Caesar's rule

From the fierce struggle for supremacy between the two greatest men of Rome, which had reached its climax in 49, Caesar had emerged victorious over his rival Pompey. Then he had crushed Pompey's adherents in Africa and Spain; he had pacified Egypt and established a secure eastern boundary for the empire on the Tigris-Euphrates River. He had earlier extended Roman sway into the remote districts of Spain. He had put down revolts in Gaul and repelled the Germanic invaders. He had penetrated beyond the Rhine and across the English Channel. The orator Cicero, no friend to Caesar, could say: "Nature piled the Alps to be a rampart to Italy . . . . Now let them sink into the earth, for beyond those mountain peaks as far as the extremest verge of the ocean there is nothing left for Italy to fear."[2] Rome was free from danger from abroad because of Caesar's military prowess.

Caesar went on to use his supremacy for the benefit of Rome. Because of his ability as a wise and just administrator, conditions within the empire were good. He seized executive power from the grasping but feeble Senate and concentrated it in his own hands. He found solutions for the problems which had disrupted the state for a hundred years: provincial misgovernment, extortionate taxes, corrupt courts, rioting in the capital. Using his fertile brain and strong will, Caesar saw to it that all classes should enjoy their just rights and their fair share in the returning prosperity of the state. He was tolerant of racial minorities. He sent out able officials to administer the provinces; they were the beginnings of a responsible, professional civil service, and they answered to Caesar for any oppression or embezzlement. He abolished tax-farming in Asia. Thenceforth, taxes were to be levied at a rate fixed in advance and to be collected by local authorities.

Citizens overburdened with debts found their obligations reduced to reasonable proportions, while creditors were satisfied that the debts were not completely canceled. The number of people receiving the government dole was limited to 150,000, a reduction of more than one half. Perhaps 100,000 others were moved to colonies outside of Italy, and a board was created to secure suitable homes for discharged veterans. The 6th Legion, for instance, was settled at Arles, in Gaul. Caesar honored Arles by declaring it a Roman city. He favored its commercial and cultural growth at the expense of nearby Marseilles which, in the civil wars, had made the error of shutting its gates in his face.[3]

Many men who needed work were able to find jobs because of a new law requiring large landholders to employ at least one freeman for every two slaves on their estates. The old Gracchan proposal that the state should assume legal title to all land in the empire not distributed by special acts was carried out, and the state was now able to afford assistance to agriculture and commerce. The calendar was corrected, to make it conform more closely to the actual seasons of the year. The colonies and provincial cities were urged to imitate the new code of laws written for the city of Rome, making provision for traffic control and street-cleaning and a police force under the supervision of a city prefect. Caesar was attentive enough to the needs of Rome, and to his own reputation, to make sure that his new measures were diligently and honestly executed and obeyed.

Plutarch says that because "Caesar was born to do great things and had a passion for honor, [he had] ideas of still greater actions and a desire for new glory."[4] Because of Caesar's foresight, projects were sketched for assuring the security and improving the conditions of the empire. Caesar was planning, perhaps to overrun Germany, more surely to subdue the troublesome Parthians to the East. Rome itself was to be physically and intellectually rejuvenated. A building program was to include a new Forum. A commission headed by Varro was to organize public libraries;

leading men of science and philosophy were to be attracted to the capital from Athens and Alexandria. Off-shore obstacles were to be removed and Rome's own port of Ostia deepened. The Tiber was to be dredged so that ships might proceed upriver to the capital. Lands around Rome were to be re-claimed by draining the marshes. Plans were laid for re-opening the famous Corinthian Canal for the aid of commerce and irrigation.

Caesar's program involved benefits for all the inhabitants of the empire—the sea-captain and the merchant, the farmer and the laborer, the small business man and the debtor, the scholar and the soldier, the citizen and the provincial. As Caesar realized, there was no one but him with the vision and the energy to put the program into effect.

2. Caesar's early career

Born probably in 102 B.C., the year Marius turned back the Teutones at Aquae Sextiae, Caesar was brought up in a Rome divided, as Mommsen describes it, into the world of beggars and the world of the rich.[5] The poor and the unemployed were most truly represented by the army; the arrogant, but weakening, Senate spoke for the rich. The individual leader, ambitious for fame, might ultimately need the consent of the Senate to give his deeds legality but he was basically dependent on the support of the army. We have noted that the army was the means by which both the great radical Marius and the great conservative Sulla maintained themselves in power.

Caesar's family was old and esteemed—the Julian tribe traced its descent from Venus—and of moderate wealth. A position of prominence seemed destined for Julius, but as a youth he showed no real desire for the fame of a public career. He chose rather to play the role of "a young man about town", spending money freely in pursuit of entertainment, accumulating prodigious debts. He preferred the company of ladies to that of statesmen. His tastes were intellectual and aesthetic, and he posed as a cultured patron of the arts. He was really a connoisseur of pleasure in all its forms. He was employed once on a diplomatic mission to the King of Bithynia, but it was extended into a pleasure jaunt and did Caesar's reputation no good.

Beneath a frivolous exterior, as a matter of fact, Caesar was developing traits of courage and strength and determination. Seized by Adriatic pirates, he first persuaded them to double his ransom. They thought he was joking when he vowed that he would soon punish them. After his friends had raised the money and bought his freedom, however, Caesar collected a force, captured the pirates while they were enjoying the fruits of his release, and promptly crucified them all.

More praiseworthy was Caesar's devotion to his first wife. She was Cornelia, daughter of Cinna, the successor of Marius. When Sulla took Rome and commenced his purge of the popular party, he had no particular grudge against Caesar. He was willing to pardon the young man and possibly enlist him as a supporter, but Caesar must first show his allegiance by discarding Cornelia. This he refused flatly to do, and finally an irritated Sulla placed his name on the list of the proscribed. But good fortune blessed Caesar. The gangster who came to murder him proved susceptible to a bribe, and with $2,000 which he luckily had at hand Caesar bought his life. When Cornelia soon after died, Caesar broke tradition by pronouncing a funeral oration over his young wife, in which he took pains to exalt the memory of the Marian party.

In the decade of the 70's Caesar began to show some interest in the service of the state. Such a course was natural, almost obligatory, for a man of his status, and his mother had ambitions for him. Furthermore, a life of leisure was growing boring, and politics offered him a challenge, like a new game in which he could display his skill. He secured election in 74 to the college of pontiffs, much to the horror of the older, more conservative candidates for this honorary religious office. The next year he was a military tribune, a post that actually required no knowledge of warfare. Caesar began gradually to awaken to the possibilities a political career could open to him. The mass of the people lacked leadership. The tribune Licinius, speaking to the Assembly, explained how they had been deceived into accepting the loss of their liberties: "All those who were elected to defend your rights have used their influence and authority against you. . . . In our civil wars neither side has fought for anything but to enslave you. . . . Your power of suffrage which formerly gave you leaders now merely gives you masters. . . . I implore you not to start changing the names of things to suit your own cowardly spirit by calling servitude tranquillity. If crime triumphs over right and honor, tranquillity will scarcely be your lot."[6] Backed by the favor of an aroused people, a man might make quite a name for himself.

His easy manner, his open friendliness to all, his courtesy, attracted the public to Caesar, and his reputation as a wastrel and rake rather charmed than scandalized them. The historian Dio accused him of capitalizing on his affability and of dissimulating the plans he was already laying for future despotism: "No one resigned himself more promptly than Caesar to courting and flattering the least esteemed people. . . . Little did he care if he had to lower himself for the moment, provided that his abasement would make him powerful later on."[7] We may doubt if Caesar yet had any serious designs for the future, agreeing at the same time that he was learning the skills of the clever politician. When he was elected quaestor, or treasurer, for Spain for 68, it was obvious that here was a man who could win votes.

Whether fully apparent or not to Caesar, the potential advantages of having a man on their side with a real ability to gain and keep the favor of the multitude were apparent to some of his contemporaries. Crassus, particularly, was anxious to build up a popular following by which to counterbalance the military reputation of Pompey, with whom he had been in constant disagreement during their joint consulship in 70 B.C. It was Crassus, the richest man in Rome, who shouldered the enormous burden of Caesar's debts so that Caesar might leave Rome and take up his task in Spain.

A taste of success, and this easily gained, whetted Caesar's appetite for more. Two stories are told illustrative of his growing ambition and perhaps of a growing awareness of his more-than-normal capacity. Passing through a mediocre town on his way across the Alps, he remarked to a friend, "I had rather be the first among these fellows than the second man in Rome." When in Cadiz he saw a statue of Alexander, he wept. "Do you not think that I have cause to weep," he asked his companions, "when I consider that at my age Alexander had conquered the whole world, while I have done nothing worth remembering?"[8]

Returning from Spain, Caesar in 65 held the office of aedile, in which he was responsible for the public games and gladiatorial shows. He was careful far to surpass all his predecessors. He decorated the buildings in the Forum, sponsored theatrical performances, and provided bountiful public feasts. On one occasion, according to Plutarch, he arranged for 320 pairs of gladiators to meet in single combat. Suetonius says he was preparing for still more but was restrained by an emergency decree limiting the number of gladiators an individual could keep in the city. These gorgeous spectacles for the diversion of the crowd enhanced Caesar's reputation as the friend of the people but dangerously augmented his debts. In 63 he became, paradoxically enough, pontifex maximus, head of the state religion. His motivation, we may believe, was more political than spiritual. This was the year of Cicero's consulate and of Catiline's conspiracy. It will be well for us to take a look at the current state of affairs.

3. The problem of government

Both in design and in actuality, the government of Rome was inadequate to the needs of a world-empire. Indeed, most Romans still refused to admit that they possessed an empire; they were at heart city-dwellers and they imagined their problems to be local. Exemplifying the narrow outlook of his fellow Romans, Cicero wrote: "In the bustle of life at Rome it is almost impossible to attend to what goes on in the provinces."9

The long-established political institutions of the Republic were not adaptable to the task of ruling extensive subject territories because they had been created for the administration of a city and the land surrounding it. In the ancient city-state, limited both in area and in numbers of people, population and power centered naturally in the city. The Roman population had long been divided into two chief groups. People of standing and property usually held the elective offices and then became senators. Government policies were normally set by decrees of the Senate. This body had often demonstrated courage, patriotism, and wisdom in the face of crises produced by external threats. Under senatorial rule Rome had managed to expand its realm and to remain firm and confident even in the presence of the all-conquering Hannibal. The solid middle classes of Rome—tradesmen, craftsmen, free laborers—had particular interests of their own: protection of their rights as citizens, fair trial in the law courts, just taxation, careers open to men of talent and enterprise. On occasion the people came together in the Assembly to vote the basic "laws of the land". At other times they depended on their tribunes to veto senatorial decrees which were obviously damaging to popular needs or desires.

Cicero praised highly the "mixed government" of Rome that had developed in the course of centuries. As he described it in his *Republic,* the magistrates exercised sufficient power, and the men of rank had sufficient influence, while the people in general retained liberty. What was desired, as Cicero saw it, was a harmony of interests and a cooperation of social classes. The wise Senate, representing merit and experience, should govern with the approval of the people, who have final power, in order to produce what all citizens wish for—"public tranquillity and private self-respect."10

By the first century B.C., however, as even Cicero had to admit, the character of both major segments of the Roman population had sadly deteriorated. With dangers from abroad declining and with new opportunities for profiteering arising in the provinces, the aristocrats sought primarily for easy chances to amass personal fortunes and to enlist crowds of clients who would obediently do their bidding and promote their reputations. Most of the aris-

CICERO

tocracy had long since given up any feeling of responsibility for
the welfare of the state. The senators seemed anxious only to maintain unchanged the traditional forms of government, to enhance
their privileges, to keep the common people in their place, and to
do as they pleased. They were unwilling to serve the state unless
thereby they could serve their personal advantage. "The fishpond
brigade," even Cicero scornfully called them; are they "such fools
as to think if the state is overthrown they can keep their fish-
ponds?"[11]

While the ability of the senators was vitiated by their
selfishness and their sense of duty by their wealth, the equites, or
upper middle class, had more to work for but seemed able to think
only of money. Both these orders were indifferent to the common
people, whom Cicero spoke of as "the wretched starveling mob,
the bloodsuckers of the treasury, the dregs of humanity."[12] The
populace had lost their independence of mind and spirit along
with their honest employment. The large proportion of slaves in
Rome—almost a third of the city's 750,000 population—enforced
a very low wage scale for free labor. The daily wage was one
denarius, or about twenty cents. It is no wonder that the existence
of the average man was wretched. His chief purpose in life came
to be self-indulgence. He called ever more insistently on the state
for free food to keep him from starvation and free entertainments
to distract him from his misery.

With the city population thus divided into selfish and jealous
factions, the just and efficient government even of Rome and its
immediate environs proved to be beyond the capacity of the people.
In the city, instead of stability, there were riots in the streets;
instead of concord among the people, there was cut-throat rivalry;
instead of mature policy, the caprices of the moment directed the
government.

Unaware of the decay of the population, the acute problems
of their agrarian economy, the threats from discontented slaves
and ambitious foreigners, the people of Rome lived in a state of
unreality and irresponsibility. The Assembly, for instance, gave no
fair representation to the large number of people who had become
citizens since the Social War. There were no proper political parties. A party, as we know it today, is organized under a recognized
hierarchy of responsible leaders; its members are agreed upon a
program of action. A party combines the thinking and efforts and
resources of many individuals to achieve a common purpose, to
contest elections, and to administer the laws. But, in Rome, neither
the "optimates", the select minority, nor the "populares", theoretically the party of the people, had any permanent organization

or concerted program. Both parties tended to fall under the domination, for a time, of an aggressive leader. Whether old aristocrats
or "new men", these leaders vied with each other in proposing
policies that would win popular favor. Seldom were they interested
in constructive, long-term reforms. For their party was really nothing more than a band, or even gang, of men who felt that their
own selfish ambitions could best be served if they attached themselves to a particular leader. In such a party there were few, if
any, bonds of shared purpose or loyalty; nor was there any real
democracy.

Where political parties were patched together and public
offices were sought and used for private gain, it is not surprising
that the typical inhabitant of Rome developed little political con-
sciousness. What did it matter to him which leader was for the time
being in control of the government? Rather than seek responsibility,
he turned away from political problems he did not understand. His
general apathy was interrupted only occasionally—by a proposed
distribution of land or money or by the opportunity to participate
in a mass demonstration.

Meanwhile, the leader, not truly representative of anyone
but himself, planned to manipulate the mob or use the party as
a weapon to force open the gates of success. Such a leader courted
personal popularity by providing immediate benefits or by promising progressive reforms. But he usually forgot his promises once he
had been voted into office. Unhappy conditions in Rome played
into the hands of such demagogues.

Just before Cicero's consulate, times had been bad. The
currency had fluctuated widely in value; debtors had refused to
meet their obligations and the government had permitted a 95%
repudiation; there had been a slave revolt; and business and industry were brought to a standstill. Catiline, disgruntled by his failure
to be elected consul, felt that conditions were ripe for him to lead
an insurrection against the regular government and to establish
a popular dictatorship. Caesar and Crassus have both been suspected
of complicity in the plot. As often happens, details leaked out.
Acting with great energy and speed, Cicero exposed the plot in
the Senate and rallied the nobles and the knights in the face of
danger. The conspirators left Rome and were defeated in battle.
Catiline was killed and a number of his chief supporters captured.

What should be done with the conspirators? The leading
citizens had been brought to a state of panic. Catiline was a bloody
revolutionary. Had his plot succeeded, the rich and the noble would
have seen their property and their lives forfeit to popular vengeance.
One after another the senators voted that it was legal for the consul
to impose the death penalty in such a case. Caesar demurred. The

captives had acted illegally, but their guilt did not amount to treason. They should be punished for reasons of state, not put to death to gratify personal prejudice. His speech is illustrative of his common sense: "Men who deliberate on difficult questions ought to be free from hatred and friendship, anger and pity. When these feelings stand in the way, the mind cannot easily discern the truth, and no mortal man has ever yet served his passions and his best interests. When you apply your intellect, it prevails. If passion possesses you, it holds sway and the mind is impotent."[13] Throughout his career Caesar was capable of this cool objectivity, but none of his contemporaries was. The captives were executed. With the fear of revolution removed, Cicero's hoped-for "harmony of the orders" broke down. Cato and the senators, scornful of the knights, refused to permit a much-needed renegotiation of a tax-contract, and the knights faced ruin. The classes fell again to quarreling and recrimination. Cicero's devotion to the tradition of political liberty won him the title of "Father of His Country" but did not relieve the economy misery of the masses.

The year after the conspiracy, Caesar was a praetor, or provincial governor. Pompey returned to Italy, having successfully concluded the war in the East with his victory over Mithridates of Pontus and the annexation of Syria and Palestine. It might be possible, thought Cicero and some others, for this famous general to inspire the Senate with new patriotism and direct it in a reformation of the Republic. So as not to appear a tyrant, Pompey dismissed his army on reaching Italy and went up alone to Rome. The Senate thereupon insolently refused to ratify his treaties, and his grants of land to his veterans, repudiating his leadership. Bitter at his rebuff, Pompey withdrew from public life.

This same year Rome was shocked by a scandal perpetrated by the young scapegrace Clodius, who gained entrance to a meeting of the Vestal Virgins at the house of Pompeia, the wife of Caesar the chief priest. The jury was so corrupt that Clodius was declared not guilty of sacrilege. Caesar divorced Pompeia, with the haughty statement, "Caesar's wife must be above reproach,"[14] and then went off to serve another year in Spain.

4. Developing ambitions: The First Triumvirate

Back for the second time from Spain, where he had gained some minor military successes, Caesar came to Rome, which he described as "the sewer of Romulus". The old Roman morality, or sense of duty, existed no longer, except in the mind of Cato. Crime and dishonor could go unpunished; poverty alone was contemptible. Every man was out for himself. Each of the leading men of Rome was nursing his pet desire. Caesar wanted to celebrate a triumph and to be elected consul. Pompey wanted recognition for his eastern victory and acceptance of his peace arrangements. Crassus wanted to extend his activities to a field larger than the money-markets of Rome. And Cicero wanted to preserve the dominance of the Senate. With Caesar probably the instigator, negotiations were opened for possible cooperation among them. Cicero decided that the Senate would be risking its independence by collaborating with such strong individual leaders; so he withdrew from the negotiations. Then, according to Plutarch, it was Caesar who proposed an alliance among the other three. With Caesar as consul, backed by Pompey's control over the soldiers and Crassus' inexhaustible resources, they might effectually smother the power of Cicero and the old guard.

This proposal brought together the ex-enemies, Pompey and Crassus, and with Caesar they formed the First Triumvirate. Cato was quick to perceive the danger in this new arrangement, but he had antagonized so many people that his influence was negligible. Cicero was suspicious of the designs of Caesar, but his vanity and sarcasm had alienated many potential adherents to his cause. There was no real opposition to the formation of the Triumvirate because its organizer, Caesar, was a "specialist in human relations." Like no one else in his day, Caesar had the supreme gift of the politician—the ability to sense the feelings and adopt the demands of the majority of the people. This also meant that of the Three Men Caesar was the most widely popular as well as the most skillful. Men only turned to Crassus when they needed a loan. Pompey had insulted too many people by his sneers at their inferiority and by his sullenness when crossed. Caesar alone had nothing serious against him. Furthermore, he naturally assumed the key role in the Triumvirate because, as consul, he was the chief executor of their plans.

There was nothing dreadfully radical in the new program. Like Tiberius Gracchus, Caesar rode roughshod over the objections of his colleague as consul, Bibulus, in order to put through a new agrarian law, to legalize Pompey's grants and treaties, and to rescue the knights from financial loss in the tax-contract. These measures he designed mainly to ease the chief causes of discontent within Rome, to keep each group from the desperation that might breed open revolt against the state. The Three Men disregarded the cost to the treasury involved in their measures and supported Clodius' bill to make the corn-dole absolutely free. This was later estimated to have cost the state 20% of its annual income.

The real danger to traditional government lay not in their

acts but in the very conception of the Triumvirate, which transferred authority and responsibility from the people's legal representatives to a junta of three men, exempt from popular control.
The two parties, headed by Pompey and Crassus, were merged, so
that there was no effective opposition. On Caesar's part, says
Plutarch, it was "a mischievous and subtle intrigue. For he well
knew that opposite parties or factions in a commonwealth, like
passengers in a boat, serve to trim and balance the unsteady motions
of power there, whereas if they combine and come all over to one
side, they cause a shock which will be sure to overset the vessel
and carry down everything." As Cato perceived, it was not the
later disagreement between Pompey and Caesar that brought
calamities to Rome; it was this extra-constitutional alliance of 60
B.C. "that gave the greatest blow to the commonwealth."[15]

Just as Caesar was the real originator of the Triumvirate,
so was he the main beneficiary from the arrangement. Its popular
reforms were carried in Caesar's consulate, and for the first time
Caesar acted on an equal footing with the older leaders. He combined the strengths and policies of Pompey and Crassus under his
direction. "Out of the three parties he set up one irresistible power
which utterly subverted the government both of Senate and people.
Not that he made either Pompey or Crassus greater than they were
before, but by their means made himself greatest of all."[16]

Thus we see that the formation of the Triumvirate was a
crucial event in Caesar's life. It elevated him to a position of the
first rank and it enabled him to make provisions for the future.
He had come to realize, in his government of Spain and in his
collaboration with Pompey, that nothing was as potent in Rome
as armed strength. He had also discovered that among the traditional orders of the Roman population he could not find trust-
worthy supporters of his policies. The aristocracy was too blindly
selfish, the knights were too exclusively interested in finance, the
people in general were too unintelligent and inexperienced in
affairs. To form a party of his own, Caesar must find employment
and rewards for men of ability from all classes. Their own success
in life must depend upon the success of their chief, so that they
would be bound to his cause both by loyalty and by self-interest.
In Caesar's day the obvious method to attract a personal following
and to make it a power in the state was to take command of an
army and to lead it to victories.

When the Three Men laid plans for the years ahead, they
decided each to take charge of a part of the empire, in which he
should have unchallenged supremacy. Command of the East was
given to Crassus that he might make his military reputation; command of Spain with its mineral wealth was given to Pompey;

Caesar was satisfied with the command of Gaul. It would appear he had accepted the least profitable command, but we may notice that his province lay closest to Rome, which maintained no army of its own.

5. *"All Gaul is divided into three parts . . ."*

The historian Sallust was an enthusiastic supporter of Caesar, who had appointed him to important political posts. He gives us this favorable view of his patron, shortly before his departure for Gaul: "Caesar was esteemed for his benefactions and lavish generosity. . . . his gentleness and compassion. . . . [He] gained glory by giving, helping, and forgiving . . . [as] a refuge for the unfortunate. . . . His good nature was admired. . . . Caesar had schooled himself to work hard and sleep little, to devote himself to the welfare of his friends and neglect his own, to refuse nothing which was worth the giving. He longed for great power, an army, and a new war to give scope to his brilliant merit."[17]

The decade of the 50's introduces to us a new Caesar—the man of action, the man with relentless "drive", the consummate commander-in-chief. His first entrance onto the stage of his new governorship was typical: hearing in Rome of the threatened invasion of Gaul by the Helvetii, Caesar traveled 700 miles in eight days—a phenomenal journey for those times—in order to take personal command of his forces.[18] It seems clear that Caesar's career in Gaul was motivated primarily by his desire to build a solid basis for power. This involved, first, creating an army with its leaders devoted to their general and, second, keeping this army available to march down and dominate Italy.

His campaigns in Gaul won Caesar a place among the great generals of history and gained him an army wholly responsive to his will. His means of making himself popular with his men were normal enough: he shared the physical hardships of the common soldiers and he appeared beside them in their posts of danger. He pleased his officers by the extreme generosity with which he distributed gold and honors among them. Caesar convinced them that his victories would benefit them rather than "feather his own nest", and thereby he won more than any amount of booty could have bought him. Caesar's real genius as a general consisted of his organizational ability—his careful attention to the details of supply, which to-day we call logistics—and of the uncanny speed with which he moved himself and masses of men. Plutarch says that he "above all men was gifted with the faculty of making the right use of everything in war, and most especially of seizing the right moment."[19] No matter how right the moment may be, you cannot take advantage of it unless you have made proper preparations and can count on the unquestioning obedience of your men.

In retrospect it becomes evident that in building his own power Caesar was also performing services of great value to the state. His victories over the Helvetii and the Belgae, his crushing of Ariovistus and Vercingetorix, consolidated the empire, Romanized the barbarians, and secured the Rhine frontier. Men will probably always debate whether or not Caesar was conscious of an imperial mission and foresaw the civilizing role of Rome, the mistress of the world. We should note several factors. His early campaigns were conducted on the extreme borders of his province so that the inhabitants of the interior should look on Rome as their protector against external foes. Once the borders were secured, the subjugation of the rest of the province should be much easier. Furthermore, he took great pains to justify his aggressions as necessary to meet threats from abroad. In Gaul Caesar acted on the principle of "aggressive defense;" he waged what we call to-day preventive war. Dio described the theory behind Caesar's tactics (and it is applicable to both his military and political careers): "We must defend ourselves not only against the actions but even against the projects of those who threaten us; we must oppose the growth of their power before it has harmed us, and we must not wait until they have injured us before we take vengeance."[20] Kill the Helvetii before they know we are their enemies; attack before your opponent is ready to fight; execute a traitor while he yet believes he is undiscovered; invade Germany before the Germans have definitely decided to invade Gaul.

The real secret of Caesar's great success in Gaul is his single-minded devotion of his faculties to the tasks he had set himself. He could adapt to unexpected circumstances without losing sight of his main goal. He could concentrate on gaining the immediate victory, without which all projects for the future might be useless. It was astonishing to many that the luxury-loving Caesar could endure the physical privations to which he was subjected, and more astonishing that he could so contentedly deprive himself of all the pleasures of the capital.

The truth of the matter is that Caesar was in his day unique in his grasp of the importance, and of the opportunities, of service away from "the hub of the universe". Cicero provides an interesting contrast. As governor of Cilicia, he wrote to his friend Atticus: "I cannot tell you how terribly I miss life in Rome and how intolerable to me is the boredom of life here." Cilicia was a far more limited field than Gaul, of course, but all Cicero could look forward to was the termination of his governorship. Again, he wrote: "The city, my dear Rufus, stick to that and live in its full light! Residence elsewhere . . . is mere eclipse and obscurity to those whose energy is capable of shining in Rome."[21] Caesar, on the other hand, made capital from his command in Gaul and insisted at the Lucca conference of the Triumvirate in 56 that his "exile" be prolonged for five years. His energy had already shone in Rome, but he was happy to let it shine for ten years in Gaul that it might later shine still more brilliantly in the capital.

For the first time in history, what went on outside Rome was of more significance for the world than any business transacted in the city. The leading men of Rome went to Lucca by the hundreds to learn the will of the man who had suffered himself to be "eclipsed" in Gaul. For Caesar did not neglect to keep himself informed of affairs in Rome. Nor did he fail to maintain agents there who might, publicly or privately, push forward the schemes he dictated to them. He was an expert in the selection of devoted and bold adherents, taking care to choose men with their fortunes to make. Cicero tacitly attests Caesar's skill as he criticizes his methods of recruiting followers: "When a man was utterly ruined by debt and in want, if he recognized in that man an audacious rascal, he most willingly admitted him into his intimacy."[22] The gangster Clodius was Caesar's right-hand man in the political turmoil of Rome. When he was killed in a street brawl with a gang of Pompey's adherents, Caesar quickly found a capable successor in Curio.

6. Tension mounts in Rome

What was happening in the rest of the Roman world while Caesar was in Gaul? First of all, the Triumvirate was disintegrating. Crassus led a great expedition against the Parthians in the East, which was to establish forever his claim to the veneration and gratitude of Rome. Instead, his army was enticed into the desert, harassed by the Parthian bowmen on horseback, and finally surrounded. The legions, paralyzed by a new type of enemy, were hopelessly defeated at Carrhae, the greatest blow to Roman prestige since the era of Hannibal. While attempting to negotiate terms for the remnants of his beaten army, Crassus was murdered.

Pompey and Caesar were left as contenders for dominance in Rome, and the only major obstacle standing in the way of either of them was the life of the other. They had already become uneasy in their collaboration, but had been kept from open enmity by their family relationship. This was provided by Julia, the daughter of whom Caesar was very fond. He had arranged her marriage to Pompey, who was sincerely devoted to her. Now Julia died, and there was nothing left to restrain the conflicting ambitions of the two remaining Triumvirs.

Meanwhile, the senatorial crowd was frantically scheming to stave off the threatened dictatorship of either of the rivals, by holding the balance of power between them. With his party, Cicero attempted to occupy a middle ground. In his speeches he flattered Caesar—"It is impossible for me not to be the friend of a man who serves his country well"[23]—but his followers grew more and more nervous at the increasing fame of Caesar's exploits in Gaul. Caesar was building his strength too well. On the other hand, the Senate was embarrassed by the continuing presence of Pompey in Rome. Instead of following custom and taking up his command in Spain, Pompey chose to send legates to administer his provinces and to stay himself in the capital. Here he handcuffed the Senate by his meddling in all political issues—especially elections. Cato severely criticized him for stirring up anarchy in order to win a monarchy for himself, but criticism could not get rid of him.

The deterioration of Roman political morality continued apace. Bad government was the order of the day. Money bribes proving ineffective, the rival factions resorted to pitched battles in the streets, like that in which Clodius was slain. The populace, demoralized by the free dole and egged on by ambitious rascals, reveled in its leisure and called for more bread and more elaborate spectacles in the arena. The maladministration of the provinces was perhaps in the long run even more scandalous and harmful than the rout at Carrhae. Even the honorable Brutus was reported to have used his official position as a cloak for collecting exorbitant interest charges. Absorbed in their petty rivalries, the politicians neglected Rome and "left the city at last without any government at all, to be carried about like a ship without a pilot to steer her."[24]

Wise men began to realize that a strong government— even one-man rule—was preferable to no government at all. Good order must be restored at all costs. "Peace is the best we can hope for now," wrote Cicero; and he saw that if Pompey and Caesar could continue in alliance they might secure peace for the people "if men will submit patiently to their domination."[25] Even Cicero was at last disillusioned as a result of the collapse of the time-honored Roman system of government with its theoretical division of powers and its supposedly concerned and thoughtful electorate. The people were too short-sighted to look after themselves and too uninformed to reach right opinions; they needed direction, and the direction could best come from a high-minded individual.

It was now that Cicero in his *Republic* was writing that more than the good-will of the optimates and the concord of all loyal citizens was required if the commonwealth was to function successfully and happily. What was needed was a virtuous and benevolent leader—a rector or moderator—who would be reasonable in the formulation of governmental policy, firm in support of his moral principles, fearless in the use of force to prevent wrong-doing, yet wise in the equal administration of justice.[26] This was a difficult prescription: it would be hard for all men to concur in any one opinion, and so the compelling power must be armed force; the wielder of this force must be motivated by *noblesse oblige*—the feeling that his power put him under obligation to those whom he controlled.

Gradually, for the leadership so desperately needed, Cicero and the Senate turned to Pompey. He was "on the spot". He boasted that "he had only to stamp his foot" and trained and ardent legions would spring from the ground to protect Italy.[27] He seemed less radical than Caesar and he enjoyed less favor with the multitude; and so to conservative elements he appeared less dangerous. Cato came to the conclusion "that any government was better than mere confusion and that . . . Pompey would deal honorably and take care of the commonwealth."[28] In 52 Pompey was made, in name, sole consul; in effect, dictator. He and the conservatives had at last struck a bargain.

7. *Caesar vs Pompey*

With Pompey sole consul, what was to become of the other Triumvir, Caesar? To him, the election of Pompey sounded illegal and was intolerable. Caesar wanted to be consul again when he left Gaul. He could not even run for consul unless he laid down his command and went to Rome. But if he gave up his *imperium*, he was sure to be arrested for improper conduct as governor before he had a chance to become consul. Caesar chafed with impatience at the legal restraints which seemed to have him caught in a maze. Sensing that they held the upper hand, Caesar's opponents in the Senate moved that he should be forced to step down at the legal expiration of his commission. But Caesar had a strong following in Rome, and he refused to resign while Pompey retained his extraordinary powers. Stalemate followed. A creature of Caesar's, the tribune Mark Antony, proposed that Pompey and Caesar should relinquish their commands simultaneously. The Assembly accepted this joyously but the Senate turned it down; and Antony, in fear for his life, fled in disguise to Caesar. Having been quite unfairly (as he thought) declared an outlaw for declining to obey the vote of the Senate, Caesar had the necessary excuse to take action. There could now be but one conclusion to the rivalry between him and Pompey—war to the death.

No high principles were at stake in the civil war that im-

mediately broke out. It was not a struggle of the Senate against
one-man rule, of the Republic trying to withstand a revolution.
It was simply a contest for supreme power between two potential
dictators, Caesar and Pompey. "Rivalry spurred them on," wrote
Lucan, "for Pompey feared that fresher exploits might dim his
past triumphs . . . while Caesar was urged on by continuous effort
and familiarity with warfare, and by fortune that brooked no
second place. Caesar could no longer endure a superior nor Pompey
an equal."29

"The object of neither is our happiness," wrote Cicero.
"Both want to be kings. . . . We can never restore our constitution
while these two are alive or with either one remaining."30 Each
of them wanted as many influential people and as much money as
possible on his side. Most of the senators decided that they would
prefer to be dominated by Pompey. Other men chose their sides
because of their personal loyalties or their hopes for lavish rewards
from their leader. Most of the dissatisfied, adventuresome, and
ambitious concluded that their best chance lay in following Caesar.
Cicero could see clearly enough that disaster was inevitable for
the believers in republican government. He wrote to Atticus: "From
a victory, among many evil results one at any rate will be the rise
of a tyrant."31 Was one faction preferable to the other?

While Cicero was never able to make a prompt and firm
decision, Caesar was, and it might have been better for Cicero
had he chosen at first to side with Caesar. For Caesar was
thoroughly prepared for the outbreak of war, whereas Pompey
was not. When the fleeing Antony reached him, Caesar was already
at the Rubicon River, the border between Gaul and Italy, with
a considerable trained army. Here on January 12, 49, Caesar
made up his mind to invade Italy and to take control of the
government at Rome which had outlawed him. Lucan puts a
florid speech in his mouth: "Here I bid farewell to peace and
outraged justice. It is thee, O Fortune, whom I follow. Away
with treaties! Let us surrender to destiny! Let war be our
judge!"32 As Suetonius less poetically reports, "The die was
cast."33

Who was this bold and accomplished man who dared to
cross the Rubicon and wage war on the Republic? Plutarch tells
us of his eloquence and affability, his tact and consideration of
other people, the splendor and munificence of his way of life.
Caesar was highly cultured; men and women both found him
charming as a companion and conversationalist. But he was also
iron-willed, contemptuous of danger, undeterred by physical hardship. He would permit no interference or delay in his plans. He

was always willing to toss aside traditions or institutions in order to accomplish his purposes.

We learn much about Caesar from Suetonius, not a great writer or profound analyst of history, but a new kind of biographer. Suetonius records human details with accuracy and gives us a vivid picture of Caesar, impressive for its mass of intimate touches. "He is said to have been tall of stature," Suetonius writes, "with a fair complexion, shapely limbs, a somewhat full face and keen black eyes." Temperate in his personal habits, he was ostentatious in dress and vain of his appearance; he tried to comb his scanty hair to conceal his embarrassing baldness, and he was always happy to wear the victor's laurel wreath.[34]

His powers of endurance and his speed of movement were alike incredible. Daring of his own person on campaign, he was cautious of the lives of his men and concerned for their well-being. Strict in discipline, he was indulgent in victory. He had gone to Gaul to enrich himself, very largely from the sale of his captives as slaves; after taking one town, he said he sold 53,000 slaves. His personal plunder, "more gold than he knew what to do with," provided "bread and circuses" and bonuses and land for his trusted soldiers. After the battle at Alesia, he gave one Gallic captive to each of his legionaries. And his exploits provided occasions for the celebrations of triumphs. "I came, I saw, I conquered," he announced after his speedy annihilation of the King of Pontus.

Whether for politics' or for mercy's sake, he was often forgiving of his Roman enemies. Conciliation of his opponents might convert them into followers, and prominent followers would lend his cause respectability. No wise political leader would choose to rule over devastated territories or disaffected citizens. But we have noted his treatment of Bibulus, which had showed that Caesar did not shrink from high-handed, unconstitutional behavior. When Bibulus attempted to obstruct Caesar's agrarian law, Caesar had him driven by force from the Forum. The fearful Bibulus thenceforth remained at home, predicting dire misfortunes, and Caesar ruled alone. He relied on the power of his personality to dominate any group or situation. His complete self-assurance was based both on the quality and versatility of his talents and on his sequence of successful encounters with less decisive rivals. But one day, Suetonius wrote, he was to grow over-fond of honors and to abuse his power, disregarding both people and laws in his arrogance.

8. Civil war

As was his habit, Caesar dumbfounded his opponents after crossing the Rubicon by the terrible speed of his movements. He allowed nothing to stand in his way. He brushed aside the Pompeian forces gathering to oppose him; he captured cities and enrolled their garrisons under his standard; he refused to be distracted from his main purpose of driving his enemy out of Italy. "Caesar moves so fast," Cicero complained, calling him "a man of frightful vigilance, rapidity, and energy."[35] Tardily aware that resistance to Caesar in Italy was impossible, Pompey resolved to withdraw to the East. Caesar advanced southward to Brundisium, arriving just too late to prevent Pompey's sailing from that port. But his failure was not crucial. Militarily speaking, Pompey was perhaps well-advised to retire to the East, where his fame would enable him to recruit very large forces. Politically, however, abandoning Italy was most unwise, for he left the capital in the hands of his enemy and the regular government at Caesar's mercy.

Nor was Caesar slow to enforce his advantage. His moral determination proved equal to his physical energy. After Pompey's departure, Caesar would have been glad to accept the willing assistance of the members of the government who had remained in Rome. At this juncture even Cicero, staunchest of defenders of the Republic and of upholders of senatorial prerogatives, wavered before declaring his allegiance. He was especially gratified by a visit Caesar paid to him at his villa. Caesar requested, if not the active support, at least the benevolent neutrality of the most eminent statesman of the day. Caesar said that he would like to avail himself of Cicero's advice, and he could expect to make political capital of Cicero's prestige. Cicero, on his side, recognized the force of Caesar's personality and glimpsed the range of his ability. He asked his friend Atticus if he understood "how clear-headed, how alert, how well-prepared" Caesar was.

Furthermore, Cicero realized that Pompey was of the same breed of potential tyrant as Caesar. Either one would overawe the Senate with his armed power and casually over-rule established laws with his authoritarian decrees. Just a few weeks before, an exasperated Cicero had criticized Pompey: He "flies before he knows from whom he is flying, or whither; he has betrayed our interests, abandoned his country. . . . He did not abandon the city because he was unable to protect it, nor Italy because he was driven from it; his idea from the first has been to stir up every land and sea, to rouse foreign princes, to bring barbarous tribes under arms into Italy, and to collect formidable armies. For some time a kind of royalty like Sulla's has been his objective."[36] Many people, like Cicero, no longer put much trust in such a Pompey.

Finally Cicero agonized his way to a decision. Personal friendship influenced him. Apparently he also concluded there was a chance for the survival of constitutional government under Pompey. Although it might be dangerous for Cicero to leave Italy, he felt he could not countenance the haughty attitudes and arbitrary actions of Caesar. So Cicero departed secretly. When he at last reached Pompey's headquarters, he would be disappointed both by the state of general unreadiness he found and by the coolness of the welcome he was accorded. But the judicious Cicero could hardly expect to be rated a potent accretion to a fighting force.

If the senators and magistrates, like Cicero, were fearful of acknowledging his leadership, Caesar would be happy to manage affairs of state by himself. The prime need, naturally, was for funds, and he demanded possession of the public treasure. The tribune Metellus protested and barred the way. Said Caesar roughly: "If what I do displeases you, leave the place. War allows no free talking. . . . You and all others who have appeared against me and are now in my power, may be treated as I please." Metellus gave in to the determined man who might more readily execute him than waste his time in argument.[37]

But the Roman state would not be secure in Caesar's grasp until Pompey's armies were defeated. First he went to Spain, Pompey's province, remarking that he was going "to defeat an army without a leader and would return to defeat a leader without an army."[38] In a rapid campaign, Caesar overcame Pompey's troops, astonishing them by setting them free on their promise not to return to Italy to fight against him, and seized Pompey's treasure. Then, after a brief stay in Rome during which he consolidated his authority, Caesar with a dangerously small force followed his enemy across the Adriatic, ordering his deputy Antony to hasten all available additional troops after him. The armies of Caesar and Pompey faced each other at Dyarrichum. Pompey struggled to organize and train his motley levies. Caesar, as usual, "dug in," attempting to hem in Pompey's larger numbers with a long line of entrenchments.

During weeks of apparent stalemate, Pompey steadily extended his fortifications so that Caesar had to stretch his investing forces more and more thinly. Early one morning Pompey mounted a fierce assault. He shattered the besieging lines and inflicted severe casualties on Caesar's legions as they were committed piecemeal to the futile combat. The situation looked desperate for Caesar. He was later to say that Pompey would have won the war that day had he known how to capitalize on his victory. Outnumbered and ill-supplied, Caesar was unable to maintain his position. Unhappily he withdrew eastward, into the hills of Thessaly.

What should Pompey do? Undoubtedly the prospect of returning unopposed to Italy and taking possession of Rome and the entire peninsula was attractive to him. To do that, however,

would mean leaving the rich resources of the Eastern Mediterranean
in the hands of Caesar, whose initiative would be unchecked and
who would one day descend on Italy with overwhelming strength.
Furthermore, it would be dishonorable of Pompey to abandon
the small army which was operating on his behalf in the back
country. Decisive in formulating Pompey's strategy, however, must
have been his clear-headed realization that his cause could never
be finally triumphant until Caesar's army was destroyed and its
leader put to death. So Pompey followed Caesar into the hills,
gradually resolving—perhaps under the pressure of his impatient
senatorial friends—that he now had a good opportunity to force
the issue.

The fateful struggle took place at Pharsalus. Caesar's
smaller force, personally devoted to their general and eager for
vengeance on their pursuers, faced Pompey's larger force of comparatively unseasoned troops, overconfident from their earlier par-
tial victory. A picked group of cohorts, which Caesar cleverly
stationed at an angle behind his right flank, routed the cavalry
charges which Pompey had counted on to carry the day. The
Pompeian infantry fought with unanticipated tenacity and skill
but finally broke before the steady pounding of Caesar's veterans.
As his footmen streamed away in disorganized flight, Pompey
rode off the field and his camp was overrun.

The battle of Pharsalus was an overwhelming victory for
Caesar. For Pompey, it proved to be the end. He fled to Egypt,
and Caesar followed to Alexandria, learning on his arrival that
Pompey had been murdered. After some desperate fighting, during
which the world-famous library was destroyed, Caesar established
his control over the disordered kingdom. Then he spent several
enjoyable months in the company of Cleopatra, its talented queen.

Pompey's followers had not given up hope of revenge for
Pharsalus. They collected a new army in North Africa, whither
Caesar pursued them. Landing from his ship, Caesar fell full-
length on the ground, but restored his companions' spirits by confidently shouting, "Africa, I possess thee." Caesar's position on the
seacoast was at first precarious, but he was aided by the division
of the enemy's forces and by his poor generalship. The battle of
Thapsus soon became a rout, and Caesar himself was unable to
stop his enraged legionaries from slaughtering their foes.

Escaping to Spain, Pompey's sons raised a new army, and it
was a tired Caesar who went there in 45 to oppose them. With
battle imminent, Caesar seems temporarily to have lost heart. He
begged the gods that he might not lose the fruit of many victories
in a single battle with mere boys. Then, when the battle began,
he plunged into the thickest fighting with a bravery bordering on

recklessness. Elsewhere he had fought for victory, but at Munda, he afterwards said, "I fought for my life."[39] The issue was long in doubt. Late in the day a column of horsemen was spied moving across the dusty field. "They fly!" shouted one of Caesar's men, and elated by that idea, his army advanced irresistibly to gain the victory. By Munda, the cause of Pompey was forever destroyed.

9. Political revolution and the reaction to it

No one could now deny that Caesar was the most remarkable of men, full of resource and vision, absolute master of his brains and his passions. By crafty plotting and daring action he had not only lived through a half-century of turbulence. He had emerged, without a rival, the master of the Roman world. To what was his success due? Partly we can say to good fortune, partly to the careful plans he had often kept concealed, but mostly to his supreme faculty for seeing clearly and grasping firmly the opportunities presented to him. Despite his long absences during his wars with Pompey and his faction, Caesar had succeeded, through Antony, in imposing his will on the government at Rome. In the Senate Cicero gave formal recognition to Caesar's predominance in the new state of affairs: "On your sole life hang the lives of us all. I mourn that while the state must be immortal, its existence should turn upon the mortal breath of a single man."[40] No one before in Roman history had wielded the power of Julius Caesar.

Cicero might praise Caesar, but he never fully understood him. He continued to express the hope that Caesar intended to re-establish a republican government. But the changes which Caesar effected in the constitution did not work the restoration of the Republic; rather they made Caesar the sole ruler, the emperor, of the world. The titles and powers of the traditional magistrates were not abolished, but the most important of them were centered in Caesar. Not satisfied to be consul, Caesar had himself declared dictator, at first for ten years, later for life. The scope of his power and the permanence of his tenure invalidated the whole system by which authority had been divided among many short-term officials. As dictator (a title formerly granted, we know, only in emergencies and for six months) his acts were not subject to the tribune's veto. As tribune, his person was made sacred and he could exercise an effective check on all popular legislation. As censor, he became supervisor of public morality and judge of the fitness of senators.

The Senate had no choice but to approve his measures; so it was reduced from a directing to an advisory body. Caesar's nominees were the successful candidates for consul and praetor, and these officials were sworn not to oppose his will. Their authority ended at the city gates in any case, for Caesar, as permanent pro-consul and *imperator*, commanded the army and was the sole executive head for all provincial affairs. To manage them, he organized a bureaucracy of men from all ranks, responsible only to Caesar. War and peace were made at his command. Appeals from the law courts might be carried to Caesar. He had personal control over the state finances and so could dispose of the treasure received from the confiscation of the vast wealth of Pompey's adherents. In all save name, Caesar was an absolute monarch.

Caesar had made himself the master of the world, and the Roman Senate had legalized his position. But he was destined to enjoy his mastery for less than a year after his final victory at Munda. Why was his power, seemingly so secure and so unquestioned, to be so suddenly overthrown?

In the first place, some Romans were not yet ready to be satisfied by a guarantee of peace and security made by an individual leader. They still resented dictatorship. Cicero, for example, although he was "always struck with astonishment at Caesar's sobriety, fairness, and wisdom"[41]—although he saw that Caesar was a 'good' dictator, yet hated the idea of dictatorship. He had warned of it when the First Triumvirate was formed: "We are tied hand and foot and no longer have spirit enough to object to our slavery, for we fear death and exile as if they were great evils, whereas compared to our abject condition they are relatively of little moment. But nobody dares say a word."[42] Now the dangers of one-man rule appeared more acute: "I see nothing to fear except the fact that when once departure has been made from law and order, one can be positive of nothing; and nothing can be guaranteed in a future which depends upon the wish, not to say the whim, of another."[43]

Did the establishment of order and the alleviation of human misery justify despotism? Cicero might be doubtful; a few others dared to say no. Cato, for instance, inflexible representative of the stern old Roman sense of duty, chose to kill himself when Utica surrendered to Caesar's army rather than to submit to a declared enemy of the state. The brave and ambitious Cassius had personal motives for hating Caesar, who had failed to procure for him the advancement in political rank that he had coveted. And the idealistic Brutus, brother-in-law of Cassius, nephew of Cato, descendant of the family which had driven the last king from Rome, proved to be Caesar's most influential opponent. Caesar had shown him great favor and perhaps considered him as his successor in power. "Whatever he wants, he wants whole-heartedly," said

Caesar of Brutus.[44] And Brutus with his whole heart disapproved of despotism. Caesar had put himself outside the law—Brutus could not be indifferent to that. Illegality must be punished. Under the old Roman code, Brutus knew, it was not only permitted, it was required, that you should kill a tyrant. Antony himself said, according to Plutarch, "that Brutus was the only man who conspired against Caesar out of a sense of the glory and the apparent justice of the action, but that all the rest rose up against the man himself from private envy and malice of their own."[45]

In the second place, judged from the standpoint of political expediency, Caesar as dictator made some mistakes. Some of these were very well-intended. As a conqueror, Caesar was lenient; as a ruler, moderate. His hope was to rise above partisanship, to weld his allies and his enemies into a strong, united state. So he wasted little time on exacting revenge. He never renewed a Sullan "reign of terror"; he pardoned the military captives of the civil wars and never thought of executing the senators who had opposed him. He recalled political exiles and put statues of Pompey back in place. To give his administration a broader base of intelligence and respectability, he appointed an ex-enemy, Pontus, Governor of Cisalpine Gaul. He did not wipe out the debts of his supporters or distribute among them the lands of Pompey's party. Even Antony had to pay for the palace of Pompey which he appropriated. Early in the conflict with Pompey, Caesar had stated his intentions: "Let us try to recover the good-will of all men and so secure a lasting victory. . . . Let us fortify ourselves by mercy and kindness."[46]

Deeply impressed by Caesar's clemency, Cicero had written to Atticus: "By heaven, if he puts no one to death nor despoils anyone of anything, he will be most adored by those who feared him most. The town-dwellers and farmers don't care a cent for anything but their lands, their poor houses, their paltry finances. Observe the reaction. The man in whom they once trusted [Pompey] they now dread; the man they dreaded they worship."[47] After Pharsalus, Caesar destroyed Pompey's files without even examining them for evidence of plots against himself. Later Cicero told him, "You never forget anything except injuries."[48] A Cicero might admire such magnanimity, but lesser men could not. They resented being under obligation to their ruler. A good deed often alienates more than an injury; and Caesar, for his own safety, might well have used harsher measures toward his enemies.

In the third place, certain of Caesar's wise reforms did not attain wide popularity. The knights objected to the abolition of tax-farming; the senators were infuriated to find outstandingly able provincials admitted to their ranks; the poor grumbled at the cut in the number entitled to the dole. So, to maintain popular support for his regime, Caesar was forced into several unfortunate expedients. He attempted to buy favor by large hand-outs to his veterans and by celebrations designed to dazzle the populace. He tried to stifle the unrest born of the decrease in the dole by suppressing the laboring men's clubs and by excluding plebeians from the courts. He increased the membership in the Senate and "packed" it with his own supporters regardless of their qualifications. He was accused of appointing additional praetors simply to add to the number of office-holders dependent on his favor, although actually an increasing volume of business required them. His luxury law, which aimed at the reduction of extravagance by setting a maximum limit on a man's daily expenses, seemed to the rich a most unfair prohibition, no less hateful because it was unenforceable. In the face of such acts, it was difficult to credit Caesar's professions of disinterestedness. He said, "I have expended for you all I possessed," and "I shall make every effort to be rich with you," but some suspected he was using the state's resources to entrench his despotism. It was natural for many to distrust his suggestion that they should not fear the army, when he kept the army in being on the excuse that "at every moment we need an army, living in a city like ours and possessing such an extensive empire." The excuse might be well-reasoned, but it was unfamiliar and therefore suspect.[49]

Too much that Caesar wanted was new. His whole idea of the empire was too revolutionary to find favor with the average Roman. Caesar planned to supercede the 'capital and colonies' arrangement by forming the world into one nation. The Senate would represent the whole people, not merely the city aristocracy. The rights of citizenship would be open to all who earned them; the barbarians should be civilized and absorbed into the Roman population. Great provincial cities, modeled after Rome in law and social organization, might grow in wealth and prestige almost to equal Rome herself. No one in the ancient world, save perhaps C. Gracchus, had ever even imagined such an empire.[50] Roman citizens did not want even to imagine it, but Caesar could not wait. His restless mind was always hatching new ideas, impatient to put them into operation. Politically, Caesar was in too much of a hurry. He did not consolidate his position. He did not permit Rome to become accustomed to his new organization of the government before he was urging her on to more extensive changes. People rebelled at his haste to overthrow their familiar privileges and prejudices. Caesar was too much the visionary.

10. *Character of Julius Caesar*

Caesar made other mistakes for which we can find much less excuse. His newly-unified world was to be totally subject to his personal rule. His title of "perpetual dictator" was hateful enough, but he aspired to be called king—to have his personal pre-eminence recognized. On at least two occasions his henchmen tried to persuade the populace to acclaim him as king, and Caesar met their rebuffs with poor grace. The Senate was convoked for March 15, 44, to vote on making Caesar *rex*. Guilty of foolish vanity, Caesar ignored the conventional abhorrence of the title king. "His desire of being king brought upon him the most apparent and mortal hatred," says Plutarch.[51] He permitted the Senate to load him with empty honors, to venerate him as though he were a god, to put his statue among those of Rome's ancient kings. He made a great parade of his personal power, not remembering that people do not like to be reminded of their slavery to an absolute ruler. Gibbon remarks that Caesar "provoked his fate as much by the ostentation of his power as by his power itself."[52] It was poor form to celebrate a triumph for Munda, a victory won over his fellow-citizens. It was an error to permit oppressive measures—the luxury law, the suppression of the laborers' clubs—to be so directly traceable to the pleasure of the dictator. Caesar should have had the sense to cloak his absolute power. He should not have tried to acquire, by senatorial decree, what most people were not yet willing for him to have.

Certain traits in Caesar's character contributed to his downfall. His habit of command made him imperious: he was impatient with excuses or delays; he was scornful of parliamentary procedures or traditional methods. He wanted action now—wise in a soldier, unwise in a politician. In his treatment of others, he grew thoughtless of their self-respect and scornful of their petty pride. He treated the Senate with contempt, failing even to rise from his chair when a deputation of senators called upon him. He acted as though he were already king. He could not even be bothered to conceal an element of fraud in his position. Surely it was scandalous for the supervisor of morality to have established his mistress Cleopatra so openly in Rome. But Caesar paid no attention to criticism.

The truth of the matter is probably that Caesar was quickly becoming bored at being the greatest living man. What was there left to prick his ambition? Plutarch thinks that Caesar, like Alexander, was motivated by a limitless desire for glory and empire, but by this time world-rule had begun to grow tiresome. Caesar was old and exhausted. He spoke sincerely when he said, "I have

lived long enough both for nature and for glory."[53] He was thinking about death, for when some one asked him what sort of end
was most desirable, he answered unhesitatingly, "a sudden one."[54]
The satirist Laberius struck home when he wrote

"He must fear many people
Whom many people fear."[55]

But, either from pride or from boredom, Caesar grew careless, both
of the feelings of others and of the strength of the opposition to
his measures. He dismissed his body guard, ignoring the possibility
of plots against his life. He was no longer the coolheaded realist,
the master of human relations; he had grown arbitrary and irritable.
Cleopatra said that only a king could conquer Parthia.

Caesar had given to Rome peace and security and the
beginnings of material prosperity. But he could not achieve a moral
regeneration. Mommsen believed that Caesar's government was "the
representation of the nation by the man in whom it puts supreme
and unlimited confidence."[56] But the truth is rather that the
whole nation was never willing to put its full trust in Caesar the
reformer or Caesar the dictator. Narrowness of outlook, selfishness
of motive, suspicion of anything new or unusual, were still widespread. Nor had nearly a century of war and destruction sated the
bloodthirstiness of the times or demonstrated the futility of revenge.

So the senatorial party hatched a plot against the life of
the dictator. Cicero was excluded, he was too old and frightened.
Cassius was the originator, but it was the participation of the
upright Brutus that lent respectability and convinced the half-
hearted. If Brutus was implicated, the assassination would take on
the character, not of a criminal conspiracy, but of "an act of devotion for the salvation of the country."[57] The Senate would concur.
Brutus had nothing to gain; but it was right to free the world of a
tyrant.

"Beware the Ides of March," the soothsayer had told a
worried Caesar, and the auguries on the morning were bad. Calpurnia had had nightmares and begged her husband to stay home;
Caesar himself felt ill. But Decimus Brutus came to remind Caesar
that the Senate was meeting to make him king, and he overbore
all objections. Caesar entered the Senate house. Senators crowded
around him to present a petition. Twenty-three daggers pierced
his body. Caesar had thought to defend himself but perceived
Brutus among his assailants. "You too, Brutus," he murmured, and
wrapped his toga around himself and died, at the base of a statue
of Pompey.

Plutarch and Suetonius are not in agreement as to the immediate aftermath of Caesar's death. Suetonius says the conspirators were fearful to carry out their intentions of confiscating

his property and revoking his decrees. Plutarch has them marching confidently to the Capitol, accompanied by an armed guard. In any case, Caesar's lifeless body was neglected "until finally three common slaves put him on a litter and carried him home, with one arm hanging down."[58] The next day his funeral was marked by an outpouring of genuine grief and of fear for the unknown future. By popular acclaim, and by decree of the Senate, Caesar was numbered among the gods.

Chaos was born again in the assassination of Caesar. The empire had grown wholly dependent on his personal rule, in whom "were combined," said Cicero, "genius, method, memory, literature, prudence, deliberation, and industry."[59] With this ruler dead, government was suspended. Cicero rationalized the assassination by declaring that Caesar had "brought a free city, partly by fear, partly by patience, into a habit of slavery."[60] But many people doubted that slavery was any worse than chaos. Slavery to a benevolent dictator, whose self-interest demanded that he make the nation prosperous, seemed less hurtful, in any case, than slavery to a small ruling class intent on making their own fortunes. Under the old system of "Political liberty" there had been much disorder and waste, and economic misery had been the common lot of the masses. The old ruling class, however, saw in Caesar's one-man rule only an insult to its capacity and patriotism. The noble and the rich murdered Caesar because they hated his despotism: "Both its outer insistence upon personal rule and its underlying tenderness for the lower orders were in constant irreconcilable conflict with every ideal of the familied oligarchy of the Senate."[61]

Caesar had always been popular with the common people. His reforms had benefited the "underprivileged." By enlarging the Senate, by giving citizenship to provincials, by civilizing the barbarians, he had worked to level society upward, to remove invidious distinctions between classes. His will, when Antony read it publicly, proved that Caesar had had a sincere interest in the welfare of the common man. To every Roman citizen he left $15 from his private fortune, and he ordered that his garden by the Tiber should be a public park. Antony described him as "the only man who has ever shown kindly feelings for the common people."[62] In the light of his solicitude for the general welfare, it would be hard for a future government to ignore the masses.

It is not easy to replace a very great man and that, surely, Caesar was. Like the Gracchi, Marius, Sulla, and Pompey, his methods had been unconstitutional and he had made his personal power greater than the Republic's. But he had taken the Roman state along the road that it would undoubtedly have followed, by peaceful means or violent, under his guidance or another's. He

had done Rome a lot of good. By his own will he had imposed
order and stability on a chaotic government. With his broad sym-
pathies he had reinvigorated the various elements of Roman
society. With his imaginative daring he was prepared to unify and
strengthen and glorify the empire. Who could fill Caesar's place?

Chapter IV

AVGVSTVS

AUGUSTUS CAESAR—FROM DICTATORSHIP TO EMPIRE

After the assassination of Caesar, a business acquaintance of Cicero asked him a momentous question: "If Caesar could not find a way out of our difficulties, who will find one now?"[1]

1. The Succession?

There were two immediate candidates for Caesar's mantle: the Senate and Mark Antony. The conspirators hoped to be generally applauded as liberators of their country from tyranny. Despite all its troubles since the days of the Gracchi, the Senate apparently had learned nothing of the need of satisfying the demands of the people. By the simple act of assassinating the dictator, it expected to restore the "good old days" of aristocratic supremacy. The conspirators made the mistake, as Appian describes it, of "counting on two incompatible things, namely, that people could be lovers of liberty and bribe-takers at the same time."[2] The Senate misread the temper of the times. Romans were no longer idealists: they were more interested in the material benefits a government might provide than in any abstract theory of how that government should be constituted. The conspirators made the further mistake of not going far enough. If they wanted Caesar's power for themselves they should sensibly have murdered also Caesar's right-hand men, Antony and Lepidus. But Brutus was as politically inept as he was strictly virtuous. There was no legal right to murder any but Caesar, he alone was the tyrant.

At first, the assassination evoked no strong feelings on either side. The conspirators, failing to be hailed as heroes, retired to the safety of fortified positions. This left the initiative to the surviving consul, Antony. He arranged the funeral of Caesar, which was turned into a vast public exhibition of affection for the dead "tyrant". From Calpurnia he secured possession of Caesar's will, his private papers, his personal wealth, and the public treasury.

Antony could thus pose as Caesar's executor, carrying out the terms of the will and giving effect to those measures which Caesar had had time only to plan. Antony already had command of the army and was popular with the soldiers, with whom he had lived as an equal. Now he had the means and the opportunity to gain the affections of the people. But he had no love for senators, and before long the conspirators found it advisable to leave Rome. Decimus Brutus, Brutus, and Cassius departed to take up their commands in Gaul and in the eastern provinces.

The assassination had accomplished nothing. Antony ruled in Rome, as Caesar's successor. "We now obey the man in his grave whom we could not endure in his lifetime," bemoaned Cicero. "The tyrant is dead, but the tyranny still lives."[3] Then, in April, 44, there appeared on the scene a new man, named Octavius.

2. *Octavius and Cicero*

Who was this Octavius? In the year of Catiline's conspiracy, 63, he was born in Rome. But his family belonged to the country town of Velitrae, where his father, a successful banker, was a respected representative of the upper middle class. Although he attained to senatorial dignity, he was not an aristocrat, and his were the bourgeois virtues of thrift, simple living, common sense, and respectability. The mother of Octavius was the daughter of Caesar's sister Julia, so that he was Caesar's great-nephew. Having achieved manhood and been elected to the pontifical college, Octavius began to attract the attention of his famous uncle, who had no sons of his own. When Caesar went to Spain for the Munda campaign, Octavius was too ill to go. He followed soon after, eluding enemies and surviving a shipwreck, "and thereby greatly endeared himself to Caesar, who soon formed a high opinion of his character."[4] The mark of this approbation was the elevation of Octavius, in 45, to patrician status and his appointment as a master of horse.

Far more important, Caesar wrote his will as he was returning from Spain. He directed the adoption of Octavius into the Julian family and designated him his heir. Therefore, the death of Caesar was a momentous event in Octavius' life. At the time he was with the army in Apollonia, and some of the soldiers urged that he should immediately lead them in a march on Rome to demand his inheritance. But his sound middle-class upbringing had made Octavius too cool and astute to give in to such mad suggestions. Nothing was to be gained by haste: a premature move, not backed up by any real force, would lose everything. On the other hand, ambition prompted Octavius not to sit idly by and watch his inheritance snatched from his grasp. The wise course was to return quietly to Italy and survey the situation before committing himself to any line of action. It was politically a clever move for Octavius to pay a call on the elder statesman Cicero before journeying up to Rome. Two aims began to form themselves in Octavius' mind: to avenge Caesar's murder, and to take up his inheritance and assume Caesar's position as master of the Roman empire.

Such aims might well have seemed absurd. What could an inexperienced youth of nineteen do in competition with the armed might of Antony and the political skill of the senators? He could not expect help from either party. Antony would look upon him as the most dangerous threat to his personal ascendancy. The Senate would not willingly accept his domination in the place of Caesar's.

But there were aspects of the situation that favored Octavius. He was the legal heir; as a Caesar, he should inherit at least some of the dictator's popularity with the masses. Then Antony was not proving to be a good ruler. His arrogance and extravagance were criticized. He listened with impatience to the requests of citizens, and he was too lazy to administer the laws properly. He seemed to care only for the soldiers, and it was becoming apparent that he planned illegally to demand the military command of Gaul without putting aside his consulship in Rome. This demand would unite against him all those who revered traditional Roman law. Meanwhile the senatorial party was weakened by being geographically separated. From their distant posts Brutus and Cassius could exert little influence. Although he had not even been admitted to the plot, Cicero was now again the master-planner of the effort to reap the fruits of the conspiracy by re-establishing senatorial government. But he could never hope to rally popular support in opposition to Antony. Some more energetic and more glamorous leader was needed.

Cicero quickly saw the possibility of finding that leader in Octavius. Too young to have any black marks against his character, and possessed of the great Caesar's blessing, Octavius could serve as the popular front against the indolent and dissolute Antony. Octavius was "at the pliable time of life," and Cicero would undertake to flatter him and mold his thinking, so that the young Caesar would be the tool of the senatorial party. Cicero was carried away by his scheme. To Atticus he wrote: "He has brains and spirit . . . but we must carefully consider the degree of reliance than can be placed upon him. . . . He must be trained and above all he must be alienated from Antony. . . . He has an excellent disposition, if it only lasts."[5] Octavius, cautious and tight-lipped, did not at once remove Cicero's doubts. He intended to keep control over his own actions, to maintain his independence, for he already realized that his purposes and Cicero's were not identical.

Octavius went on to Rome, to try his luck with Antony. It immediately became clear that there could be no wholehearted cooperation between them. Antony laughed at the idea of the delicate-looking Octavius as Caesar's successor: such a boy could never command the support of the soldiers. Antony treated him with studied discourtesy and spoke of him with contempt. But Octavius was not to be bullied into inactivity. Quietly he began to distribute money according to the instructions in Caesar's will and to win over, as a Caesar, the loyalty of some of the veteran troops. Nevertheless, Octavius realized that his inheritance—even his life—would never be secure until Antony's power was broken. The first necessity was to build up his own resources to rival Antony's. Perhaps the senatorial party could be induced to help.

So negotiations with Cicero were reopened in a friendly spirit on both sides. It was against the advice of Brutus that Cicero indulged himself in intrigues with Octavius. But all Cicero's hesitancy was overcome by Octavius' responsiveness and by the obvious unfriendliness between him and Antony. Cicero, therefore, employed his eloquence to persuade the Senate to work with Octavius. He was, of course, guilty of double-dealing, for he planned now to compliment Octavius so that he could make use of him, and then, when Antony had been discredited, to discard Octavius. For the present he praised Octavius to the senators: "Nothing is dearer to him than the Republic, nothing more important than your authority, nothing more desirable than the favor of good men."[6] Brutus was not convinced; he said: "The boy's ambition and unscrupulousness have been rather provoked than repressed by Cicero. . . . Though Octavius call Cicero 'father', consult him in everything, praise and thank him, nevertheless the truth will come out that deeds do not agree with words."[7] Brutus, himself incapable of political trickery and not advised of Cicero's duplicity, was wise enough to retain his doubts of Octavius' honesty.

But Brutus, far away, could exercise no control over events in Italy. These events now hastened to a crisis. The uneasy truce that had existed between Antony and the conspirators came to an end. Antony openly demanded dictatorial powers and left Rome for the army in order to enforce his demands. The Senate declared him an enemy of the state and began to make preparations for war. Any soldiers disaffected from Antony would be likely recruits for the senatorial army. And by now, as the result of his carefully scattered gifts, Octavius had several legions "in his pocket". The logical course for the Senate was to appoint him to a command against Antony. This it did, and Cicero hailed the action in a self-satisfied speech: "I know all the thoughts of this young Caesar; and I will go so far as to answer for him with my own person. No one compels me to assume so dangerous a responsibility, but I take it upon myself; I vow and protest that Caius Caesar will, throughout life, remain the worthy citizen he is today."[8]

The alliance was of Cicero's making. Confident that Octavius would act as it directed, Cicero spoke extravagantly to the Senate, "What god has given to Rome this god-like youth?"[9] Brutus, unimpressed, continued to believe that Cicero was Octavius' dupe; instead of working for the Senate, Octavius could use it as a legal cloak for his own climb to personal power. Brutus wrote to Cicero: "You fancy that this young Caesar is less bloodthirsty than Antony; perhaps under his rule it will be possible to cling to life, to style oneself consul, and to become rich, but one would never be a free man. My motto is that Rome exists wherever there is freedom."[10] Cicero knew, at last, that Brutus' thinking was out of date.

Events were soon to tell whether Cicero or Brutus was correct in his judgment of Octavius. Antony was besieging the troops of Decimus Brutus in Mutina. The senatorial army, under the two consuls and Octavius, marched to raise the siege. In the resultant battle, Antony was badly defeated and forced to flee northward; the two consuls were killed, leaving Decimus Brutus and Octavius in joint command. They disagreed. Octavius refused to lead a vigorous pursuit of the retreating Antony, who might now have been disposed of for good. D. Brutus complained to Cicero, "Octavius will take no orders."[11] Suspicions formed again in the mind of Cicero, who wrote to Brutus: "I seem scarcely able to make my promise good [of Octavius' devotion to the state]. . . . He seems to have a character of his own, and there are many prepared to corrupt him."[12]

There could be little question of Octavius' intentions when, two months later, he sent his officers to demand that the Senate give the consulship to their commander, aged not yet twenty! The threat of the centurion Cornelius was open: he touched his sword and said, "This will make him consul if you do not." With his eyes opened, Cicero bitterly tried to make the best of a bad bargain. The Senate named Octavius consul.[13]

3. The Second Triumvirate

Meanwhile, Antony was able to rally his army. Lepidus joined him and, one by one, provincial governors fell into line.

Cicero might plead, as he did to Plancus in southern Gaul, "What hope can there be in a state in which everything is held down by the arms of the most violent and headstrong of men; in which neither Senate nor people has any power to control; in which there are neither laws nor law courts—in fact no trace even of a constitution?"14 But Cicero was growing as old-fashioned as Brutus, and Antony had the present strength to compel support. The Senate had one hope left: Antony and Octavius would fight and destroy each other. As the armies approached each other in northern Italy, however, Lepidus hastened back and forth between the two leaders. When the soldiers met, they mingled together in comradeship. Instead of war between Antony and Octavius, there was friendly agreement and unity based on the watchword, "Vengeance for Caesar". Their joint task would be to hunt down the conspirators and degrade the Senate. To accomplish it, they formed, with Lepidus, the Second Triumvirate, with five years in which to reconstitute the commonwealth.

The formation of the Triumvirate attests the shrewdness of Octavius—his calm self-control, his patient opportunism, his skill at dissimulation. He had never lost sight of his goal. He had proved himself a far more clever—and unscrupulous—intriguer than Cicero. He had now effectively undermined the senatorial party, after having maneuvered them into assisting his own rise. He had made his own power great enough so that he could treat on equal terms with the Antony who had laughed at him eighteen months before. For Octavius, however, that was only the first step. The Triumvirate was to serve his purpose of taking revenge on Caesar's murderers. But neither he nor Antony was going to be satisfied in the long run by any division of authority. The future was to determine whether Octavius or Antony should be the first man of Rome.

The history of the Triumvirate does not make wholly pleasant reading nor does it reflect much credit on the personalities of the leaders. If it records the progressive deterioration of the physical and moral characteristics of the once-able Antony, it must also include the callous inhumanity and calculated deceitfulness of Octavius. The Triumvirate was founded on base motives—greed, self-love, revenge. Its story begins with the collaboration of Antony and Octavius in the proscription of hundreds of prominent Roman citizens. The Triumvirate was illegal and, therefore, could not tolerate honest opposition. The best way to dispose of the senatorial faction was to wipe it out, and the three men placed the names of their particular enemies on the list of those marked for destruction. It has been estimated that 300 senators and 2,000 knights were murdered. The confiscation of their property provided convenient replenishment for the Triumvirate's treasury.

It is reported that Octavius tried to save Cicero, whom he described years later as "a learned man and a lover of his country,"[15] from the fury of Antony. If so, his efforts were not persistent enough to succeed, for a price was put on the statesman's head. Cicero was tracked down at one of his seaside villas and, when he put his head out of his traveling litter to find the cause of the commotion around him, the ruffians severed it from his shoulders. Octavius has been excused for his part in the proscriptions on the basis that his cruelty was not natural to him but was evoked by the reasons of politics. But the cruelty remains and Suetonius says that after the murdering began, Octavius "carried it through with greater severity than either of his associates."[15] At least, Octavius was thorough.

Expediency also triumphed over principle in regard to finances. The Triumvirate was backed solely by military strength. If the soldiers were to be counted on, they must be amply paid. Antony and Octavius joined in promising them large booty from their campaigns and generous land-grants in Italy when the fighting was over. The land, however, was not available, and so plans were laid for the eviction of long-established farmers and the depopulating of eighteen Italian towns. No sympathy for the feelings or misery of those evicted was to be allowed to obstruct this forcible expropriation of private property.

The only purpose on which Antony and Octavius were fully agreed was to take revenge on Caesar's murderers. This was accomplished in 42 at the battle of Philippi. In the Greek peninsula the conspirators had collected a sizeable army, and the Triumvirs marched to the attack. Both armies were divided in two sections with co-equal commanders. The advantage of position was with the senatorial force, and on the seaward wing Brutus decisively defeated Octavius. Suetonius records the fortunate escape of Octavius from an early death. Brutus' troops swarmed through his camp and thrust many swords into his litter, where he was supposed to be lying ill. But Octavius, warned by a dream, had risen from his sick bed shortly before.[17] Meanwhile, Cassius and Antony clashed in indecisive combat. Amid the dust of the field, and lacking reliable communications, Cassius conceived the idea that all was lost and fell on his sword, leaving Brutus as "the last of the Romans". The next day his over-anxious army compelled Brutus to abandon his works and advance. The veteran legions of Antony smashed this attack, gaining for him the military honors of the victory. With freedom lost forever, Brutus committed suicide.

Caesar was avenged. The soldierly Antony took upon himself the task of pacifying the rest of the East. Octavius, ineffective in war but skilled in politics, went back to the unsympathetic jobs of governing Italy and supervising the settlement of the soldiers demanding their rewards. Antony's wife Fulvia, resentful of the dominance of Octavius, raised a revolt which was finally crushed at the siege of Perugia. When the city fell, Octavius permitted the butchery of hundreds of citizens, no doubt to serve a warning against further rebellion. A new accommodation between Antony and Octavius was clearly called for, and the Triumvirate met at Scutari. There they divided the world so that each might enjoy an undisputed command. The shadowy Lepidus must content himself with Africa. Antony took the East with its wealth and its field for military glory—and its corruption. To Octavius was left the more difficult, but ultimately more fruitful, control of Italy and the West. A marriage bargain sealed the agreement. Fulvia having opportunely died, Octavius gave his sister, the virtuous and highly-respected Octavia, to be wife to Antony.

4.   *Rivalry of Octavius and Antony and the outcome of it*

The next decade provides a startling contrast between the constructive activity of Octavius and the profitless indolence of Antony. The latter fell a prey to the lures of the East—its warmth, its wines, its perfumes. He was ensnared by the wily Cleopatra, who saw in his prowess a chance to revive the majesty of Egypt. He wasted his time, his strength, and his reputation in luxurious living. He made a miserable failure of his half-hearted expedition to conquer the Parthians. He ignored Octavia for Cleopatra; even when the long-suffering Octavia traveled to Athens to take him a gift of supplies, he rudely departed before her arrival. Nothing stimulated Antony from his sloth: he added neither to his own power nor to the glory of Rome.

Meanwhile Octavius was occupied with a host of tasks. The business of ejecting peasants from their farms—the poet Virgil was a victim in Mantua—was highly unpopular, but Octavius found ways in which to rebuild his credit. The prime need was to restore order, so that the people might find profitable outlets for their energies and cease political disturbances. Octavius' measures are reminiscent of Caesar's. Public works were undertaken, to provide employment: a building program, improvement of the water-supply and drainage-system of Rome. Taxes were reduced, disbanded troops settled, robbery curtailed by a new police system. Agriculture was thus encouraged and commerce rendered safer. While rumors spread of Antony wallowing in oriental splendor, Octavius began the restoration of the temples of the ancient Roman gods.

Octavius' outstanding achievement in these years was the suppression of the Sicilian pirates, whose skillful commander Sextus, the one remaining son of Pompey, had made them the scourge of Roman merchants and captains. Their existence athwart the sea-lanes from Africa constantly threatened the interruption of the corn supply on which Rome's life depended. Octavius' first attack on Sextus at Messina failed, but it taught him valuable lessons. He now entrusted the active command to his friend Agrippa, a genius in war. The Roman fleet was equipped with grappling-irons, by which the small, fast pirate vessels might be immobilized. The attack of 36 was a joint operation. Octavius landed with an army on Sicily, but his efforts were inconclusive. The issue was decided in the sea-battle of Naulochus, in which the pirate fleet was destroyed. In the meantime, Lepidus had come to Sicily with an army from Africa but had failed to cooperate in the attack, perhaps hoping that Octavius and Sextus would so maul each other that he could assert his supremacy over both. He had so little purchase with his own men, however, that Octavius won them over and had Lepidus at his mercy. He spared him because of his position of pontifex maximus, by appointment of Caesar, but from then on Lepidus counted for nothing in affairs of state.

So the Triumvirate was reduced to two, and the showdown between Octavius and Antony would not be indefinitely postponed. Octavius must make preparations. Some steps had already been taken. By this time he had been twice married. His first wife, the rich widow Scribonia, had established his private wealth. His second, Livia, the daughter of Livius Drusus who fell by Brutus' side at Philippi, had given him an alliance with the old aristocracy. Also, the people had favored him with an election as tribune. But the personal glamor that had won for Caesar the popularity with the common people which was his most durable asset, had so far escaped Octavius. It would be proper to speak with horror of the approaching conflict, but he must be sure to educate public opinion to be on his side when it inevitably came. Support for Octavius against Antony must be interpreted as natural patriotism—support for Roman nationalism against a foreigner, for Roman morality against vice, for Roman government against despotism.

Fortunately for Octavius, Antony had chosen to reside in Alexandria, and war against him could be depicted as war against Egypt. Fortunately again, Cleopatra was both cordially hated and feared in Rome. Many remembered her as the demon who had ruined Caesar. To all, she was the personal embodiment of oriental monarchy, its bottomless corruption, its blatant wickedness, its thoughtless tyranny. Bribery and treachery were commonplace in an oriental court, ruled by favorites who yet prostrated themselves abjectly before their monarch. And Antony's folly made it possible to criticize him (as Horace later did) as the "passionate slave of that woman." Had he not spread the trophies of his wars, scant though they were, at her feet and celebrated a triumph in Alexandria instead of properly at Rome? Had he not spoken of himself and Cleopatra as king and queen and even given the dreaded royal titles to their children? Did not Antony's will, which had so luckily come into Octavius' possession and been published to the world, did not this will indicate that Antony looked on the East as his private domain to be parceled out for the benefit of Egyptian princes? If Antony were to prevail over Octavius, would not Alexandria replace Rome as the capital of the world, and senators take orders from Egyptian eunuchs?

These were the questions which Octavius' propagandists, under the sponsorship of his friend Maecenas, asked the Italians. When threatened by the debauched monarchist Antony, surely Roman prestige and independence could only survive if entrusted to the hands of Octavius. It was only logical and proper that every Roman individually should swear an oath of loyalty to Octavius as the leader of the national forces against a foreign monarchy. The war would be declared against Cleopatra, not against Antony.

Even with the minds of the Italian populace thus turned against him, Antony's cause was not yet doomed. Octavius was still unprepared to fight. In 32, as always in time of war, he raised taxes and required of all free men $\frac{1}{4}$ of their income and of all freed men $\frac{1}{8}$ of their property. Had Antony possessed his youthful vigor of mind and body, he might have invaded Italy and, aided by popular discontent at the heavy taxation, won the war. But he loafed in Alexandria and lost his opportunity.

The next summer Octavius was ready. Though his forces both on land and on sea were fewer in number than his opponent's, they were more energetically and ably led. Antony found himself surrounded on land and blockaded by sea at Actium on the Adriatic. He must break out or be starved into surrender. It was probably foolish for the foremost general of the day to choose to fight at sea, but there he would have the aid of Cleopatra's sixty powerful vessels. As the great ships of Antony came out of the harbor, they had to break formation to have room to fight and they were hampered by contrary winds. Suddenly the Egyptian ships broke off the engagement, made all possible sail, and fled southward. Inexplicably, Antony followed them in flight. The rest of his fleet was sunk or beaten ashore and his army, demoralized by the precipitate departure of their general, surrendered to Octavius' discretion.

After Actium, Antony and Cleopatra hoped perhaps to be able to hold Egypt, but Octavius gave them no time to recover. His strength was too great for the paltry troops Antony could muster, and the Egyptian navy again chose not to fight. When Octavius pounded on the gates of Cleopatra's palace, resistance was out of the question. The queen's efforts to charm Octavius into leniency failed. Hearing that she was dead, Antony killed himself, and Cleopatra—proud and brave even in failure—followed his example with the aid, according to Horace, of two poisonous snakes.

Octavius stayed some time in Egypt. To ensure that there remained no center of revolt, he ordered the murder of all Cleopatra's sons, including Caesarion, her child by Caesar. He decided to retain Egypt as his personal estate. He would be responsible for its administration; he would control the indispensable corn exports; he would be the beneficiary of its wealth. So he set to work to reorganize the government and to dredge the canals, in order that his power might always have a solid base in Egypt. At last he was ready to cope with his major problems: to bring order and prosperity to Rome; to give wise and honest government to the empire. Actium had given the Roman world a new master, if he could maintain himself.

5. Character and policies of Octavius

Octavius now stood on the threshold of his real career, that of ruler of the Roman Empire. He was proud of what he had done already; he wrote later in his own account of his accomplishments: "I raised an army by which I restored to liberty the commonwealth which had been oppressed by the tyranny of a faction."[18] But at this time the 'liberty' would have seemed doubtful, and Octavius had not yet done anything of permanent value. His first thirty-three years of life had all been by way of preparation. He had had to win his way to his supreme position, outwitting the Senate, defeating Antony, gaining popular favor, himself learning through experience the arts of politics and statesmanship. Now that he had reached the top, people must have wondered what sort of ruler he would prove to be.

Let us pause to consider Octavius the man. In appearance, he was not quite as imposing or awe-inspiring as statues and busts of him suggest. Suetonius describes him as mild of countenance,

with a nondescript complexion and rather prominent nose, careless of the style of his hair. His teeth were too small and set wide
apart. His eye-brows met and beneath them were clear, bright eyes.
Octavius was proud of the special radiance of his eyes, before
which other people often dropped their gaze. On the other hand,
he was short of stature, so that he sometimes wore shoes with built-
up soles. Octavius was not especially healthy. He did not like
extremes of climate, and so he wore four tunics and a toga on
top of woolen undergarments in winter and a large-brimmed hat
to shield him from the sun in summer. He suffered from rheuma-
tism and a variety of internal complaints. Yet Suetonius speaks
of "the fine proportion and symmetry of his figure," and calls
him "unusually handsome and exceedingly graceful."[19]

In character, Octavius had certain outstanding talents.
First, perhaps, was his tenacity of purpose. He had seen from
the beginning that the work of delivering Rome from the economic
and political confusion into which she had fallen could not be
done by squabbling factions. The re-ordering of Rome would be
done by the genius of one man, who must have the backing of
the army. Octavius had decided at the outset that he would be
that man and that nothing would divert him from his goal.

In pursuing his chosen end, Octavius showed great powers
of self-command. Thus he could resist, early, the arguments of
Cicero and, later, the blandishments of Cleopatra. He had a brilliant sense of timing. His brusque demand of the consulship was
made when the Senate must give in, but he refused to hasten the
final contest with Antony until he had made all possible preparations. He suited his actions to the moods of the people of Italy.
His judgment of men was no less brilliant. He penetrated the
intrigues of Cicero and perceived the weaknesses of Antony. On the
other side, aware of his own deficiencies, he supplied them by
choosing able helpers who gave him the utmost loyalty. Such were
the diplomatic Maecenas, who handled his public relations, and
the steadfast Agrippa, who was his capable military executive. At
all times, Octavius was adaptable to existing conditions, even if
unpleasant, and resourceful in the selection of his own best course
of action. And he had confidence in himself.

Octavius rose to power in trying times, and it would be
miraculous if he could escape harsh criticism. He was a master-
opportunist, and he chose his methods without much regard for
the morality of them. He resorted to bribery and deception; he was
willing on occasion to break his own word. In short, he was unscrupulous. His cool head was matched by his unfeeling heart. His
own and his sister's marriages were the results of political bargain-
ing. His cruelty in the proscriptions cannot be explained away.

Gibbon accuses him of conducting his whole life behind a "mask of hypocrisy,"[20] and we must agree that often he concealed his true intentions for reasons of policy. There can be no question that the rising Octavius was convinced in his own mind that to achieve his end he was justified in the use of any means, fair or foul.

Many people deplore Octavius' character, but no thoughtful person now regrets his victory. Pharsalus, Philippi, and Actium have been described as three great battles determining the fate of our civilization. All were fought in the Greek peninsula, where West and East then merged. In each, the better trained soldiers of the West triumphed over the more numerous levies of the East. Each victory preserved Rome from the horrors of a potential invasion. Each was a victory for the cause of patriotism and constructive reform. Had Rome fallen before the East, ancient civilization would have decayed far sooner than it did, and the development of Europe would have been far different. It was much better for Rome to be controlled by the ambitious and clear-headed and still youthful Octavius than by an aging Antony whose judgment and moral sense had been corrupted by his years in Alexandria.

Octavius was no paragon of virtue and he lacked the personal magnetism of Caesar. But no serious or widespread conspiracy was ever made to assassinate Octavius. In his career we see a perfect example of the meeting of the man and his times. Rome cried out for assured leadership. Octavius provided it and went on to direct Rome along certain new paths. He did exactly what the Roman citizens wanted him to do, and he did it better than they could possibly have done it. Both leader and followers were satisfied, and both achieved greatness.

After Actium, no revolutionary ardor burned in the hearts of the Roman people; they were inspired by no zeal for any cause or principle. Radical reform had lost its appeal. All classes were exhausted from years of chaos, insecurity, and civil war. Their one desire was for a breathing spell—a period of peace and orderly government in which they could settle down and look after their private affairs. Their property, even their lives, had been too long in danger. They had had their fill of confiscations and assassinations. Dio quotes Maecenas' description of Rome at this time: "Our city, like a great merchantman manned with a crew of every race and lacking a steersman, has now for many generations been rolling and plunging as it has drifted this way and that in a heavy sea, a ship without ballast."[21]

Octavius presented himself as the pilot, and the people offered their allegiance to any one who could give them security and repose. They elected Octavius consul year after year, confirming him in his extraordinary power to purify and reorganize society. The process seemed painless because his private wealth, augmented by the revenues of Egypt, made it possible for him to start a program of rehabilitation without new taxation. There were no rivals left to raise a following and compete for his post of leadership, no widely or deeply believed political doctrines for him to outrage. Octavius had a clear field in which to operate. He imposed his will on a people content to be subjugated if only times became good again. As Tacitus rather bitterly described it in his *Annals,* "Octavius won over the soldiers with gifts, the populace with cheap corn, and all men with the sweets of repose, and so grew greater by degrees, while he concentrated in himself the functions of the Senate, the magistrates, and the laws. He was wholly unopposed, for the boldest spirits had fallen in battle, or in the proscription, while the remaining nobles, the readier they were to be slaves, were raised the higher by wealth and promotion, so that, aggrandized by revolution, they preferred the safe present to the dangerous past."[22]

Having entrusted the protection of the state to Octavius, the people now looked upon him as their savior and placed in him the unlimited confidence which they had denied to Caesar. Octavius had the practical intelligence not to abuse that confidence. With no dangerous rival threatening him, he could safely put aside the inhumanity and double-dealing which had characterized his self-seeking climb to power. He had earned for himself the good fortune of being able, in his years of personal ascendancy, to treat most people with thoughtful kindness and generosity.

To gain power, Octavius had found it necessary to take radical measures. Now that power was his, he developed the conservative spirit that accorded with the temper of the times. His life and habits seem to have been directed by what we might now well call "middle-class values"—sobriety and moderation, honesty and decency, duty and perseverance. His style of living was unaffected and he seldom presumed on his unique rank or authority. Modest and approachable in manner, he permitted freedom of speech and even considerable criticism of himself.[23] He objected to undue attention or flattery. When he moved around the city, he traveled on foot or in a closed litter, to prevent unwonted commotion. His tastes were simple. He chose to continue living in an ordinary house on the Palatine Hill rather than in a magnificent palace. His household furnishings were commonplace, scarcely fitting for a prosperous citizen. Save for formal public functions, he dressed simply, and he relaxed at home, often taking a nap after lunch without bothering to undress. Seldom was there anything extravagant in the food or drink that he served to his friends.

Even in his pleasures and minor vices, Octavius was typical of the substantial member of the bourgeoisie. He enjoyed sports as a spectator; probably boxing was his favorite. He attended the games with regularity and enthusiasm. He liked to gamble, for moderate stakes, and he was fond of the company of women. Although he declined personal bequests, he was especially pleased when his friends said good things about him in their wills. He tended to be somewhat superstitious.

In speech and in writing Octavius expressed himself with clarity and directness, without affectation of elegance. His tone was frequently moralistic, as he tried to impress people with precepts and examples of good behavior. He inclined to be puritanical in his demands on others. With all his seriousness of purpose and demeanor, it was lucky that he had a sense of humor. When a humble man advanced fearfully and hesitantly to present a petition, Octavius laughed at him for approaching as though he were giving "a penny to an elephant."[24]

Unlike Caesar, Octavius was not impetuous; one of his strongest traits was self-restraint, and he did not overwhelm Rome with a spate of proposals for reform. After all, he was not trying to create a perfect world, he was merely seeking workable solutions to current problems. He had great political tact: he realized he must accept existing conditions and habits and modify them only slowly. From the beginning, he had acted from the motive of ambition. His victory at Actium had established his personal preeminence. To retain it, he now realized that he must use his authority, not to defeat opponents in a particular battle, but to benefit the whole Roman world. No unwise haste or foolish adherence to special doctrines should be allowed to alienate groups of people from him. Ambition demanded that he serve the whole empire. The historian Bury quotes this description of the development of Octavius into a leader whom all could follow: "His intellect expanded with his fortunes, and his soul grew with his intellect."[25]

As Octavius was not flamboyant in manner or personality, there was little to call exciting in his political leadership. He adopted the sensible policy of making as few changes as possible in the structure of Roman society, so that the people could more readily feel secure again in their accustomed ways of life. He abandoned what some had censured as the "wild schemes" of Caesar. No more talk was heard of wholesale grants of citizenship or of a reconstruction of the Senate into a body representative of the talents of the whole empire. The idea of a unified empire, composed of many great, equal, self-governing cities, might one day be desirable. But for the present it was impractical: conditions such as the extent of the empire and the slowness of communications, or the diversity of the population and its lack of experience in self-government, were unfavorable. Therefore, Octavius, in line with the Italian nationalism which he had fostered before Actium, reverted to the older concept of an empire governed by an Italian elite, with its cities subordinated to the great capital, Rome. Octavius realized that revolutionary upheavals destroy much that is good along with the bad they are intended to destroy. His solid business sense told him that debtors, clamoring for relief, could not be satisfied completely without wiping out the capital of their creditors. The solution was the revival of Caesar's sound bankruptcy laws, permitting perhaps a 25% reduction in debts. Both debtors and creditors benefited in the long run.

Octavius had the wisdom to realize that no single panacea —such as the Agrarian Law of the Gracchi—was sufficient to restore Roman prosperity. His reforms must be moderate and reasonable, must provide assistance for various elements in the population, if his rule was to command broad popular support. The aristocracy were given a chance to rebuild their fortunes in security; the commercial activities of the middle classes were protected, and they were given a larger and larger share in the government; the efficiency of the government preserved all the people from excessive taxation. The provincials breathed more easily because they were no longer unfairly exploited. Young men rejoiced that careers were open to them in the administration and that their advancement depended on their abilities. The more puritanical elders were pleased at the restoration of the ancient religion and of a sense of service to the state. Octavius was successful in satisfying almost everyone.

Whereas Caesar can be remembered as the daring originator of new ideas, Octavius is rather known for his conservative reforms. The younger took much of his inspiration from the older dictator, but Octavius profited from Caesar's experience to make his own administration work with less friction and less opposition. Both men realized that the old Roman Republic was incompetent to govern an empire. To Caesar's dream of personal rule, Octavius applied his practical genius, making allowances for the stubbornness of human nature and for the inevitable difficulties to be met in the reorganization of a great state. Octavius was polite to the Senate Caesar insulted; Octavius gave just rule to the provinces not yet ready for the privileges Caesar would have given them; Octavius never made Caesar's mistake of yearning publicly for the title of king. Where Caesar planned to extend the empire, Octavius was content to consolidate what he had. Where Caesar flaunted his personal power, Octavius chose rather to keep his concealed. Politically, Caesar was much the more naive. He was a strong man, who took what he wanted and planned to reorganize the world according to his will. Octavius, also strong and ruthless, realized that the world would have to be persuaded to accept his plans. Caesar expected men to catch the inspiration of his vision and live up to their better selves. Octavius was more cynical, expected men's actions to be dominated by their worst motives. Octavius proved the better judge of human nature, and he was clever enough to avoid Caesar's fate.

6. The Principate: Augustus Caesar

Whereas Caesar ruled for less than a year after Munda and was assassinated as a tyrant, Octavius ruled for forty-five years after Actium and has gone down in history as the first Roman Emperor. What were the accomplishments of his long reign? First of all, he re-ordered the government of Rome. Caesar had thought that his authority was sufficient to over-rule the old system. Octavius faced the problem of how to reconcile his tremendous power with the traditional constitution. The best proof of his abiding genius is that he succeeded in this difficult task by devising a new system, which is called "the principate". In 27 B.C. Octavius felt it both safe and wise to "lay the ghost" of the Triumvirate. So he went before the Senate as "the champion of the liberties of the people", to follow his "duty and inclination" and surrender the extraordinary powers, legal and extra-legal, which he had been exercising since 42. He "gave back the Commonwealth into the keeping of the Senate and people." The old magistrates should recommence administering the laws passed in the time-honored way. "The times of danger are over," he said. "The day has come on which I can return to the Senate the powers it granted me, but I shall continue to work as a faithful servant of the republic."[26]

The last sentence, of course, is crucial. Neither Octavius nor the Senate was foolish enough to believe that the old machine, which had broken down so disastrously, could begin to function smoothly again just because Octavius gave it permission to do so. His guiding hand must remain at the helm. By acclamation, the Senate re-appointed him consul and reserved for him for ten years his rights of *imperium*. Then, to indicate its recognition of his position as supreme director of state affairs, the Senate voted him a new title, "Imperator Caesar Augustus". Thenceforward Octavius was Augustus, and so he has remained throughout history.

In 23, under Augustus' direction, a final reorganization established the lasting framework of the principate. Augustus resigned the consulship and ceased to be a magistrate. From this time on, he seldom condescended to occupy any post in the regular hierarchy of Roman officials. But because he was Augustus, the victor of Actium, the savior of the state, he retained his real authority. Although he was not in name consul, tribune, or censor, yet he could exercise the prerogatives of all those offices. The Senate voted him a *maius imperium,* a greater power of command than that held by any magistrate; and the power was voted not for a term of years, or for the duration of any emergency, but for an unlimited period. His command was effective both in Rome and throughout the empire. He was authorized to call a meeting of the Senate and initiate business and nominate candidates for the magistracy. He was empowered on his own authority to issue edicts which should have the effect of law. All the outlying provinces of the empire were placed under his personal rule and he appointed the officials to govern them. Thus the effective direction of foreign affairs was in his hands, and war and peace were made at his will. Taxes were collected in his name and disbursements made at his order. As commander-in-chief he could levy troops and negotiate treaties.

"I declined to accept any office inconsistent with the customs of the country," Augustus could later write. "I stood before all others in authority, but of actual power I possessed no more than my colleagues in each separate magistracy."[27] His tribunican powers, to be sure, did not exceed those of the duly-elected tribunes; his consular dignity was not greater than that of the consuls. But Augustus held all their powers at once. This combination in his hands of consular authority in Rome, proconsular authority in the empire, tribunican and censorian powers, raised him to a position outside and above the constitution. It required a new title, and Augustus began to be called *princeps senatus*—the leading man in the Senate, the first citizen of the state. This new title did not designate a particular office, for Augustus had ceased to occupy an official position. It marked rather the respect which people paid to Augustus' primacy in the state. *Princeps senatus* was not an office-holder; he was the unofficial premier, in whom all powers were vested, as they had formerly been entrusted, for brief periods, to the Gracchi and to Pompey.

Naturally Augustus overshadowed the entire constitutional system of government. The popular magistrates were reduced to local officials, and even in Rome Augustus could veto any of their acts. The Senate retained its traditional prestige, had executive control over all the peaceful, interior provinces, and was, in theory, the main law-making body in the empire. But Augustus had the power to control its deliberations and to regulate its membership. His censorial authority permitted him to revise the whole system of class distinctions on which the senatorial privileges were based. The senators were still unable to forget their personal interests and take the broad view of the welfare of the whole state. They were unwilling to shoulder the executive responsibilities and the unpopular expense of provincial government, and so they turned over to Augustus the control of more and more provinces, until three-quarters of the empire was subject to his personal rule. Impressed by the greatness of the *princeps,* the Senate passed only those laws that were satisfactory to him. It provided him with advisers, but its independent authority was gone. Meanwhile the Assembly continued to elect officials and vote on legislation proposed by the Senate. But Augustus had the right to nominate candidates for office and to preside over elections. Directly or indirectly, all the officials of the empire owed their appointments to him. Appearances of popular rule were maintained, but actual sovereignty had passed from the people to Augustus. The votes of Senate and Assembly merely gave the sanction of legality to his commands.

In theory, the *princeps* had been given his wide powers by the Senate, expressing the will of the people. In theory, therefore, his powers could be revoked. In actuality, however, both Senate and people were powerless, because Augustus' authority was based ultimately on the army. His supreme command was beyond the control of the civil authorities. The Senate could neither dictate to the commander-in-chief nor control the army in contradiction of his orders. Augustus was careful to keep the army satisfied by making military service the path of advancement for citizens and the path to citizenship for non-citizens. In fact, Augustus was a military tyrant, and he created for the protection of his person a praetorian guard of 9,000 men. But so great was his personal prestige that he was able to keep the army in the background.

The fame of his military victories and the success of his management of the empire put Augustus' authority beyond challenge. The state was safe in his hands. There was no one else who could possibly fill his place. The Senate, therefore, bent to his will, and the Assembly was the rubber stamp for his desires. The people happily acknowledged his supremacy, for he was the only guardian of their peace and well-being. They were glad to grant to Augustus an unlimited power of command because they were confident that it would be exercised in their behalf. Behind a front of constitutional form, therefore, Augustus was able personally to rule Rome. He had, in fact, changed everything without, in appearance, changing anything. Bury praises the skill with which

Augustus imposed a military tyranny on a constitutional state: "No statesman has ever surpassed Augustus in the art of withholding from political facts their right names."[28]

7. Accomplishments of the Principate

Arbitrary power must not be applied to foolish or wicked ends. The principate could justify itself only by efficiency, and the personal authority of Augustus could be maintained only if its benefits for the people continued to win for it popular approval. Its first contribution was a real and lasting peace, spreading out from the golden milestone set up in Rome over the imperial highways to the farthest bounds of the empire. Epictetus wrote that Augustus "has won for us a profound peace. There are neither wars nor battles, robbers nor pirates, and we may travel at all hours and sail from east to west."[29] The empire was so vast, its population so diverse, that it could only maintain its equilibrium under the guidance of a strong and good ruler. The political reconstruction which Augustus accomplished prevented it from being split up into quarrelsome segments.

The principate once established, Augustus for nearly a decade devoted most of his energies to the problems of the administration and prosperity of the provinces. His appointees composed an expert and professional civil service, and Augustus himself traveled throughout the empire to ensure the justice and efficiency of their rule. The knights were the backbone of the imperial bureaucracy. Augustus cultivated them as a makeweight against the senators, from whose pride and jealousy they were free, by giving them the principal administrative posts—even that of his viceroy in Egypt—and they repaid him by loyally serving his personal interests. Experienced career men replaced senatorial amateurs and advanced their own interests by efficiently enforcing —for the welfare of the governed—the old republican laws. There was also a slight re-adjustment of the system of provincial government. Military and economic authority were separated: legates ruled, while procurators administered the finances. Independent of each other, they were both subject to Augustus' supervision.

Augustus caused a census to be taken of the population and the resources of the empire. On the basis of this enumeration, it was possible to estimate the income available from the two main taxes Augustus imposed—on land and on other personal property —and to assess each province its fair share. The injustices of tax-farming disappeared. Nor were Roman citizens entirely exempted from contributing to the costs of imperial government. The old tax on the freeing of slaves was revived. New taxes of

5% were levied on inheritances and on sales. In colonies such as Spain, government was unified and simplified and money was spent to construct a network of roads. In Gaul, the growth of cities was forwarded and the use of the Latin language and Roman law was encouraged. All the provinces were bound together in their joint reverence for Rome and for the ruler who provided peace and good government. This veneration of the ruler of imperial Rome developed into the cult of Augustus and was later formalized as Caesar-worship. Augustus refused to be deified, but the cult was politically useful in imparting a personal focus to the allegiance of all the provinces to his rule. In truth, he interfered little in their particular customs or local self-government. The aim was not to impose a deadening uniformity of method, but to inspire the provinces with a unity of spirit as parts of the great Roman Empire.

From provincial affairs Augustus turned his attention to domestic reform. The Senate had never been efficient in its handling of specific executive jobs, and now Augustus assumed responsibility for more and more of them. The haphazard administration of the aediles was replaced by the careful work of experts, who served on commissions appointed by the *princeps*. A commission maintained the roads in Italy and ran the government's postal service over them. Other commissions took charge of the administration of Rome itself. Seven thousand men were enlisted in new police and fire departments under equestrian prefects who reported directly to Augustus. Because the people were frightened of the danger from "fire and falling houses", he issued an ordinance limiting the height of buildings in the city to seventy feet. A commission was appointed to collect, store, and distribute the state's corn supply. The dole did not derange the government's budget because the costs of it were paid out of Augustus' private purse. To improve the water supply, Agrippa was appointed head of the water commission, and new aqueducts and sewers were built. A department of public works laid down a building program for Rome, and the capital was beautified by the use of Carrara marble to face the less sightly brick and cement. So Augustus grew to be the active executive of the city as well as of the provincial government, and the ancient magistracies were subordinated to his power.

Far more than the senators was Augustus actively concerned with the welfare of the city proletariat. Civic improvements were helpful but specific provision must be made for the comfort and contentment of the common people. They must not be permitted to sink into unemployment and starvation. To give the poor a fairer chance to earn an honest livelihood, Augustus re-

stricted the number of slaves in Italy and discouraged the widespread freeing of slaves. He permitted the reopening of the trade
guilds and from his own wealth often made money gifts to the
poor. The people felt that he was their protector.

Augustus was also a patron of learning and the arts.
Suetonius says, "He gave every encouragement to the men of
talent of his own age."[30] He founded two libraries in Rome; built
the huge and magnificent theatre of Marcellus; planned, constructed, or restored forums, temples, basilicas, and other public
structures. He commissioned the graceful sculptures that adorned
the Altar of Peace, which was erected after his return from a
triumphal tour of the western provinces in 13 B.C. Virgil said
that Augustus made of Rome the fairest place in the world.
Meanwhile, Agrippa had built the earliest temple on the site of
the still-standing Pantheon, and artists were developing the special
Roman skills in portrait statuary, bas-relief, and wall-painting.

We, of course, know the Augustan Age best from its
literature, which has most successfully survived the ravages of
time. The stable government of Augustus provided the conditions
necessary for a flowering of the arts—peace, economic security,
and the return of self-confidence. The taste and liberality of
Augustus, directed by his friend Maecenas, attracted poets and
historians to the ruler, who welcomed them as additions to his
cultivated society. He made few demands on them, but he enjoyed
their company and praised their works. The ideals of Augustus
became the themes that enlisted the enthusiasm of the writers:
morality, law, duty, patriotism, reasonableness.

In literature, the age was predominantly one of poetry,
and Virgil was the leading figure. He took delight in the countryside, the farms and animal life of Italy, the abundant harvests.
It was owing to the intervention of Augustus that Virgil's *Aeneid*
was published, rather than burnt, at the time of the poet's death.
It is not surprising that this greatest of epic poems in Latin, which
delves into the mythical past to celebrate the glory of Rome,
should have been written during the rule of Augustus. Virgil
told the story of the growth of Rome in the light of the grandeur
of the Rome he himself lived in, recounting the noble destiny of
a great people. "Thine it is, Roman," said Virgil, "to rule over
the world." He spoke of Augustus as the son of a god and the
founder of a golden age.

Virgil introduced Horace to Maecenas. Horace had fought
for Brutus at Philippi but had been pardoned. Maecenas now
gave him his beloved Sabine farm.. Horace celebrated the joys of
every-day life as lived with moderation and common sense. The
master alike of lyrical form and of social comment, he wrote

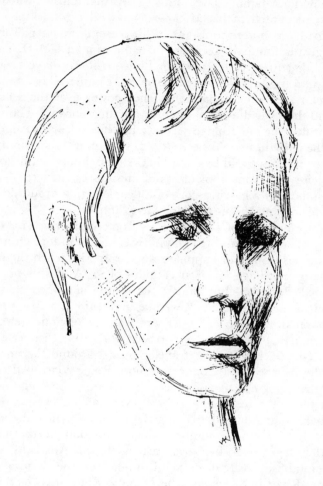

VERGIL

with urbanity and compassionate understanding in his *Odes* and *Epistles* about the desires and foibles of mankind. His good-natured tolerance softened the incisiveness of his satire.

The most famous poet of love in its many forms was Ovid, who also recounted in his *Metamorphoses* all the tales of mythology. Ovid was not circumspect in his personal manner of living, and Augustus found it necessary to exile him in 8 A.D. and to resist all his entreaties for pardon. Livy's *Histories* have been described as a prose epic. With patriotic eloquence he narrated the Roman past—the expansion of her power over the whole of Italy and her steadfastness against the invasions of Hannibal. Livy glorified the old Roman virtues; he believed, with Augustus, that if these virtues could be restored, the luxury and corruption of their own times could be abolished. Although modern historians can criticise Livy's incompleteness of analysis or naivete of interpretation, he told a moving story of a people with a proud destiny; his is a history of heroes teaching by example.

Improvement of conditions in Rome and in the provinces was only possible because the empire was safe from foreign attack. There is no assurance of happiness and prosperity when the threat of invasion or pillage hangs over one's head. Augustus not only maintained the army but built a navy and stationed it, under independent command, at Ravenna and Misenum, to prevent sea-raids on the Italian coasts. There was one obvious weak spot in the empire. Journeying to northern Italy and then eastward towards Greece, the Roman traveler passed around the northern end of the Adriatic Sea. Along the shore Rome controlled only a narrow strip of land, the province of Illyricum; beyond that lay the territory of often-hostile tribes. Two dangers were present: that a barbarian raid might reach the coast and cut the empire's east-west line of land communications, and that northern Italy would then lie open to barbarian attack. It was Augustus' intention to establish easily-defended frontiers for the empire. Like the Rhine River in Germany, the Danube River was the natural boundary for this section of the empire. So, in campaigns of 16 and 15 B.C., Roman troops swept the area from the Adriatic to the Danube. The territory was annexed and organized into the three provinces of Roetia, Noricum, and Pannonia.

Augustus sought the solidity of the empire. He was not at first interested in extending Roman conquests. There was no talk during his reign, for instance, of reviving Caesar's plans for the conquest of Britain or Parthia. With the Rhine-Danube line fortified, however, the prospects of further advance proved irresistible. Augustus sanctioned the crossing of the Rhine, with the aim of extending Roman rule to the Elbe, and the crossing of the Danube, in order to conquer Bohemia. But we may notice that the now-aging Augustus took no active part in these campaigns. He gave command of them to younger members of his family—notably Livia's sons, Tiberius and Drusus—that they might gain experience in command and win the sort of personal prestige which had been of such value to him in establishing his rule.

Although Augustus began gradually to delegate certain authority to his relatives or his loyal lieutenant Agrippa, he continued to work very hard himself at the business of administering the empire. We might say that Augustus made a profession of ruling. He realized that the efficiency of his provincial bureaucracy and of his government by commission would be proportional to the closeness of his interest and the carefulness of his supervision. If his rule was strict and honest, he would succeed in his mission of building an orderly world out of the chaos which had existed after the assassination of Caesar. As ruler of Rome, his attitude was that of the Stoics: "We also must be soldiers, and in a campaign where there is no intermission and no discharge."[31] He worked tirelessly. "No man in history was ever forced to labor so continuously and decide daily on graver issues," says his biographer Buchan.[32] His will dominated the whole civilized world of his day, and he took keen pride in every one of his achievements. He expected neither unfailing success nor universal concurrence in his policies. But he wanted to be allowed to accomplish his task of rebuilding Rome. To Tiberius he said in common sense fashion, "Don't be carried away by the ardor of youth or take it too much to heart that people speak evil of me; we must be content if we can stop them from doing evil to us."[33] The principate must be strong enough to discourage any subversive conspiracies.

8. A look to the future

The Augustan principate left certain problems to future generations of Romans. No more than Caesar was Augustus able to renew the morale of Rome or revive that spirit of unselfish service to the commonwealth which had made the Republic great. His promises of generous pay and advancement did attract many able men to public careers, but it was Augustus' state they served, not their own. The difference is subtle but important. An abyss began to open between the government and the people. Instead of being responsible for their own welfare, the people gained efficient administration at the price of subjecting themselves to a ruler. The old patriotic enthusiasm, the old sense of corporate achievement, the old pride in Roman citizenship, were gone. If the credit for Rome's progress was to go to Augustus, then the thought and the worry and the responsibility should be his also. Each individual could safely concentrate on his private affairs so long as there was an Augustus to look after the welfare of the state. More and more did the edicts of Augustus and his cabinet of advisers supercede the decrees of the Senate as the law of the land. More and more were the decisions of the regularly-constituted courts called into question by appeals to the *princeps*. It is a dangerous habit to put too much reliance on a government, especially a one-man government.

Here we meet a second problem. The principate was Augustus' own creation, and it worked as well as it did because Augustus developed into an able administrator and genuine lover of humanity. But the principate was essentially a personal and temporary form of government. It had been designed to meet a particular emergency; it was not based on any established constitutional principles. Was the *princeps* to exercise as much power as he could, or was his power in some as yet undetermined way to be restricted? Augustus had made himself *princeps;* who was to be *princeps* after him? The *princeps* was not a king and his office was not hereditary; the principate has been described as dying with each particular *princeps*. But clearly a successor must somehow be chosen, and equally clearly the ruling *princeps* must have the decisive voice in the selection.

Augustus recognized this problem, of course, and early sought a solution by making his potential successor an equal colleague in his rule. Thus, during the reign of the elder *princeps,* the successor would be established in pre-eminent rank and given the necessary practical training. But Augustus' own experience showed the difficulty and uncertainty in this method. Naturally enough, he was ambitious to find his successor among his own descendants. During the Triumvirate it became clear that Livia could give Augustus no male heir. His son-in-law Marcellus appeared the most likely candidate for the succession, but he died unexpectedly. We have seen that Tiberius and Drusus, Augustus' stepsons, were favored with independent military commands and early distinguished themselves. But Drusus died in 9 B.C., and Tiberius and Augustus had a disagreement which resulted in Tiberius' long banishment from Rome. Meanwhile Augustus' daughter had two sons by her marriage with Augustus' old colleague Agrippa, who had since died. The favor of the *princeps* was now turned on these two grandsons who showed signs of marked ability. But they died within a year of each other, shortly after the turn of the century.

Augustus was forced to take an interest again in Tiberius,

with whom he was reconciled in 4 A.D. Fortunately, Tiberius was a man of very great talents, although somewhat embittered by his years of exile. But was not the burden of the duties and responsibilities of the *princeps* entirely too onerous to lay on any one man unless he were a genius comparable to Augustus? For the principate to function properly, the *princeps* must be a man of surpassing ability and of extraordinary devotion to Rome. Suppose the designated successor should prove to lack intelligence or nobility of character. How would Rome then prosper? Suppose the *princeps* should die young before there was an heir-apparent. How then would a new *princeps* be chosen? By the Senate, which had granted Augustus his powers? By the army, which had won him his supremacy? The Augustan principate set up no standards by which these questions could be answered.

A third problem was more immediate and more material. We have mentioned plans for the expansion of the empire into Bohemia and across the Rhine. Revolts in Dalmatia, not finally quelled until 9 A.D., interrupted preparations for the Bohemian campaign, and Augustus was happy to rest content with his advance to the Danube. But in Germany Drusus had earlier launched an aggressive campaign and taken possession of the Rhine-Elbe area. Fortified posts were built there, preparatory to the erection of a new province, and Varus was sent out as governor. This was an unwise appointment. Varus had earned a bad reputation as legate in Syria: every one agrees that when he went, he was poor and Syria was rich; but when he departed, he was rich and Syria was poor. Varus failed to perceive that the Germans were restive under the Roman occupation and that Rome's grasp of the new territory was not yet secure. In 9 A.D., moving his main force toward winter quarters, Varus let his German adviser Arminius lead him into an ambush in the dense Teutoberg Forest. There three legions—the 17th, 18th, and 19th—ceased to exist. All save one of the Roman posts were subsequently lost to the barbarians. The story is that thenceforward the aged Augustus, tormented by nightmares, used to rise up in the darkness pleading, "Varus, Varus, give me back my legions!"[34]

The significance of this one real check to the plans of Augustus was far greater than the story of a bad dream or even than the termination of Augustus' policy of expansion. Although the reliable Tiberius hastened northward to hold the Rhine frontier, the defeat of Varus was a portent of the future. The Roman expansionists had misjudged the nature and the strength of the Germans. These barbarians did not want peacefully to accept Roman domination; they were not willing to be assimilated into the Roman empire. They would cling to their own government, their own religion, their own customs. At Augustus' death, these proudly irreconcilable and valiant barbarians were left unconquered on the Rhine frontier. They had shattered Rome's reputation of invincibility. They were a new force; Rome would have to learn to deal with them.

Today we cannot give unqualified approval to the principate as a form of government. It was a dictatorship masquerading as a democracy. Its democratic forms lacked lasting vitality: Assembly elections, senatorial law-making, popular sovereignty, were shows. The power of the *princeps* was the reality. Rome became a one-party state; there was no effective opposition to Augustus. The dictatorship was strong and absolute, even if it was efficient and benevolent. But we must remember that Augustus was not able to put into operation a perfect scheme of government as it might have been conceived in an idealist's imagination. Rather he had to devise political expedients to meet the requirements of the moment. Practical minds must deal with the world as it is. Augustus was looking for a system that would work, and the principate was the best that he and the Roman world of his day were capable of. Like all the effective governments Rome ever produced in her long history, it resulted, as Polybius might have said, from the struggles and troubles that tested the minds and hearts of the citizens. It was shaped by the experience gained in the disasters of the previous century and a half of civil disturbance.

Under Augustus, the principate achieved great popularity because it was so successful in meeting the needs of Rome. "Never," says the geographer Strabo, "had Rome and her allies enjoyed richer blessings of peace and prosperity"[35] than under the rule of Augustus. Then did the provinces flourish and commerce expand in the security granted by Rome's victorious armies. Then did Rome substitute for the unruliness of gang wars an orderly existence under a just government. Then was peacefully achieved the sound political reconstruction of the empire. Then occurred the golden age of Latin literature. Then did every class in the population find a profitable occupation, achieve reasonable contentment, and contribute to the stability of the whole state.

Horace described the life of his age. Devoted though he was to Augustus, we doubt if he has much overstated the popular veneration of the ruler. In the *Odes* he wrote: "With vows and prayers his country calls for Caesar. . . . For when he is here, the ox roams the fields in safety, Ceres and bounteous happiness enrich our farms; our sailors sail peaceful waters; public honor stands inviolate; pure homes are stained by no adulteries, custom and law have vanquished sin, and punishment follows swift on crime. . . . Who fears Parthian, Scythian, German or Spaniard, if Caesar be safe? Each man sees day close in peace on his native hills, and trains his vines to the trees, and returns home light of heart to drink his wine and bless him as god indeed."[36]

"If Caesar be safe. . . ." But Augustus' long and fruitful life drew gradually to a close. In 14 A.D., returning to Rome from a meeting with his heir-designate Tiberius, he halted at Nola on the seashore and could go no further. As he lay dying, he asked those about him, "Don't you think I have played my part in life's masquerade rather well?"[37] There are episodes in the masquerade he might well have been willing to forget—the murder of Cicero, the slaughter at Perugia—but there was good cause for his over-all satisfaction with his life. As he had hoped to do, he had attained —or surpassed—the standards set by the worthiest rulers in Roman history.[38]

The sensible and substantial Augustus had been able to effect that re-ordering of the Roman world of which the imaginative and brilliant Caesar had been able only to dream. And he could die now quietly—admired, respected, even worshiped as "Pater Patriae", the Father of his Country. Suetonius has ascribed to Augustus this statement: "May it be my privilege to establish the state firm and secure and to reap the fruit of my toil, so that I may be called the author of the best possible government, and, when I die, the foundations which I have laid will remain unshaken."[39] If this was indeed his purpose, Augustus had masterfully achieved it. He had triumphantly reached the end of the path on which he had been set by the vision and the victories of his great uncle.

The monument of the combined genius of Caesar and Augustus was the Roman Empire.

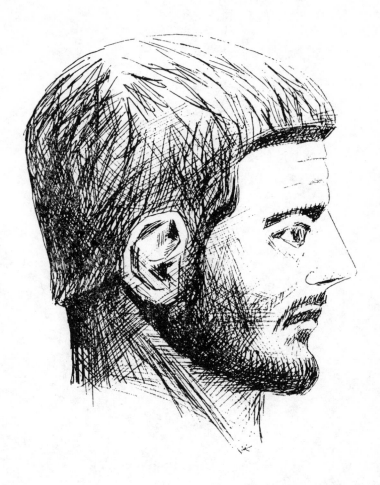

Chapter V

DIOCLETIAN

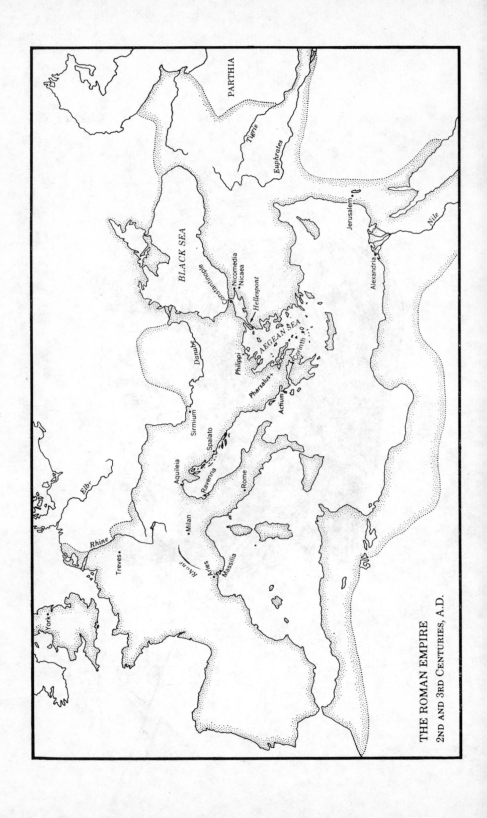

THE ROMAN EMPIRE
2ND AND 3RD CENTURIES, A.D.

DIOCLETIAN REGENERATES THE ROMAN EMPIRE

Augustus' reorganization of the state proved satisfactory and his system of government remained in effect for about three hundred years. The name "principate" fell into disuse, however, and was succeeded by the name "empire", and this is indicative of certain changes which took place in the course of time.

1. The Empire to 284 A.D.: decline in power and wealth

The *princeps*-become-emperor freed himself more and more from even the theory or pretense of constitutional restraint. Both Caesar and Augustus had risen to power as champions of the lower classes against the aristocratic clique. But instead of representing the common people, the emperors dictated to them. The government became a tyranny; the emperor's power increased while the Senate's declined. It was quicker, easier, and more efficient for the emperor to issue an edict than for the Senate to pass a law. And the emperor had a trained staff to execute his edicts. So the status of the emperor changed. No longer "the first of the senators", he grew into a being apart, isolated from the crowd, a master, even a god. His absolute power resulted in an increase in the importance of the army as an active participant in the government. If the emperor wished to over-awe the Senate, he could best do so by having at hand a military force sufficient to compel agreement. In the last analysis, then, the Empire grew to be based on the power of the sword. Citizens, even senators, became less and less significant. High rank in the army meant real power in the state. Naturally the most convenient force for the emperor to employ was his private army, or praetorian guard, stationed in Rome. The commander of the praetorians had influence second only to the emperor's.

123

These changes did not occur all at once, and the full effect of them did not become apparent until the 3rd century.

In the years following the death of Augustus the imperial power was a monopoly of the Julian family. Tiberius and Claudius were able rulers, but the dangers of hereditary dictatorship were exposed in the reigns of Caligula and Nero, who lacked both intellectual capacity and moral strength. When Nero was finally murdered, the succession was for the first time a matter of dispute. After a year of civil war, a capable general named Vespasian secured the throne. He was succeeded by his son, Titus, and there followed a golden era in ancient history.

Vespasian's successors are called the "Good Emperors". They reigned for a century of security, prosperity, and contentment. The skill of the Roman builders was employed in the provinces as well as in Rome; the land, as Homer had hoped, seemed to be the common possession of all men. Trajan, the first provincial to wear the imperial purple, extended the Empire by conquests in Britain, across the Rhine, and beyond the Danube. If his successor Hadrian abandoned these out-lying conquests, it was only to solidify the Empire behind his famous walls. Under the Good Emperors the civilized world enjoyed the benefits of the unbroken Roman Peace.

It was of this era that the Greek philosopher Aristides wrote to the Emperor:

> Now any Greek, or non-Greek, can travel wherever he likes as easily as if he were passing from homeland to homeland. Neither the sandy approaches to Egypt through Arabia cause terror, nor inaccessible mountains nor immense stretches of river nor inhospitable barbarians; it is enough to be a Roman citizen. You have measured and recorded the land of the entire civilized world; you have spanned rivers with bridges and hewn highways through mountains and have filled barren stretches with posting stations; you have accustomed all areas to a settled and orderly way of life. . . . Cities gleam with radiance and charm; the whole earth has been beautified like a garden. . . .[1]

But the defense of the frontiers and the maintenance of effective government grew increasingly expensive. To be a substantial member of middle-class society in the Roman Empire was to be faced with an ever-growing burden of taxation. The task of supporting the Empire was beginning to become heavy. Sufficient recruits for the army were hard to find among the provincial peasantry. Sufficient funds to meet the imperial expenses were hard to collect from the provincial bourgeoisie.

When the philosopher-emperor Marcus Aurelius died in

180, his worthless and brutal son Commodus succeeded him. Later a group of senators carried out their plot to murder Commodus. This murder opened the critical struggle which was to rage throughout the next century—the contest for the control of the emperor between the new army and the old senatorial and moneyed classes. The army was the rising element, men with their fortunes to make. The wealthy city-dwellers were the conservative element, trying to hold on to their estates and rights of local self-government. If the army won, the emperor could impose uniformity on the various parts of his realm and the soldiers would occupy a privileged position. If the conservatives won, the localities would retain their independence and their diversity of customs and a limit would be set on the powers of the emperor.

This internal conflict in the 3rd century brought the Empire to the verge of ruin. To begin with, the conspiracy against Commodus gained the Senate nothing. The imperial power required a strong arm to wield it and was usurped by a general, Septimius Severus. He proscribed a number of "opposition" senators and introduced army officers into the government on a large scale. For the first time, the imperial power was openly based on military might. To pay the army, the provincial municipalities were taxed more heavily than ever. Although a wise and humane ruler, Severus left to his sons the advice, "Please the soldiers". Next, Caracalla attempted to satisfy Rome with a magnificent building program and the provincials with a universal grant of citizenship. But his benefits to the soldiers were largely confined to the praetorian guards. The armies on the frontiers were discontented, and Caracalla's murder was arranged. In the following reigns the bonds between emperor and army were drawn closer, and the middle classes fought a losing battle for political rights and lower taxes. Maximinus relied wholly on the army and impoverished the bourgeoisie. He "would have no man of noble rank in his entourage." He confiscated so much personal property that "every day one could see the wealthiest men of yesterday beggars."[2] A few years later Gallienus prohibited men of senatorial rank from holding any command in the army. The old rulers of Rome were degraded by exclusion from all responsibilities. The new rulers had risen through the ranks, and their barbarian and oriental habits of thought came to dominate the government, as they already dominated the army.

These new rulers had vigor and ambition. But naturally they had little awareness of Roman tradition and little respect for any constitution. Contemptuous of "right", they were accustomed to taking what they could get, by force or bribery. But they could not insure their enjoyment of the prize. Before a new emperor could even begin to rule, plots were hatching for his overthrow. Of the twenty-three emperors who actually reigned in the period 211-284, not a single one died quietly at home. This is not to mention the host of disappointed pretenders to the throne who were murdered by their disgruntled supporters or executed by their successful rivals. It must scarcely have seemed worthwhile to try to become emperor or to rule well, for, as Gibbon says, "Such was the unhappy condition of the Roman emperors, that, whatever might be their conduct, their fate was commonly the same. A life of pleasure or virtue, of severity or mildness, of indolence or glory, alike led to an untimely grave."3 As soon as some of his soldiers murdered the brave Aurelian, they repented their hasty act, but it was hard to put aside the habit of assassination.

While the army was making and unmaking emperors, the need for strong government at Rome grew more pressing. Trouble was brewing on the borders, and the safety of the Empire was at stake. Invaders pushed across the Rhine and the Danube, and the pressure was too great to be appeased by grants of land or wholesale enlistments in the Roman army. The barbarians wanted parts of the Empire for their own. And the reviving power of Persia threatened the eastern provinces. With the authorities at Rome apparently powerless to halt the marauders, the provincial commanders acted on their own initiative and established little empires of their own, such as the one which flourished in Syria, 259-273, under the leadership of the remarkable Queen Xenobia. Repelling the invaders, they also flaunted the power of Rome. The Empire showed signs of falling apart from its own unwieldiness. Aurelian had enough military genius to crush these "splinter" empires and to hold back invasion in his too-brief reign of five years, but it is significant that he saw fit to construct fortifications for the city of Rome itself.

The weakening of the frontier defenses and the rapid turnover of emperors both contributed to the internal decay of the Empire. The Roman Peace was broken. Towns were abandoned. Land was permitted to go to waste. Plagues, invasions, and civil wars took their toll. The population and resources of the Empire steadily decreased. Occupied with constant warfare, plots and counter-plots, and the unending problem of satisfying the soldiery, the emperors had little time—even when they had the capacity—for good government. The administration during this chaotic period was never established on a firm basis. Rome was in a perpetual state of emergency. It was always necessary to think of the army first, and the army demanded the ruin of the old privileged classes. The taxpayers were gradually squeezed to death. With their capital seized by the state, they shut down their industries and curtailed their trade. Unemployment spread and tax receipts went down. The emperors resorted to debasement of the currency. The silver *denarius* which had been worth at least sixteen cents under Augustus was worth only half a cent under Aurelian. Such inflation forced all save the richest buyers out of the market. Barter began to replace money-trading. When money was unavailable for tax-payments, property was requisitioned and labor was forced.

The decline in material well-being and the collapse of orderly government were matched by a deterioration in moral standards. Rostovtzeff gives a vivid summary of the dreadful conditions of the 3rd century:

> Hatred and envy reigned everywhere: the peasants hated the landowners and the officials, the city proletariat hated the city bourgeoisie, the army was hated by everybody, even by the peasants. . . . Work was disorganized and productivity was declining; commerce was ruined by the insecurity of the sea and the roads; industry could not prosper, since the market for industrial products was steadily contracting and the purchasing power of the population diminishing; agriculture passed through a terrible crisis, for the decay of commerce and industry deprived it of the capital which it needed, and the heavy demands of the state robbed it of labor and of the largest part of its products. Prices constantly rose, and the value of the currency depreciated at an unprecedented rate. The ancient system of taxation had been shattered and no new system was devised. The relations between the state and the taxpayer were based on more or less organized robbery: forced work, forced deliveries, forced loans or gifts were the order of the day. The administration was corrupt and demoralized. A chaotic mass of new government officials was growing up, superimposed on and superceding the former administrative personnel. The old officials still existed but, foreseeing their doom, strove to avail themselves to the full of their last opportunities. The city bourgeoisie was tracked down and persecuted, cheated, and maltreated. The municipal aristocracy was decimated by systematic persecution and ruined by repeated confiscations . . . . The most terrible chaos thus reigned throughout the ruined empire.[4]

The system established by Augustus was out-of-date. The very survival of the Empire, challenged from without and stagnating within, was doubtful. The question of the hour was, How could the Empire be saved? Everyone—aristocracy, bourgeoisie, army— was agreed that the first need was the protection of the Empire. The survival of the state assumed larger importance than the welfare of its individual inhabitants. It seemed proper for resources to be concentrated for the maintenance of an efficient army. Then only could the Roman people seek their fortunes in security. Once again, as in Augustus' day, chaos threatened to engulf Rome. "The Roman Empire bitterly needed peace and was ready to accept it from the emperor at any price."[5]

2. *Diocletian gains the throne*

In 284 the Empire acquired a new emperor. At first it appeared that there was little to distinguish him from his predecessors, little reason to suppose that his reign should be longer, more settled, more fruitful than theirs. Diocletian had been born in 245 in a small town in Dalmatia, the son of a freed slave. Like many other ambitious provincials, he entered the army as the most likely pathway to advancement. He served under Aurelian and held minor commands against the Germans. In 282 he went with Carus to the war which recovered Armenia and Mesopotamia from the Persians. By this time he had shown such ability and trustworthiness as to be given the command of the household guards, and he had broadened his vigorous mind by contacts with all sorts of men. By this time, also, he had had an experience of deep significance to a person of superstitious nature. While in the army, the story goes, Diocletian spent a night at an inn whose landlady was a Druid priestess. The next morning he was slow to produce the money for his lodging. "Don't get stuck to it," she said. He replied laughingly, "I'll part with it quicker when I'm emperor." "You'll be emperor," she said, "when you have killed the boar." Diocletian later murmured to a friend, "I always kill the boar, but someone else gets the skin."[6]

These cryptic words take on meaning when we learn the events that occurred at the end of the Persian war. The Emperor Carus died in his tent during a thunderstorm. His son Numerian died in an unexplained way, and his death was for some time concealed. Then the praetorian prefect Arrius Aper—"the Boar"—was accused of murder. Without giving him any opportunity to protest his innocence, Diocletian himself killed Aper, saying "Great Aeneas slays you!" Diocletian not only got away with his high-handed assumption of judicial power but he was promptly elected emperor by the troops. This record persuades some historians to accuse Diocletian of having plotted the series of deaths in order to grab the throne. Circumstantial evidence points to his guilt, but his later behavior makes such cold-blooded cruelty seem unlikely, and Aurelius Victor, the most reliable of the ancient narrators, asserts his innocence. It will probably remain forever impossible to ascertain the truth.

Whether or not Diocletian plotted the murders, he possessed the energy and decisiveness of mind and will necessary for him to take advantage of the opportunity they offered. Numerian's brother Carinus collected an army in the West and met Diocletian's forces in Illyria. Diocletian was no military genius, and his army was being defeated, when the news spread that Carinus had been murdered. Both armies then accepted the leadership of Diocletian, who was thenceforward generally acknowledged as emperor. Not only had Diocletian been a good enough opportunist to gain the throne, but also he had the wisdom to grasp the magnitude of the task facing the ruler of the Empire. He later declared that he had hoped for the death of Carinus, not out of ambition for himself, but out of concern for the welfare of Rome. He knew that Carinus was a foolhardy wastrel. His deep insight into the problems of the day informed him that the Empire could not survive unless it were removed from the control of irresponsible emperors who catered exclusively to the soldiers and lost their thrones as soon as they lost the favor of the military. The army must protect Rome, of course, but it must not be permitted to control all government policy and personnel. Perhaps we may agree with the 19th century historian, Burckhardt, that Diocletian understood the paramount need of the Empire for permanence of rule and that he was "driven inexorably to the throne" to accomplish such permanence in his own person.[7]

3. *Reorganization of the political and economic systems*

However we judge Diocletian's phenomenal rise, we cannot but praise the political courage with which he at once proceeded to effect his plans for the salvation of the Empire. Despite the frequent changes in the occupant of the throne, the people still had respect for the position of the emperor. The population in general—with a very large proportion non-Roman in origins—was very different from the population with which Augustus had to deal. The people had no experience, and therefore no jealous pride, in self-government; they were accustomed to obeying orders. The quarrelsome population groups were unable to save themselves. So Diocletian saw that a movement for reform must be initiated from above; it must stem directly from the emperor and be in the form of an order rather than a suggestion.

It would be impossible to persuade the different elements in the Empire to cooperate for their mutual benefit. Class interests were divergent, inter-class hatreds intense. Augustus had been able to rely on a solid core of bourgeois support, and the provincial cities had been for him "little Romes"—subsidiary centers of the

Augustan system. But Diocletian lacked these advantages: by his time the cities were decaying and the middle classes had been all but obliterated. He could find no natural allies, for the Senate had been discredited and there were few conservative citizens left. Fortunately, Diocletian saw that with cooperation unavailable, compulsion became necessary. Instead of being "first among many", as Augustus had modestly styled himself, the emperor must be lord of all, absolute master, with no limitations on his power. Only such an emperor could dominate the army and compel universal obedience. The closer the monarch came to resembling a god, the quicker could he expect his commands to be executed.

The chief dangers facing Diocletian were those which had ruined his predecessors. Now that the Empire had expanded so far, especially to the East, the emperor was too remote from many of his subjects to exercise effective control over them. If he was at Rome, he could not command his armies. If he was with the army on the frontier, he could not supervise the ordinary administration of the Empire. If he should be killed or captured, as Valerian was by the Persians, the army might have settled the succession before even the news of his fate had reached the capital. The personality of the emperor was the sole cement holding the disintegrating state together. He was also the sole obstacle standing between an ambitious usurper and the throne. The emperor made too good a target for the assassin's knife. To dispose of him, with the connivance of a part of the army, was too easy, and his murderer might then occupy his throne. The death of an emperor in the 3rd century always entailed at least a short intermission in the regular processes of government, when the executive ceased to function. So many emperors succeeded each other in such a brief span of years, that these periods of anarchy were more extensive than the periods of orderly administration and regular tax collection. And they were often concluded by orgies of proscription and confiscation, which further weakened the basic structure of the state.

Diocletian was not a visionary idealist. Instead of attempting a bold reform of society or politics, he proposed simply to make the existing organization function efficiently. His thought was to make the power of the emperor secure and constantly effective throughout the Empire. One man could not do the whole job. He could not be at once successful general and competent administrator. He could not at the same time be on the Rhine and on the Danube, govern Rome and treat with the Persians. So Diocletian conceived the idea of a "board of emperors". Less than two years after his accession he selected a colleague, Maximian, to share the imperial duties and honors. Diocletian kept the East under his personal rule. It was the larger and richer section of the Empire, as well as the more troublesome.

Diocletian made his capital in Nicomedia, an Asiatic city not far from the Hellespont. This change in the location of the chief capital of the Empire was significant. Diocletian was the first ruler to establish his official residence outside of Rome. The ancient capital had declined in value as the Empire expanded: it was now geographically inconvenient and strategically unimportant. It is doubtful if Diocletian had yet even visited Rome. He entrusted control of the western part of the Empire to Maximian. He, too, ruled from a new capital—Milan. It would have been dangerous to surround him with the prestige of the old capital, which might have prompted him to attempt to make himself sole emperor. Milan was a busier crossroads, also, and closer to the problems of the barbarians. Diocletian's arrangement effectually degraded once-proud Rome.

Before many years Diocletian realized that he and Maximian could not govern well if they must give so much of their time to keeping peace on the frontiers. Gaul and Dalmatia were currently the trouble spots. They required the presence of physically energetic commanders to maintain border security and establish firm provincial government. So, in 293, Diocletian increased his "board" from two to four. He and Maximian, the seniors in age and experience, retained their full authority. They were to be called "Augustus". The new appointees were their assistants, their military executives, with special responsibility for the outlying provinces. Their title was "Caesar". Each of them, however, maintained his own staff and held his own court. Constantius Chlorus guarded the Rhine from his capital at Treves; Galerius the Danube from his capital at Sirmium.

Diocletian had not lessened his own prestige or authority. As originator of the scheme, he held plenary power over his three colleagues. He was "chairman of the board", with the right of final decision in disputes. His superior wisdom and will power held even Maximian in line. An illustration will serve to show that none of the lieutenants thought to challenge his supremacy. Following an unsuccessful campaign against the Persians, Galerius awaited a visit from Diocletian. When the latter arrived in his chariot, he did not halt but motioned Galerius to accompany him. Clothed in the imperial purple, Galerius had to run a mile in the dust of Diocletian's chariot, before Augustus would deign to pause to converse with Caesar.

In dividing the imperial authority, Diocletian's first aim was to make that authority more effective. With four emperors in widely-separated capitals, every part of the Empire could be closely and continuously supervised. Each ruler would naturally become an expert in the particular problems of his section. There would be much less chance for disorder or rebellion to spread while the emperor was engaged in other affairs. Diocletian's second aim was to maintain the unbroken continuity of the imperial authority. When an Augustus ceased to reign, he would automatically be succeeded by his Caesar, who would in turn select his own second-in-command. Any ambitious "tyrant", any one provincial army, would now find four emperors standing in the way of a usurpation of the throne. Four simultaneous assassinations would be difficult to engineer. Diocletian's plan should end the sudden and violent changes of government which had so disrupted the Empire for a hundred years.

Several other aspects of the plan deserve notice. The Caesars have been described as "apprentice emperors". While serving as lieutenants to Augustus, they gained political experience and acquainted themselves with the policies of their superiors, so that those policies could be carried on even when the imperial personnel was changed. Diocletian intended to set a term of twenty years to the reign of an individual Augustus. He knew that young children and old men were alike unfitted to manage the complex affairs of the Empire. The Augustus should be in the prime of life. The Caesar, somewhat younger, should have his ambition satisfied by the assured prospect of achieving the supreme power. Thus the succession of emperors would be regular and legal, according to prescribed "right". Finally, this succession should not be based on heredity. The Caesar should be appointed to his office not because of an accident of birth but as the result of his proved ability. The Augustus should adopt him as his successor because he was the best man available. Diocletian hoped by this new system to give to the Empire efficient government and a secured and peaceful succession of emperors.

Diocletian reorganized the imperial structure in order to achieve administrative stability within the Empire and a successful defense of the frontiers. But these goals must be reached at a cost which the Empire could afford to pay. It was inevitable that the Emperor had to give his attention to the economic condition of the realm. The immediate problem was inflation, which may be described with equal accuracy as a decline in the value of money or as a rise in the price of goods. Diocletian attempted to attack this problem from both angles—that is, to raise the value of money and to cut prices. He had to accept some depreciation of the money values of the principate, even though this worked severe hardship on creditors and on those living on fixed incomes or trust funds. But Diocletian tried to halt further depreciation by re-establishing a stable currency. He issued gold *aurei,* silver *denarii,* and copper *folles,* with their value determined by the ratio between the cost of the metal contained in the coins. Diocletian's currency won popular confidence. Unfortunately, the supplies of the precious metals were insufficient. As the expenses of government increased, the emperors could not resist using their control of the mint to meet their new expenses, even though the currency was further debased by the reduction of its metallic content.

Price-fixing is another governmental expedient with which the 20th century is familiar. In his Edict of 301, Diocletian proclaimed "ceilings" on both prices and wages. Harvests had been poor, speculation had been rife, and prices had risen sky-high, as a result of "measureless avarice" and "unprincipled greed". Said Diocletian: "Our law shall fix a measure and a limit to this greed."[8] There must be no further profiteering in foodstuffs, clothing, building materials. Eggs could be sold at no more than 5¢ a dozen, ham at 12¢ a pound, wheat at 75¢ a bushel, boots at 52¢ a pair. These prices might seem absurdly low until we realize that an unskilled laborer could only be paid 11¢ a day, a carpenter or mason 22¢, a painter 33¢.[9] The wages for every trade and profession were similarly limited. Offenses against the Edict were punishable by death.

Diocletian's Edict was well-intended. But it did not take account of local differences in conditions, and it condemned as "lust for plunder" the normal profit-taking of the middleman. Instead of bringing down the high cost of living, it encouraged hoarding. Goods were not offered for sale, except on "black" markets. Producers saw no reason for doing business at a loss; so no business was done. Even the elaborate machinery of Diocletian's powerful government was unable to enforce the decree. Faced with impoverishment and starvation, the Romans ignored the Edict.[10]

4. Success and failure of Diocletian's reforms

To what extent was Diocletian's reorganization of the Empire successful? Just what did he accomplish? To put it briefly, Diocletian was responsible for keeping the Empire alive. This involved, first of all, the protection of the unity and integrity of the Empire against internal and external foes. Firm government replaced civil disorder in Gaul, which had recently been on the verge of making good its independence. In Egypt, Diocletian put down rebellions and restored respect for the paramount authority of Rome. Under Diocletian's orders, the frontiers were once again rendered secure. Galerius was finally able to establish Armenia as a buffer state, effectively reducing the Persian threat. Similarly, Constantius reduced the Frankish threat on the German border. His outstanding feat was the overthrow of Carausias, a "tyrant" who was attempting to build for himself a kingdom in Gaul and Britain. So well did Diocletian's lieutenants do their work that the Empire could enjoy a generation of freedom from foreign invasion.

The Empire had been militarily weak because it had grown to resemble a hollow shell. Isolated armies had held the frontiers, with no adequate reserves behind them. Centralizing command had been lacking and there had been no core of power on which the emperors could call in emergencies. All this Diocletian changed. The borders could be garrisoned by militia, with strictly limited areas of responsibility. Then the flower of the soldiery need not be dispersed among the frontier armies but could be concentrated into a "mobile striking force". This enlarged and highly-trained army was directly under the emperor's orders, quickly responsive to the particular needs of the moment. It became the main support of the imperial authority. Instead of being the weapon by which a usurper might unseat the emperor, it was the chief agency by which the emperor could enforce his commands.

But Diocletian is known as a statesman rather than as a general; he preferred persuasion to force. He did not, therefore, base his control solely on the army. Instead, he created a parallel civil organization for ordinary administration. These civil authorities were kept carefully separate from the military; command over men was strictly divorced from control over money. There must be no question of any one becoming too powerful by engrossing both civil and military power. But there was a marked similarity between the organization of the civilian officialdom and the military. At the top were four prefects, each responsible for the government of one of the four major divisions of the Empire, called prefectures. Under them were a dozen vicars, who administered the somewhat smaller dioceses. Under them were a hundred or more governors, who administered the individual provinces. An almost military discipline was required of this civilian hierarchy. Each official reported to his immediate superior. At every level there should be an official directly responsible for executing the imperial will. At every level, also, the civilian vicar or governor had his counterpart in the military duke or count.

Diocletian thus secured the imperial authority, not only by enlisting colleagues at the top but also by dividing the administrative powers among a host of officials, who would supervise and check each other. These officials were his appointees, his servants; they hedged him off from the dangers and pressures of everyday politics. Only the very highest and most loyal among them ever saw the chairman of the board of emperors. They formed his council of advisers, and even they stood respectfully in their ruler's presence. Each had his own clearly-defined area of authority. No rich or aristocratic amateurs were entrusted with vague grants of responsibility which they might use to build up their own personal prestige. There could be no disunion in Diocletian's Empire. His political system was constructed on strict subordination; under his simplified constitution everyone from senator to peasant was treated equally, as a subject of the emperor.

Diocletian had created for the Empire new administrative machinery, and under him it functioned smoothly. Peace was attained; within the Empire there was good order. Careers in the public service were open to all men of ability and loyalty. The imperial office itself took on new stature. There was revived respect for an Emperor whose power had some permanence and who seemed to sense his obligation for the welfare of the state. From the *Historia Augusta* Burckhardt quotes, about Diocletian: "He was an outstanding man, clever, zealous for the state, zealous for those under his protection, prepared for any task; always unfathomable in his thoughts, sometimes foolhardy but otherwise prudent; the stirring of his restless spirit he suppressed with inflexible perseverance." And Burckhardt calls him "one of the greatest of the Roman emperors, the savior of the Empire and of civilization, the shrewdest judge of his time."[11]

But Diocletian has not been universally praised. He replaced anarchy with stability, but he failed to make any real improvement in the lot of the common man. The fabric of his government had in it certain flaws. First was its high cost. The mere substitution of four emperors for one, of four courts for one, was a tremendous expense. The enlarged army of soldiers and army of clerks had to be paid, or their services would be lost. Government is always expensive, and the multiplication of officials provided a new burden for the taxpayers as well as a new field for corruption. Diocletian made a drastic increase in taxation. The basic tax unit was the *annona*, a sum to meet the cost of a year's essential supplies of grain, wine, meat, oil, and salt for one soldier. An annual assessment specified the number of *annonae* which must be paid into the imperial treasury. Every five years a survey was made to determine the taxable population and the extent of their resources, so that the government could get its share from any increase in private wealth. The size of a man's liability depended on the amount and productivity of the land he owned. The unit here was the *iugum,* the area of land which could be cultivated by a single worker. This land tax was always a heavy obligation, the more burdensome because you could not estimate in advance the number of *annonae* which your *iuga* must produce. Surprisingly enough, Diocletian permitted exemptions to certain privileged groups, such as senatorial families, and teachers, doctors, and priests appointed by the state. But this loss of revenue was compensated for by special taxes on senatorial property and the businesses of the bourgeoisie.

The land tax, nevertheless, was the chief support of the state, and the heaviest imposition on the taxpayers. The landowners could hope to meet their obligations only by maintaining maximum productivity on their land. They dared not lose any of the workers from their fields. And the government could not afford smaller tax yields. So legislation was proposed requiring farm-laborers, *coloni,* to remain on the farms for their lifetimes. Sometimes a landowner who allowed some of his fields to revert to wasteland found his taxes too heavy. He was apt to transfer the burden of them to a stronger landlord and accept for himself the status of a *colonus.* Even the large landowners were unable to find the ready money with which to pay taxes. The government had to accept payment in kind—that is, in grain or oil or wine—or in labor. This in turn added to the costs of government, for storehouses must be built and overseers added to the payroll, calling for additional *annonae* the coming year. Placing his main reliance on the land tax, Diocletian simplified the imperial tax system. But the new system was too rigid and placed oppressive loads on the farming population.

Increased expense was only one of the faults of Diocletian's government. It stifled initiative and limited freedom. In quest of efficiency, a bureaucracy likes to make uniform rules. The same order from the central authority must be executed in the same way throughout the realm. Local customs are ignored; local problems cannot be considered. Local self-government is abolished, for all provinces must be treated uniformly. Every official finds himself curbed by the orders of his superior in the imperial hierarchy. From the top issue the orders of the absolute monarch.

Under Diocletian, all traces of republicanism vanished from the Roman government. The despotism which had been increasing from the days of Augustus was now asserted as the proper basis of government. Diocletian was not *princeps,* but *dominus,* lord. He wore the crown and the robes of an oriental monarch and surrounded himself with an elaborate court ceremonial. Augustus had enjoyed the company of his patrician "equals"; Diocletian demanded that all men prostrate themselves before him. Even in the coinage of their reigns is this contrast between Augustus and Diocletian evidenced. The coin portraits of Augustus had represented the almost breathing vitality of the graceful and vigorous human being. Those of Diocletian seem the abstraction of power, with the hair stylized and the personal emotions hidden behind a conventional mask.[12]

Where Augustus had striven to conceal, Diocletian openly

displayed the enormous powers of the emperor. To be sure, it was politics rather than personal vanity which inspired Diocletian thus to pose as an oriental potentate. By so doing he thought to impress the multitude with the splendor of the Empire and the greatness of its ruler, thereby fostering submission to imperial dictates. He had too much sense to be affected by the adulation given his person. As Aurelius Victor says: "He suffered himself to be called lord but behaved like a father; doubtless he wished to show, in his wisdom, that not evil names but evil deeds are what matter."[13]

Diocletian was neither unreasoning nor cruel; he was vigorous and efficient, and he wanted to create a durable system. The "government he imposed upon a suffering world" was, Frank complains, "utterly un-Roman," compounded of "despotism, elaborately systematized espionage, and unabating suppression."[14] Hadas, on the other hand, praises Diocletian for his "true statesmanship in shaping the Empire according to the realities" of his era. In the preamble to the famous Edict of 301, the Emperor explained that "public decency and the dignity and majesty of Rome demand that [the state] be organized efficiently and managed successfully."[15]

So Diocletian could readily justify his taking the Senate, the one remnant of the old Republic, and reducing it to a nonentity. Augustus had destroyed its actual supremacy; Diocletian now removed even its formal authority. No longer did ratification of laws depend on the Senate. No longer did the Emperor at Nicomedia consult with the Senate at Rome. Honors still came to the senators, but overmighty individuals might find themselves accused of disloyalty to the Empire and their property or lives sacrificed at the will of the Emperor.

Diocletian's reorganization of the state marks a fundamental change in the relations of the Roman people with their government. Ancient Romans of wealth and standing—like Cato—had served the state as a matter of course, as their natural duty. But under Diocletian, to rise in the world was only to increase your obligations to the tax-collector, and to hold office was to add to your own the heavy obligations of others. Here is an example. The local aristocracy, or decurions, in a provincial city—comparable in prestige to the senators in Rome—were held liable by Diocletian for the entire tax assessment on the city. They were responsible even for the lands within the city which might have been deserted. Therefore, from their own resources they had to make up the inevitable deficits. And at the very time that such increased burdens fell on substantial citizens, incentive was taken away from them. What they accomplished was for Diocletian's benefit, not for their own or their city's. They came to feel they were nothing but "slaves" to the emperor. No wonder that people sought to avoid decurion status, even by leaving their native cities or fleeing from the Empire. The expense and trouble of holding office had come to outweigh the attendant honor and dignity. This effort of the citizens to evade public service at all costs is often considered the surest sign of the decay of a state.

We can see then that Diocletian had not easily or cheaply brought uniformity and efficiency to the Roman government. There were critics aplenty who felt that peace was not worth the price. For instance, the Christian historian, Lactantius, wrote of Diocletian:

> That inventor of crimes and deviser of evils . . . was the man who overturned the whole world, dividing the Empire into four parts so that armies were multiplied . . . . Thus the receivers of taxes began to be more in number than the payers, so that by the excess of land-taxes, the farms were laid waste and tilled lands turned into forests. In order, too, that all places might be filled with terror, the provinces also were cut up into fragments, and many . . . officials lay heavy on every territory.[16]

Lactantius condemned the "continual confiscations and requisitions . . . whenever Diocletian saw a field more carefully tilled or a house more elegantly adorned than usual." Then the historian described the results of the Edict of 301: "Again when by various evil deeds he caused a prodigious scarcity, he essayed by law to fix the prices of goods in the market . . . so that the scarcity was made much worse, until after the law had ruined multitudes it was of sheer necessity abolished." Lactantius accused Diocletian of ruining the provincials to satisfy his tastes for building, "here public offices, there a circus, here a mint, there an arms factory, here a palace for his wife, and there one for his daughter . . . in his endeavor to make Nicomedia equal to imperial Rome."

5. Diocletian abdicates and confusion ensues

Whether our final estimate be that Diocletian had a good or bad effect on Rome, we must all admit that he built a strong government. While he reigned no one openly questioned the wisdom of his imperial system. His personal authority was unchallenged, even by the aggressive Galerius, and no dissensions split the board of emperors.

In 304 Diocletian went to Rome to celebrate a triumph for the successes of his twenty years of rule. This may well have been, as Gibbon suggests,[17] his first visit to the ancient capital, but Diocletian had not ignored the welfare and happiness of its

inhabitants. Following the precedents of earlier rulers, he had ordered the construction, as a new center of community life, of
spacious and magnificent baths. Diocletian's are reputed to have
accommodated more than three thousand patrons at a time. His
triumph was another ritual act. It was performed now, however,
not—as was customary—to glorify a new conqueror in the eyes
of his subjects and to confirm their loyalty, but rather as a prelude
to his retirement. Diocletian had reached the decision that the
proper time was at hand for him to abdicate his power.

His contemporaries and later historians have suggested
many reasons for his abdication. Some ascribe it to a collapse of
his physical health, others to a mental breakdown, still others to a
plot of Galerius. Diocletian is said to have simply grown contemptuous of material grandeur and bored with the magnificence of
his court or to have been overcome by remorse for his cruelty to
his Christian subjects. It is true that illness had caused Diocletian
to withdraw from the public eye during the last year of his reign.
But in the period immediately before his abdication, when rumors
were spreading and people were uncertain if he were still alive,
the imperial decrees were still quietly obeyed. There was no unrest,
no murder, no military coup d'etat. Diocletian was not being
forcibly removed from the scene; it was willingly and purposefully
that he laid aside his supreme power.

"It wanted a lofty character," wrote Aurelius Victor, "to
despise all pomp and to step down to ordinary life."[18] Diocletian
must have realized that his work of stabilizing the imperial authority and regularizing the succession was still incomplete. But he
was somewhat disillusioned by the failure of his economic measures
and by his experience with human weaknesses. After his retirement he said, "A monarch can see only with the eyes, and hear
only with the ears of his ministers; and they take a great deal of
trouble to deceive him. So he advances bad men, and neglects
good ones—to the profit of those who are arranging the graft."[19]
Unknowingly perhaps, he thus put his finger on the chief weakness
of an absolute government—the ruler badly advised by self-seeking
counselors.

But it seems that most of the truth is on Burckhardt's
side when he says that Diocletian abdicated in order to show that
the system of government he had devised would actually work.[20]
The system—with its four rulers chosen for their ability—was un-
natural to Rome. Unlike Diocletian, his "junior partners" were
ambitious for themselves and their sons. So he was trying to set
them a good example, which he persuaded Maximian to follow.
Their voluntary retirement opened the way for their colleagues to
move upward and for new Caesars to be chosen. Here was the

chance to establish the order of succession. The dynasty, although recruited by adoption rather than by birth, would calmly continue to exercise the supreme power, and the internal peace of the Empire would be undisturbed. Diocletian was loyally living up to the rules he himself had set for the conduct of the emperors.

No matter the worthy intentions of their action, the withdrawal of the two Augusti in 305 was disastrous. Diocletian's successors proved to have neither the patience nor the vision to abide by his rules. His system had not had time to take root, and without his masterful authority, it would not operate. It was too elaborate, too artificial, too utopian in concept. As Gibbon pointed out, with more than a trace of scornful irony, it required "two emperors without jealousy, two Caesars without ambition, and the same general interest invariably pursued by four independent princes."[21] Such conditions and such men were simply not to be found. The abdication of Diocletian was the signal for the resumption of internal strife. Order once again gave way to chaos.

The new line-up of the board of emperors found Constantius and Galerius elevated to be the Augusti of West and East, with Severus and Maximin Daia as their respective Caesars. Especially notable among those who were excluded from the succession were Constantius' son Constantine, and Maxentius, the son of the retired Maximian. Both of these young men were ambitious. Several years earlier, Constantine had been sent to the court at Nicomedia for training and experience and also, no doubt, so that Diocletian could keep his eye on him. Then he had served under Galerius on the Danube frontier, and he was in Galerius' retinue when Diocletian abdicated. Should any antagonism develop between Constantius and Galerius, whose policies were by no means the same, the western emperor would be fatally handicapped by the presence of his son—virtually a prisoner—in Galerius' court. The danger was clear to Constantius, the advantage he possessed clear to Galerius. The father more and more ardently requested the return of his son, but Galerius invented excuses for postponing consent. At last he gave permission for Constantine's departure. Constantine was off at once, before Galerius could revoke his grant. The story is that, to prevent pursuit, Constantine first disabled all the posthorses in the imperial stable. He rode across the Empire to join his father in Gaul and then accompanied him to Britain to repel the raids of the Picts and Scots. At his provincial capital of York, Constantius died in 306.

Here was the first critical test of the new imperial system. Theoretically, Severus should become Augustus and have the choice of his Caesar. But York was a far outpost of the Roman world, and the army in Britain needed a supreme commander. Constantius had gained great popularity with his soldiers and subjects by the justice of his humane rule, and this popularity his energetic son inherited. Meanwhile, Galerius' severity had gained for him the nickname, "the Beast", and it would be good sport to flout his authority. The sequel was obvious. The army enthusiastically acclaimed Constantine as Augustus. Sending the news to Galerius, Constantine disclaimed all responsibility, but certainly he would not voluntarily resign his new powers. Equally certainly Galerius could not come to Gaul or Britain to intervene, and so he accepted the *fait accompli,* though recognizing Constantine only as Caesar, under Severus. This reservation in no way irked Constantine: the power, not the title, was what mattered. So, at its first test, Diocletian's system was severely shaken. Heredity had dictated the selection of Constantine, and it was the military faction which had procured his elevation.

6. *Emergence of Constantine, as sole emperor*

Actually, not Diocletian himself could have chosen a more able or vigorous Caesar than Constantine. Returning to Gaul, he defeated the invading Franks and pursued them across the Rhine, re-establishing the frontier defenses. Then he moved southward to be ready to take part, if expedient, in the disorders newly arisen in Italy. There Maxentius, wrathful over not succeeding his father in power, had found support among the Romans, who were jealous of Milan and fearful of Severus' expected demands of tribute. Initially, the revolt of Maxentius was successful. The death of Severus was treacherously contrived; and Galerius, marching into Italy to punish the usurper, was turned back by a mutiny of his troops. The ex-emperor Maximian strongly supported his son and arranged for the cooperation of Constantine, to whom he gave his daughter Fausta in marriage. But Galerius, as senior emperor, could not countenance this bare-faced overthrow of the imperial system. He played his trump card when he called for the assistance of Diocletian, whose prestige was undimmed by the recent turmoil. In conference together, Galerius and Diocletian rearranged the personnel of the western government. Constantine they had to keep as Caesar, but they passed over the rebellious Maxentius. As Augustus, they appointed an experienced Dacian general named Licinius. Nothing was accomplished, however, toward the practical suppression of Maxentius' power at Rome.

Only the aging but restless Maximian was seriously dissatisfied with the existing situation. He had never wanted to retire in the first place, and now he gave way to an irresistible desire to regain power. He applied to his old colleague Diocletian. Together,

he said, it would be easy for them once again to dominate the
Roman world. But Diocletian was not interested, for he was enjoying his retirement. "Were you but to see the cabbages which I
raised in my garden with my own hands," he wrote the scheming
Maximian, "you would no longer talk to me of empire."[22] Re-
buffed by Diocletian, ignored by Maxentius, Maximian went to
live with his son-in-law Constantine, against whom he was promptly
plotting. When his guilt was disclosed, Constantine arrested him
and ordered his death. Then, in 311, Galerius died. Become Augustus, Maximin Daia grew ambitious for still wider power. He opened
negotiations with Maxentius, looking to the expulsion from the
board of emperors of Licinius and Constantine, whom this plot
now made allies.

Of all the rulers in 312, Constantine was the best prepared
for immediate action. In his own domain he had popular support.
His veteran army was loyal to its skilled and successful commander.
Secure at home, Constantine had a potent striking force ready at
hand. Equipped by nature with a capacity for rapid decision, at
this juncture in world affairs Constantine knew exactly what he
wanted. The first step must be the downfall of the upstart Maxentius. In southern Gaul Constantine was poised for the descent into
Italy. The Italians, resentful of the high taxes by which Maxentius
supported his lavish living, were ready to welcome him. To the
rich of town and country alike, Constantine entered Italy as a
liberator from tyrannous misrule. He had laid careful plans. His
march southward was bold and swept all obstructions from his
path. Desperately, Maxentius made a stand on the Tiber River
outside Rome. Constantine's attack was successful, and in the panic
of the retreat across the Milvian Bridge Maxentius was plunged
into the river and drowned. In Rome Constantine was a gracious
victor. He freed political prisoners and recalled political exiles, restoring their confiscated estates. He abolished the praetorian guards
by which emperors had been able to impose their will on the people. The Senate had visions of a return to the rule of law. Within
two months Constantine made himself the effective, and popular,
master of Italy. The West was his.

Shortly afterwards, in the East, Licinius won a comparable
victory. Defeated at Heraclea and unable to collect a sufficient
force to halt Licinius' further advance, Maximin Daia committed
suicide. There were no other claimants to the supreme power.

Diocletian's board of emperors was thus reduced to two.
The victorious survivors met in Milan in 313 to organize their
rule. They issued proclamations jointly, and to seal their alliance
Licinius was betrothed to Constantia, half-sister of Constantine.
But what would Diocletian think of their forceful modifications of

his scheme of government? We have seen that the abdication of the old Emperor had not deprived him of influence. Now his approval was deeply desired, and probably he was invited to the marriage of Licinius and Constantia. But he did not go, and he died not long afterward. It may be that he killed himself, perhaps distressed by the failure of his system of voluntary renunciation of the imperial power, or possibly fearful of the machinations of Constantine and Licinius.

Diocletian's death occurred at Spalato on the eastern shore of the Adriatic, in the palace he had built as a refuge from the world's cares. Although Gibbon declared that Diocletian's mind "was totally uninformed by study and speculation,"[23] this palace was a monument to his interest in the decorative and building arts. Just its vast bulk was another affirmation of the absolute power of the emperor, and in later centuries would provide habitations for the people of a whole town. The frank repetition on the facade of the Roman arch, supported on Corinthian columns, was monotonous but structurally honest. The exterior magnificence impressed the spectator with the greatness of its owner, as the books and statuary on the interior indicated his intellectual alertness and good taste. At his death, Diocletian had long abandoned his imperial dignities. Nevertheless, he was enrolled among the Roman gods, the first private citizen to be so honored.

Constantine and Licinius cannot fail to remind us of Octavius and Antony. They divided the Roman world between them, and each was the sole obstacle in the other's path to supremacy. Rivalry between them was inevitable, and it did not long remain secret. Licinius exposed his ambition to be sole emperor by the cruelty of his wholesale political murders. It was legitimate for him to execute the family of Maximin. But desirous of removing all possible rivals, he had the sons of Severus and of Galerius murdered, and even the wife and daughter of Diocletian. When the conflicting purposes of Licinius and Constantine produced open warfare in 314, the more humane and tolerant western ruler enjoyed the bulk of popular support. He was the better general, too, and defeated Licinius in Pannonia. Generous still, Constantine granted to Licinius peace and continuance in power. But Greece and Illyria were transferred to the western ruler. Constantine now made the Danube frontier secure, driving the Goths deep into Dacia. Jealousy drove Licinius to make war again in 324. After two victories, Constantine moved across the Hellespont and made Licinius prisoner in the eastern capital of Nicomedia. A year later Licinius was executed, as punishment for his "treasonable correspondence with the barbarians."[24]

So the Empire was again at last united under a single ruler. The years since Diocletian divided his power had been costly, and the years since Diocletian retired had been filled with bloody civil wars. One by one the aspirants to the supreme power had met defeat and death, until Constantine alone survived. He had attained the undisputed mastery of the entire Empire—the goal which had been since 306 both the object of his undivided ambition and the sole means by which he might assure his personal safety.[25]

Chapter VI

CONSTANTINE

CONSTANTINE LEADS THE EMPIRE INTO A NEW ERA

It was as a conquering hero that Constantine assumed the imperial rule. Still in the prime of life, he was impressive in stature and gracious in manner. Hardened by his years of campaigning, he was vigorous and resourceful. Scornful of luxury and inactivity, his energy made him seem to be always in motion. He had pursued his policies with cold intelligence and unswerving determination, yet with unusual forbearance. He had proved himself skillful as a military leader and had infused his intrepid spirit into his followers. Victorious in every contest of war or diplomacy, he had earned the acclaim of the crowd.

Constantine seemed a compendium of the traditional Roman virtues—courage, manliness, perseverance, temperance. Like many of the earlier heroes of Rome, he had come through troublous times unscathed, almost by magic, as though unseen powers had watched over him. In his character was a typical Roman strain of fatalism, a conviction of his great destiny. He had trusted in his "star" and had set his course unerringly, confident that in striving to realize his personal ambition he would be at the same time benefiting the state. And now that his hands had grasped the supreme power, he would carry himself in a manner befitting the great station thrust upon him. "To become emperor is a matter of destiny; but if the power of fate has imposed the necessity of rule on a man, he must strive to appear worthy of the *imperium*."[1] At the outset, therefore, Constantine was a magnanimous conqueror. He had delivered Rome, and Italy, from tyrannous misrule and ruinous taxation. Or so people thought. Recalling exiles, freeing slaves, returning property, he established himself in popular favor. Above all else, he restored peace.

1.   Continuation of Diocletian's policy

Constantine was a shrewd politician rather than an inventive statesman. He made no startling innovations in the government of the Empire, retaining the elaborate bureaucratic machinery devised by Diocletian. But he made one significant change, at the very top. There would be only one emperor. On paper, the division of the imperial power and the choice of successors by merit had looked reasonable and wise. But, in practice, it had proved contrary to human nature; and it had not worked. So Constantine returned to the older system, risking the vagaries of heredity. Thus he would discourage civil wars at the same time that he enhanced the future of his own family. And he had a talented son, Crispus, who would be a worthy successor.

Constantine's victory had not, of course, solved the social and economic problems of the Empire. The progressive deterioration of the commercial classes, the high level of government expense, the decline in agricultural productivity, continued as sources of weakness. To counteract these, Constantine issued a mass of decrees similar in purpose to Diocletian's.

We have seen that both rulers frankly accepted absolutism as the central principle of the government. The old pretenses of divided powers, local self-government, and constitutional checks on the emperor's authority were finally abandoned. The emperor's word alone had the effect of supreme law; it was recognized that his prerogative was unlimited. The emperor was the absolute lord, *dominus*, of the Empire, which now resembled a vast private estate. All men were his to command; all lands his to distribute. He alone disposed of the army, which owed loyalty to him rather than to the state. The cabinet of chief imperial officials was made a permanent body, but it functioned as a group of personal agents of the emperor rather than as a body of responsible statesmen. To support the pomp of imperial majesty, a new aristocracy was created, carefully graded in rank as in an army and bearing the titles of Illustrious, Respectable, and Honorable. To insure the loyalty of the authorities in the provinces, the emperor dispatched private espionage agents among them.

If he would achieve efficient administration, a dictator cannot afford to permit exceptions to his decrees. In the 4th century this meant that neither Italy nor Rome could be allowed any extraordinary privileges. We have already noted that Constantine had disbanded the praetorian guards, Rome's private army. And the old urban aristocracy had been further humiliated when the formal consent of the Senate to an imperial edict was no longer required. The senators enjoyed no automatic membership in the new hierarchy of rank. Although they were again made eligible to hold administrative posts in the provinces, they were to be subordinate to the provincial governors. They were made subject also to the regular imperial courts, losing their right to being tried only in the Senate. Like those of Rome, the privileges of Italy were cut away. Italy was treated no differently from the other provinces, administered uniformly with them and subjected like them to the imperial tax-collectors.

The inhabitants of the Empire directed their loudest complaints against the oppressive taxation, but there seemed no remedy for it. Constantine's early wars and later extravagances, added to the annual expense of the cumbersome administrative and military machines, kept the government constantly in need of more money. The basic land tax and poll tax on laborers began to drain capital as well as income from the provinces, so that Constantine had periodically to remit these taxes in order to maintain popularity; but the imperial purse remained empty. Taxes were imposed on inheritance and on the use of various commodities. Gifts from the cities, which had once been requested only in emergencies, were now demanded as regular imposts. And Constantine decreed two new taxes, on the property of senators and on the profits of businessmen. Truly, the taxes of this era were too high: they were so burdensome to the people as to tend to dry up the sources of wealth on which the tax-revenue depended. The individual was losing his incentive to accumulate wealth; it seemed worse than useless to work hard or to increase output.

More and more people sought to escape their duties. Diocletian had unwisely imposed back-breaking responsibilities on the decurion class. Now Constantine made the error of granting immunity from taxation to certain groups in the population. The new court nobility was thus exempted, and their extravagance unchecked. As we shall see shortly, Constantine favored the new Christian religion and granted tax-exemption to its clergy. Entering the clergy became a most convenient escape route for an ordinary citizen. The government soon had to compel clergymen with property to give up their religious posts, and to prohibit decurions from assuming clerical orders. This interference by the government in the lives and occupations of its subjects was another instance of a policy noted under Diocletian and intensified under Constantine, the so-called "closing of the castes".

The aim of this policy was to stabilize the social organization of the Empire and to maintain high economic productivity. It involved fixing and perpetuating the status of every citizen so that he could not avoid his obligations. Every citizen was of importance not so much as an individual but as a member of a certain class, which must perform certain vital functions to keep the state healthy.

From the standpoint of the imperial economy, the three most valuable classes were the landlords, the farm laborers, and the craftsmen. No member of these classes could be allowed to forsake his proper calling. The landlord must work his estates to capacity so as to be able to pay annually the full tax levied on them. Successful management brought him no relief from work and worry but only heavier obligations. The farm laborer must not be free to migrate into the cities in search of a better job. He must be kept at work on the land, tied to it as closely as though he were a building, so that the land could not be sold without him. To be sure, this law protected the laborer from rent-increases or eviction, but it restricted his freedom to move, his right to do as he pleased. The craftsman must be kept at work at his particular trade. His normal output was a necessary part of the product of the Empire, and he must forego the risks of invention and the rewards of successful experiment.

The barriers between classes grew ever higher and harder to surmount. Then class distinctions were made hereditary. Not only was the farm laborer attached to a particular acreage but his son was automatically attached after him. The farmer was degenerating into a mere appurtenance of the soil. The imperial authorities were apparently unconcerned that limiting a man's horizon undermines his will to work. Production enforced by decree never equals production encouraged by hope of future prosperity.

The army was, of course, another vital element in society and it too came to be included in the caste system. It was hard to keep up the number of the military forces. A traditional inducement to enlist was the promise of land to be granted at the time of discharge from the service, but now the veteran found that he could not keep his land unless his son was willing in his turn to join the army. This matter of "forced" enlistment was not the only change in the armed service. The number of citizens available for duty as highly-trained and patriotic legionaries had been fatally reduced. To fill the ranks, greater and greater reliance was placed on barbarians from the borders, especially Germans, and some of them rose to high rank. The size of the individual legion, and with it the power of its commander, was drastically reduced, and the so-called auxiliary troops came to outnumber the legionaries. Thus the old citizen army was transformed into a mercenary force. The new army was kept efficient, ready to march at the emperor's command, but at the cost of a reduction of its will-to-fight. The military reforms and the "closing of the castes" were criticized by Gibbon as "timid policy"—dividing what was united, reducing what was eminent, dreading what was active, and expecting the most feeble citizenry to be the most obedient.[2]

Constantine's motives were noble. He had a sincere desire to reorganize the society of the Empire, and the number of his decrees testifies to his diligence. Several of his edicts are notable for their humaneness. He ordered kinder treatment for civil and military prisoners. He decreed that the courts should remain open on Sundays for the freeing of slaves.

It is said that he even desired to abolish gladiatorial shows because he was repelled by the physical and emotional violence they engendered. If this seems doubtful in the light of the military exploits of Constantine's youth, it is even more doubtful if he succeeded in wiping the cruel streak out of the Roman character. As a landlord, Constantine was a model of decency and efficiency. He understood that the way to maintain the productivity of his enormous estates was to make fair contracts with the laborers and to deal justly with them so that they would not be tempted to run away.

2. Errors of Constantine's later years

Unfortunately, Constantine proved somewhat less just and active in enforcing his laws than he had been in making them. The mature Constantine as Emperor often appears less admirable than the youthful Constantine who sought the throne. The internal decay of a state is frequently evidenced in history as the decay in the character of its ruling class, and the centuries of declining Roman power provide vivid examples of this moral deterioration at the very top of the social ladder. The emperors and their chief officials fell into the habit of acting selfishly and violently, in response to their inflamed passions and in disregard of the consequences of their rash deeds. Diocletian was an outstanding exception to this tendency, but Constantine—especially in his later years —was not. He grew distressingly fickle. His opinions changed overnight and he was sadly subject to outside influence. An imperial policy was often determined by who held the emperor's ear at the particular time. Constantine was prone to play favorites. He spent money so lavishly for the adornment of his court that he has been described, in the latter part of his reign, as a robber of the people's goods and a spendthrift.

The most tragic episode in Constantine's life occurred in the summer of 326. His oldest son Crispus had developed into an attractive and capable prince, and in him Constantine had centered all his dynastic ambitions. In the mind of the still-vigorous ruler, however, lurked some shadow of envy of the success of the

younger man. And Crispus was hated by Constantine's second
wife, Fausta, jealous of his favored position and anxious for the
future of her own three sons. She went to work ingeniously to in-
sinuate suspicion into the heart of her husband, and the very charm
and promise of Crispus played into her hands. The prince, she
said, was plotting to displace his father in the popular affections
and then to push him from his throne.

Constantine's earlier experiences surely had given him little
cause to trust in people's friendship and loyalty. The most outstanding men of his time—like Galerius and Licinius—had tried
to play him false. Was there any reason to suppose that his own
family should be free of treacherous impulses? He was convinced
by Fausta's wiles, and in a fit of fury he ordered the banishment,
and then the execution, of Crispus. Almost as soon as the sentence
was carried out, Constantine had a change of heart. Sure now of
Crispus' innocence and aware of the enormity of what he had
done, he turned against the scheming Fausta and had her put to
death. But it was too late to undo his earlier crime: the killing of
his heir was his greatest single mistake.

Gibbon is a severe critic of Constantine. The evidence we
have suggested of the Emperor's impulsiveness, of his unevenness
of temper, perhaps of his moral decay, gives some support to the
most unfavorable comparison which Gibbon draws between Constantine and Augustus. In Augustus, "the tyrant of the republic
was converted into the father of his country."[3] In Constantine, on
the other hand, the hero loved by his subjects degenerated into a
cruel and dissolute monarch corrupted by his fortune. The wisdom
and clemency of Augustus as *princeps* erase the memory of his
earlier cold-blooded ruthlessness, whereas the savagery of the older
Constantine tarnishes the lustre of his youthful accomplishments.

"Power corrupts" is the best-remembered aphorism of Lord
Acton, and the possession of absolute authority has often worked
the downfall of the possessor. His head is turned by immoderate
praise, his passions cloud his judgment, and he follows the vicious
promptings of self-interest. Constantine "abandoned himself, without moderation, to the abuse of his fortune," says Gibbon. "As he
gradually advanced in the knowledge of truth, he proportionably
declined in the practice of virtue."[4] One can almost sense the
physical and spiritual deterioration of the youthful into the older
Constantine, that Gibbon hints at on numerous occasions: the
vigorous energy of the strapping physique softened by luxury; the
frank ambition perverted into vengeful jealousy; open affability
supplanted by a taste for finery and contrived pomp; simple living
replaced by extravagance; and straightforward policies confused
by crafty dissimulation.

But the "power corrupts" theory is not the whole explanation of Constantine's inhumanity and injustice. He was born in a rude age and passed all his younger years in army camps. From the beginning his life was insecure, and there were strains of suspicion and superstition in his character. His education, cursory and narrow, gave him little in the way of standards by which to regulate his own conduct or judge wisely the motives and behavior of others. The complexity of human nature was beyond his understanding, and he was liable to be deceived by clever argument or seeming virtue. Avid of glory, he was at times unstable in temperament, given to excesses and sudden anger. Rather than condemn Constantine for jealousy or cruelty, we may wonder that he so rarely lost control of himself and regret only that he was not able always and unfailingly to rise above the limitations of his age and his environment.

The murder of Crispus left the future of the Empire in doubt and led ultimately to a fatal error in policy. Here again Constantine allowed himself to be guided by the foolish custom of his times. Renewed turmoil on the northern border, fomented by the unruly Goths, and a rebellion in Cyprus, engineered by the son of Licinius, led Constantine to worry about the solidarity of his realm. In 335, feeling that he himself was growing older, he took the familiar step, fraught though it was with danger, of dividing the Empire. To each of three sons and two nephews he granted immediate authority over a part of the Empire, although personally retaining his supremacy over these junior rulers and over the whole state. Constantine should have sensed the folly of such a step. He may have been planning more for the good of his family than of the Empire, hoping to provide a satisfactory inheritance for each of his descendants, or perhaps to discover, by trial and error, which of them was the worthiest to succeed him in the arduous tasks of government. Whatever his motive, he divided what he himself, at tremendous cost, had united. And the results were bad, both for his family and for the Empire.

3. The beginnings of Christianity; its rivals

Both Diocletian and Constantine used their absolute power in an attempt to halt the disintegration of the Empire and to reconstruct its society and reanimate its economy. Diocletian had been the originator of the new policies, Constantine his apt imitator and successor. But in one outstandingly important respect Constantine reversed the policy of Diocletian. He embarked on an original course in dealing with the new Christian religion.

Even though the way had been prepared for it by the historical experience of the Hebrew people, by the written evidence of their Scriptures, and by their faith in one just and merciful God as preached by their greatest prophets, there would be no Christianity without the life and death story of an individual man, Jesus Christ. It is the perfect example of what we call an historical religion, not primarily because it conceives of the world as created by God who accomplishes his purposes through the medium of human history, but because its whole meaning and power depend on certain actual events which occurred in Palestine in the reigns of Augustus and Tiberius.

The Christian creed is not a collection of abstract philosophical principles explaining purity of thought or righteousness of life, nor is it a compilation of the wise teachings of an exalted prophet. Instead of these, it is, in great part, a brief story of the life of an apparently simple man—what we might glibly call a "thumbnail biography" of Christ, emphasizing his birth and his death. The "good news" which the disciples of Christ carried into the world was not some new magical formula of how to lead a moral or religious life. It was the straightforward, although wonderful, report of a few historical events, supremely the incarnation and the resurrection. The essence of the Christian faith is the confident knowledge that in Christ God put on mortal flesh and came down into the world, reaching out to man, and that this same Christ, having suffered crucifixion for the sins of the whole world, was raised from the dead into life everlasting. The early Christians taught no special virtue by which man can achieve his own salvation. Nor did they boast of the mighty power of their God. Said their greatest teacher, Paul: "We preach Christ crucified."[5]

The "good news" recounted vividly by convinced and enthusiastic men met with an immediate response. It was given to a world ripe to receive it. It came at a time when most of the peoples of the world (including the Jews) had lost their independence to an increasingly autocratic Rome, when for most individuals life was hard and opportunities were limited, when the future looked bleak. It came at a time when to most thoughtful people life seemed fleeting and futile. The vaunted "reason" of classical civilization had brought Roman citizens of the first century B.C. to economic collapse, political impotency, and moral depravity. They had lost their self-reliance.

The earliest Romans had taken their religion seriously, for religion involved critical relationships with powers outside of, and stronger than, themselves. Their divinities were the spirits that resided in natural phenomena and that protected their households. They worshiped their ancestors, respected their elders, and strove to fulfill their duties to the city-state, in which each member played an

integral part and each might climb to a post of highest honor.
Heroism for the early Roman meant restraint of himself and loyal
service of the state. The original creation of Rome was "due to the
Fates," Livy said. The survival and growth of the city were events
over which some gods must have watched with particular care.

From Etruscans and Greeks and other people whom they
conquered, the Romans learned new customs and new ideas with
which to augment their tribal religion. They built temples, developed ceremonials, resorted to divination and prophecy, depicted
divine spirits as human beings of surpassing strength or beauty.
They trained priests to conduct rituals and Vestal Virgins to keep
alight the flame that symbolized the spirit of Rome. They consulted
the Sybilline oracles. But the religious traditions gradually came to
be nothing more than rituals, without meaning, and the Empire
grew far too large for the individual citizen to have much sense
of personal participation in its destinies. Under Augustus and his
successors, as we have seen, there developed the worship of the
emperor. The emperor had power, to be sure, but often he was far
from admirable, and the people could scarcely think of him as a
friend or helper.

Despite the efforts of an Augustus to rekindle the ancient
Roman "piety", to revivify Jupiter and Juno, to enforce emperor-
worship as the universal state-religion, increasing doubts seized
the people of Rome. On the one hand, skepticism spread; on the
other hand, a desperate sense of emptiness and spiritual hunger.
The cult of the emperor was a mere convention, a political ges-
ture. It produced no exaltation, no internal "lifting of the heart".
Religious observances were formalized, lifeless, impersonal. They
offered no saving consolation in times of sadness or suffering. They
answered no anxious questions about the value of existence or the
promise of the future. Now that Rome had survived and grown
and mastered the world, what *was* the purpose of life?

The crucial test of any religion, says Goodenough, is whether
or not it offers men what they feel they deeply need.[6] Does it satisfy
their emotional longings? Does it provide spiritual sustenance? Inspiration in moments of uncertainty? Comfort in adversity? A feeling of safety amid the tumult of a weary world? In the early years
of the Empire, believer and skeptic alike would welcome a freshen-
ing of religious spirit, a renewal of faith, a confidence in personal
worth, a discovery of purpose, and—above all—a promise of immortality.

The lonely individual is conscious of his sinfulness, frightened by his incompetence, helpless before the massive forces of
the world, threatened with extinction. He cries for help—for conviction and courage—from a source outside of himself. He has a

vague sense of the existence of some spiritual force, more powerful and more permanent than he, and he feels a vague capacity to respond to it. How can he find that spirit? Comprehend it? Converse with it? Intensify it within himself? This was the religious quest of first century man.

Some people turned to the new Stoic philosophy. It taught that a single mind guides the world and that a life lived in harmony with natural law will produce contentment. The individual must order his life by reason. Self-discipline and self-denial will enable him to overcome the difficulties and unpleasantnesses he must inevitably confront. Strength of character will render him self-sufficient. But we can readily see that the intellectual emphasis and the stern demands of Stoicism disqualify it as a religion for the "masses".

Other people turned to "mystery" cults, old or new. The secret rites, into which only a select brotherhood were initiated, might be especially pleasing to the gods, bring the participants close to them, and reveal their spirit. But, again, the "masses" cannot be exhilarated or satisfied by secret mysteries from which the great bulk of them are excluded.

There was far more deep and widespread appeal to the common man in certain religions that had been developing in the eastern parts of the Empire. These religions responded to emotional needs; they had the power to attract large numbers of people, and they proved to be keen rivals of Christianity in winning the hearts of men. Each of these theologies sought to define the supreme power which ordered the universe, created a hierarchy of priests, and evolved the magical or sacrificial or ceremonial means by which the divine spirit might be disseminated among its votaries.

There was, for instance, the worship of the Great Mother, the life-giving force of all Nature. She might be adored in the person of Cybele, the fertility goddess, by means of abandoned revels, dancing, and bloody self-mutilation. Or in the person of the gentle and compassionate Isis, whose devotion restored to life her slain lover. The rites or revels devoted to these goddesses were held to heal and purify and redeem the participants, bringing them into close communion with the supreme divinity who ruled the world, freeing them from some of this world's wretchedness, giving them a claim to immortality.

There was, for another instance, the worship of the sun-god, Mithras. This religion was popular among men and, especially, among the soldiers. Mithras was valiant and vigorous. He represented good in its conflict with evil, light in its conflict with darkness. To devote oneself to the service of Mithras was to choose to defend the right, to be willing to undergo severe physical torment, and to seek release from misery at the hand of the unconquerable sun.

So we find paganism, like Stoicism, tending toward monotheism—the worship of one dominating force—and recognizing the need of living according to conscious moral standards. Unfortunately for the devotees of the mystery cults, the trances they induced were of temporary duration. The enthusiasm engendered by the rites of Cybele produced oblivion from woe, even—on occasion, perhaps—an exaltation of spirit; but this could be only a transient feeling, and afterwards the woes and problems of life might seem worse than ever. Even Mithraism proved ultimately disappointing. Evil and darkness do sometimes have their victories. Humans are never as good as they ought to be, and men needed not simply a just cause to fight for but acceptance of, and forgiveness for, their failures, their inadequacies, and their selfishness.

The yearning, therefore, persisted. More help was necessary than Isis or Mithras or the Stoics could provide. The thirst was unquenched—for sure knowledge, for unquestioning faith, for confident expectation of future happiness. This thirst Christianity could assuage. As Burckhardt says, it had "utterly simplified" the problem. A "triumphant conviction" of eternal life "permeated each individual Christian."[7] God had come down to earth to help the poor and suffering. People had seen and talked to him. He had sacrificed himself for mankind but then had risen from the dead. With the aid of his spirit, ordinary mortals could share in his redemption and rebirth.

We can easily imagine that the appeal of Christianity must have been irresistible for many people. It gave them something to live by—the moral example of Christ's life—and something to live for—the promise in his resurrection that they could be redeemed in the Kingdom of God from the wickedness and tragedy of this guilty world. The downtrodden and oppressed found themselves borne up in their present sufferings by the hope of a blessed state to come.

Christianity appealed also to educated people who could find little reassurance in conventional polytheism and little fervor in Greek philosophies. Paul the Apostle, an extraordinarily understanding man, afire after his conversion with the love of God, was a compound of the Hebrew spirit and the Greek intellect. He and John, the author of the fourth Gospel, were able to explain the meaning of Christ's life in terms that made sense to a sophisticated, cosmopolitan world. The Hebrew Messiah, the Son of God, became one with the Greek Logos, the Word of God, the central force of the universe.

The new religion spread widely and rapidly. Socially, the "good news" attracted all classes. The love of God was universal; Christ had died for *all* men. "There is neither Jew nor Greek, there is neither bond nor free, there is neither male nor female, for you are all one in Christ Jesus," Paul wrote to the Galatians.[8] Neither wealth nor rank, not even "good works", enters the account at the final judgment. For, in sin, all men die. But in Christ, all men live.

And geographically, the "good news" spread into every corner of the Roman Empire. Indeed, in the process by which the sect of a small, subject people expanded into a world religion, the existence of the unified structure of the Empire was of marked value. The excellent network of Roman roads made communication among the early converts rapid; habitual use of the Greek and Latin languages made their message understandable among many peoples; and ways of thought and life held in common provided a common ground to receive the seed of the new faith. Paul himself was a Roman citizen, which gave him a certain prestige wherever he might go to preach. There were no national barriers to the spread of the Christian faith. The Roman world was one; it was logical that it should accept a universal creed.

4. *Further history of Christianity; persecution, then toleration*

Despite the deep need for a concrete and living faith to give meaning to their individual lives, we have seen that at first there was no general agreement among the people that Christianity was the best way to meet that need. Opponents of the new religion were many, and often among the most influential elements in the Empire.

For centuries Rome had been tolerant in matters of private belief, but there had always existed the official religion by which the welfare of the state was considered dependent on the favor of the gods. We have noted that this state-religion had become fused with the worship of the emperor as a god and as the protector of the state. Now along came the Christians who not only chose to worship their particular God but who refused to take part in the state-religion. They would not worship the emperor, they would have no other gods but God. Thus they defied the authority of the state and violated the principle of unity which the imperial and Stoic Rome of the 1st century had come to revere as the basis of politics and philosophy. Because a multitude of private cults flourished within the Empire, the Christians were not dangerous as heretics; but they were dangerous as potential traitors. Their crime was not that they worshiped God; it was that they refused to worship the emperor. Their highest loyalty was to a power outside and above the state; therefore, the majority of sound citizens suspected their loyalty to Rome. They were regarded as little gangs of criminals who might be bent on undermining the state.

The emperor who chose to cast the blame for any misfortune on the Christians and to attack them as a disruptive force threatening the security of the state, would merely be catering to this popular prejudice. Official persecution of the Christians began in the 60's, under Nero, when hundreds were "thrown to the lions" in the arena or burned as torches to illuminate the evening sky. Nero, of course, accused the Christians of setting the great fire which came close to consuming Rome. It was a dubious accusation, however. Tacitus writes: "Even though these Christians were malefactors who deserved severe punishment as public examples, general sympathy grew up for them, since they seemed punished not to protect the public welfare but simply to satisfy the ferocity of one man."9

Christians denied their duties to the state and were not patriotic; it was, therefore, not legal to be a Christian. But few emperors were as unjust and unbalanced as Nero. Early in the next century, a provincial governor named Pliny wrote from Bithynia to inquire of his friend, the Emperor Trajan, whether or not he was according fair and proper treatment to the Christians. He had questioned those accused "whether they were or were not Christians. To such as professed that they were, I put the inquiry a second and a third time, threatening them with the supreme penalty. Those who persisted, I ordered to execution. For, indeed, I could not doubt, whatever might be the nature of that which they professed, that their pertinacity, at any rate, and inflexible obstinacy, ought to be punished." But if they were willing to revile Christ and to offer wine and incense at the statue of the Emperor, "these I deemed it proper to dismiss." Pliny admitted that the new religion was infecting large numbers of townsmen and countrymen alike.

He must have found Trajan's reply reassuring: "You have followed the right mode of procedure, my dear Pliny. . . . These people should not be searched for; if they are informed against and convicted, they should be punished; yet he who shall deny being a Christian and shall make this plain in action, by worshiping our gods, even though suspected on account of his past conduct, shall obtain pardon by his penitence. Anonymous informations ought not to be allowed a standing in any kind of charge; this course would not only form the worst of precedents, but it is not in accord with the spirit of our age."10 Hadrian later issued a decree: "If anyone accuses Christians and shows that they are breaking the law, pass judgment according to the seriousness of the crime. But if anyone accuses another falsely to do him injury, arrest the accuser and see to it that you punish him."[11]

Sporadic persecution of the Christians continued and was, in fact, intensified under the good Marcus Aurelius. But persecution strengthened the resolve of the Christians, and their courage in the face of adversity and death impressed others with their faith. We have grown accustomed to hearing that "the blood of the martyrs was the seed of the Church." The persecutions seemed rather to hasten than to halt the spread of Christianity. By 300, perhaps one-tenth of the population of the Empire was firmly converted to Christianity. In cases of conflict they might obey the orders of the Church before those of the state.

Such a situation was intolerable to the authoritarian Diocletian. There must be no breach in his absolutism. No rival institution could be permitted to distract the subject from his supreme duty of service to the state or to challenge the wisdom and justice of any imperial decree. But the Christian Church was precisely such an institution. It had a devoted membership and a compact organization; it was constantly growing in wealth and influence and reputation. It was, in fact, "a state within a state". Christian insistence on the brotherhood of man made a "caste system" seem ridiculous; Christian stress on the freedom of the mind and will of man opened the path to criticism of imperial edicts, and perhaps to disobedience to them. The existence of the Church was a living symbol of Diocletian's failure to bring the entire Empire into uniform dependence on the Emperor and a continuing threat of rebellion against the "divine" monarch.

To degrade the officials of the Church and to scatter its rank-and-file members would be to complete the work of unifying and strengthening the Empire. Diocletian was not one to shrink from necessary action, however arduous. In 303, even though his own household had been infected with the new faith, he decreed a severe persecution that was finally to destroy the organization, and thus the independent power, of the Church. Says Eusebius:

> Royal edicts were published everywhere, commanding that churches should be razed to the ground, the Scriptures burned, those who held positions of honor degraded, and the household servants, if they persisted in the Christian profession, deprived of their liberty . . . . Not long after, the Emperor commanded that all the rulers of the churches in every place should be first put in prison and afterwards compelled by every device to offer sacrifice . . . . [These] were followed by other commands that those in prison should be set free, if they would offer sacrifice, but that those who refused should be tormented with countless tortures . . . .[12]

There followed prohibition of public worship, confiscation of property, loss of citizenship. Christians were placed outside the law.

Diocletian's motive was political, not bloodthirsty. Despite popular murmurings against him, he enforced his decrees vigorously. But his persecution was unsuccessful. The best Christians did not recant; they held to their faith more fervently than before. They upheld the principles of their moral law against the power of the civil law and defied Diocletian's magistrates. The state failed to destroy the Church.

The Emperor Galerius confessed this failure when in 311 he halted official action against the Christians. They would not participate in the state-religion but formed their own congregations, made their own laws, and enacted their own ceremonies. They could not be broken to the imperial will. So Galerius announced:

> Many were subdued by the fear of danger, many even suffered death. And yet since most of them persevered in their determination, in view of our most mild clemency and the constant habit by which we are accustomed to grant indulgence to all, we thought we ought to grant our most prompt indulgence to them, so that they may again be Christians and may hold their meetings, provided they do nothing contrary to good order.
>
> Wherefore, for this our indulgence, they ought to pray to their God, for our safety, for that of the state, and for their own. . . .[13]

This decree of Galerius is only a grant of indulgence. It tolerates Christians but gives them no new privileges and in no way favors their doctrines. Galerius is not concerned for their welfare, but only for the cessation of disorder in the state. And yet, at the end, there is just a hint that perhaps the Christian God is worth something after all in the suggestion that he might affect the safety of the Empire.

5.   Constantine accepts and favors Christianity and seeks cooperation of Church and State

Meanwhile, what of Constantine? In the North his father and he had declined to carry out the harsh provisions of Diocletian's edicts of persecution. Not later than 312 Constantine and his army were marching under the banner of the Christian God. But 313 was the critical date in the relations between the Empire and the Church. Constantine and Licinius, fresh from their respective victories over Maxentius and Maximin, issued the Edict of Milan, famous in history as the earliest official pronouncement of complete religious toleration:

Among the steps likely to profit the majority of mankind,

nothing is more necessary than to regulate the worship
of the Divinity.
We have decided, therefore, to grant both to Christians
and to all others *perfect freedom* to practise the religion
which each has thought best for himself, that so whatever
Divinity resides in heaven may be placated, and rendered
propitious to us and to all who have been placed under
our authority . . . . [This] policy is demanded by healthy
and sound reason—that no one, on any pretext whatever,
should be denied freedom to choose his religion . . . .
Henceforth, in perfect and absolute freedom, each and
every person who chooses to belong to and practise the
Christian religion shall be at liberty to do so without let
or hindrance in any shape or form. . . .[14]

This is specific and definitive. The Emperors publicly acknowledge the existence of a new God, and give formal recognition to Christianity. The new religion is granted full equality with
the official state-cult. The grant of toleration, to be sure, is general,
but Christianity is singled out and placed under the protection of
imperial authority. In his own western realm, Constantine went
further in benefiting Christianity, restoring property confiscated
by Diocletian and, most significant, recognizing the Church as a
corporate institution legally entitled to own property. There is a
world of difference between the edicts of 311 and 313: the earlier
is negative in spirit, defeatist in tone; the later bravely charts a
new course in human affairs. The tired Galerius had said to the
Christians, We won't persecute you any more, unless you prove
troublesome. Constantine said, We grant you unconditional toleration, imperial protection, and special privilege.

Why was Constantine, alone in his day, so wise in his
attitude and so bold in his action toward the "traitorous" Christians? The answer to this question establishes Constantine's best
claim to creative originality. In three hundred years of persecution
Christianity had proved itself too durable to be stamped out. Now
it had become the most vibrant spiritual force within the Empire.
People obeyed the Church's precepts gladly. For their God the
Christians were ready to serve, to sacrifice, even to suffer martyr-
dom. In this same era, the subjects of the Empire reluctantly obeyed
its harsh dictates or wilfully disregarded its exorbitant demands.
Where the Church inspired veneration, the Empire inspired fear.
If only the Church could be aligned with the state, if only the
decrees of the government could be supported by the moral power
of religion, if only the Christians' enthusiastic love of their God
could be carried over into a love of their country, then truly the
ancient glory of Rome might be revived. The Empire ruled by
force; the Church by persuasion, by example, by the power of

love. A common faith in Christianity might serve as the inspiration for new and magnificent achievement.

Constantine might almost be credited with coining the phrase, "If you can't beat 'em, join 'em". Diocletian had scorned popular opinion; he had resented the strength of the Church; he had tried to "beat 'em". Constantine, more sensitive and flexible than Diocletian, saw that persecution was no longer either effective or popular; he determined not to resist the tide, but to swim with it. Rather than beat the Christians, he would "join 'em". And further, dealing with them as equals, accepting their Church as a reputable institution and making no effort to undermine it, he would grant them privileges and responsibilities which would attach them indissolubly to himself. Impressed by the growing strength of Christianity, Constantine recognized that it was "the wave of the future". He perceived the potential value of the Church to the Empire. He determined to effect an alliance between them. To the Church he would grant toleration, privilege, prestige; in return he expected the Church to exert its spiritual influence on behalf of his imperial policies. Durant calls it "a stroke of genius" for Constantine to have seen the possibilities of the union of Church and State.

It is clear from his official actions that Constantine as Emperor was favorable to Christianity. It is more difficult to judge how greatly Christianity affected him as a private person. We can ask the question, Was Constantine a sincere, a "good" Christian? Indeed, Was he really a Christian at all? The account of Constantine's "conversion" to Christianity is among the most appealing of our early chronicles. In 312 he was leading his army southward before his crucial battle with Maxentius. There was widespread Christian sentiment in Constantine's force, but the leader's religious conviction was wavering. Maxentius was still a confirmed pagan, trusting in the Sun God, whose worship was very popular in the Roman army. On the eve of the battle of the Milvian Bridge, Constantine's troubled sleep was interrupted by a vision. In the sky he saw a cross, and the inscription, "In this sign, you shall conquer." Constantine embraced the new faith, marched his Christian army forward, and—with God's help—swept the pagan forces of Maxentius into the river.

We do not have to accept this story of the vision, although its narrator, Eusebius, affirmed that Constantine himself told it.[15] A recent biographer believes that Constantine was identified with Christianity as early as 306. A variety of pressures impelled him toward the new faith. Both his father and he observed the moral, law-abiding character of their Christian subjects. The Christians were notably obedient to the authority of their bishops. Clearly their God must have some power. Constantine was superstitious enough to have felt the need of supernatural assistance and to have feared lest by alienating the power of the Christian God he doom himself to a crushing defeat. After his conversion and victories in the civil wars, he would have been ungrateful not to have ascribed some credit to the God who had fought on his side at the moment of crisis.

His public acceptance of the Christian faith, sad to say, did not transform Constantine into a wholly wise and good man. His worst sins were those of his later, "Christian" years. Religious conviction was not a decisive element in Constantine's personality. It is so difficult to define his beliefs partly because they fluctuated so radically. There can be little doubt that Christianity seemed to Constantine much preferable to paganism. He wanted to believe in God, but he was not quite positive that he had found the proper God to believe in; and he had a lingering doubt as to the advisability of abandoning the traditional ways. Scorning paganism, he yet allowed the old rites to be celebrated. In 321, on the very occasion when he decreed that the Sabbath be kept for slaves and soldiers, he ordered that the auguries be consulted. Constantine was not interested in the complex details of Christian doctrine. Nor did he think that doctrine was a matter of much importance. He was always a man of vigorous action rather than of reflective thought.

Whether or not there was any causal relationship between them, much of Constantine's social legislation gave effect to ethical principles the Christians supported. The laws concerning the Sabbath are a case in point. There was a new spirit of humanity abroad, a concern for people just as people. Some of the cruel practices of earlier times were discouraged—the separation of slave families or the killing of unwanted children. Laws against the unmarried state were relaxed; and the celibate life, devoted to God, was, of course, a Christian ideal. Stricter penalties were enacted against divorce, adultery, and rape, which are moral crimes. Meanwhile, additional privileges were bestowed on the Church. The clergy were exempted from military service. Church courts were declared equal to the civil courts of the Empire. The Church was permitted to acquire, by bequest, ever larger tracts of land.

Gradually, perhaps almost unconsciously, Constantine turned more and more to the Church. But he delayed formal acceptance of Christianity as his personal faith until the very end of his life. When he was dying near Nicomedia, in May 337, he received the sacrament of baptism from Bishop Eusebius. Christian historians have placed great emphasis on his "deathbed conversion", hailing Constantine as the first Christian Caesar. In his imperial crown and purple robe, the ruler had given his favor to the

Church, proving its material strength as an institution. Dying in the white dress of baptism, this same ruler evidenced the spiritual strength of Christianity as an inward faith. But this is probably to read too much into the story. It is doubtful if Constantine should ever be called a devout, penitent Christian. His religion was always subordinated to his statesmanship. Hodgkin perhaps came closest to the truth when he wrote, "Constantine was half convinced of the truth of Christianity and wholly convinced of the policy of embracing it."[16]

6.   Church unity is maintained in the face of challenges

Constantine's real goal was to unite Church and State in an Empire that would be physically impregnable and spiritually indivisible. The Emperor should exercise final control over both the religion and the government of his subjects. The state must be able to regulate the Church, which consequently had to sacrifice its total independence; on the other hand, the Church might be able to humanize the decrees of the state, so that both would be working to establish the Kingdom of God. But the Church would only be of value to the Emperor's ideal of centralization if its own internal unity could be permanently maintained. Unfortunately, there were signs of division within the Church; under Constantine, division in the Church meant division in the state. It was logical, therefore, that Constantine should be concerned in church problems.

For the solution of such problems he had neither doctrinal subtlety nor deep conviction but only his shrewd sense of the practical needs of his time. At all costs, the single-mindedness of the Church must be preserved, within the larger unity of the Empire. The Emperor could not tolerate a schism in Christianity. As early as 314 we find Constantine intervening in a church quarrel with which we should expect a civil governor to have nothing to do. It was a matter of defining the rightful authority of a bishop. A group of Christians in Carthage were dissatisfied with their bishop. Called Donatists, after their leader, they maintained that a bishop who had in any way surrendered to the demands of Diocletian's persecutors was neither holy nor worthy to be obeyed. In opposition to the regularly-consecrated Catholic bishop of Carthage, the Donatists put forward their own candidate, unspotted by the sin of weakness in the face of persecution. The Catholics maintained that the holiness and authority of a bishop derived from the holiness of the Church which Christ had founded, not from his own personal virtue. Constantine appointed a commission to investigate the dispute. Fearful no doubt of undermining the entire church hierarchy, the commission pronounced for the Catholic bishop. So likewise did the other western bishops in their Synod at Arles, speaking officially for the united Christian Church.[17] When the decision was appealed to Constantine, he promptly directed the use of the state's power to coerce the troublesome Donatists. The existence of the Church was more important than the purity of its individual representatives.

Still more important was the doctrinal dispute which soon threatened to dismember the Church. This was the Arian heresy. Here was not a matter of the calibre of church personnel in a particular locality; here was a matter of asserting the one true doctrine which all Christians should believe. Arius was not a dangerous radical; he was a learned theologian who had meditated long on the basic story of Christ's life on earth. His speculations produced the first real example of the conflict between reason and faith with which the Christian world has since become so familiar. If Christ had really come into our world as a human being, said Arius, he could not be God, for God is superhuman. And if Christ were really God, then he could not have suffered death upon the cross, for God is immortal. God and Christ could not reasonably be one and the same. Christ could only be the messenger of God, less holy, less divine than the God who sent him. Christ was *like* God; but he was not God. Otherwise we must worship two gods instead of one.

The Church held, on the other hand, that it was a divine not a human being who had taken upon himself the sins of the whole world and sacrificed himself for mankind. What made Christianity unique was that God had been willing to come down to man. This position was eloquently upheld by Athanasius, who explained that the whole meaning of Christianity depends on our accepting the idea of the unity of God and of the divinity of Christ. Christ is not only the Son of God; he is not only like God; he *is* God. Even if this is hard to understand, what we know of Christ's career on earth compels us to believe it. Faith goes beyond reason.

Now Constantine was not interested in dictating the beliefs of the Church but only in controlling its actions. He was not concerned with what Christians should think but with whom they should obey. The niceties of the quarrel were probably unintelligible to him. The whole dispute seemed petty, nothing but a verbal quibble. What difference could it make whether God and Christ were "*like* in substance" or "of the *same* substance"? But to the followers of Arius and Athanasius it did make a great difference. They held their divergent views passionately because they thought (and rightly so) that the essence of Christian belief was at issue. Unaware though he was of the vital importance of the dispute, Constantine was irritated by it. He wrote petulantly to both disputants. He told them that the cause of their quarrel was insignificant, that there was no material difference between their views. Why should they, with their silly arguments, disturb the composure of the Emperor and the peace of his realm? But Constantine's wish did not abate the quarrel. And he was aware that the threatened split in the authority of the Church might easily extend to a split in the authority of the state.

To Constantine dogma was not so much a matter of profound conviction as a political expedient—a means to his goal of unity. He *desired* a compromise settlement of the Arian controversy, but he *insisted* on an immediate settlement that would leave the Church united. In ancient pagan Rome a multiplicity of beliefs had been tolerated so long as lip-service was paid to the state-cult. But now the religious institution was the partner of the political. Constantine could permit no variations in the Christian creed. So there should be no minority report when the differences between Arius and Athanasius were resolved. The Church must present a unanimous decision which the state might then enforce. Here was a new idea: a single belief within the Empire, the worship of a God which prohibited the worship of any other kind of god.

To reach this settlement, Constantine in 325 called a conference of the leaders of the entire Church from East and West, which became the world-famous Council of Nicaea. And, wonder of wonders, the Emperor determined that he would attend it in person. The Council must be sure to reach a decision satisfactory to the government. So an imperial decree summoned the church potentates to Nicaea, and their travel expenses were paid from state funds.

The Council of Nicaea, the high point of Constantine's relations with the Church, was one of the few most important events in the history of Christianity. The manner of calling the Council, the magnificence of the delegates, the presence of the Emperor, impressed the world with the new status of Christianity. The bishops deliberated for two months. They finally decided in favor of Athanasius. The doctrine of the Holy Trinity was enunciated as the orthodox—and universal—belief of the Church. There is one God, in three Persons: God the creator of the world and Father of mankind; God the Son and redeemer of a sinful world; God the Holy Spirit who lives eternally in the heart of every individual man. And the cooperation of Church and State was definitively established. The decrees of the Church were inscribed as the law of the state. Arius, condemned by the Church, was banished by the state. Church and State were the two instruments by which Constantine could rule his Empire.

Gibbon rather ironically describes Constantine at Nicaea as seated on a low stool in the middle of the Council, where he "listened with patience and spoke with modesty."[18] We may doubt whether Constantine was comfortable for two months in such a humble position; but his presence at the conference served to remind the bishops of the task before them. His influence may have been decisive in preventing the early dismemberment of the Church into warring sects. Be that as it may, Constantine gave a sumptuous banquet for the bishops when their work was done. What a revelation it was of their new prestige for the Emperor to entertain at dinner the Christian bishops some of whom, but two decades before, had been fugitives from Diocletian's persecution! But the Emperor *presided* at the banquet. He was rewarding the bishops for having established the unity of doctrine which seemed at the moment as vital to the future of the Empire as it would prove to be to the future of the Church. The Church was no longer wholly free to determine its own policy; the state had won the right to interfere in religious matters.

So the settlement reached by the Council was not perfect. Constantine hoped that fanaticism was now finally discredited and orthodox doctrine permanently fixed. "Peace might seem to be restored," Milman writes realistically, "but the Arians were condemned, not convinced; discomfited, not subdued."[19] Furthermore, in demanding unanimity of faith, Christianity having just earned toleration from the state, seemed to be denying toleration within its own boundaries. In its hour of prosperity, the Church hardened its heart and closed its mind. Actually, toleration was not abolished. In his speech to the bishops at the end of the Council, Constantine warned against extremism and urged a reasonable spirit of compromise. Both tolerant and changeable by nature, Constantine in his later actions to some extent undid the work of Nicaea. He conciliated the Arians instead of annihilating them. He even temporarily banished the too-influential Athanasius whom he now found to be haughty, inflexible, and troublesome. Although we find Constantine lacking in doctrinal consistency as in personal piety, we must give him credit for his vital contribution to Christianity. Without his driving desire for unity in the Church, it might not have survived its early divisions; it might have dissolved before ever it was firmly established.

7. *Constantinople*

Aside from his critical decision to make his Empire Christian—a decision which made Christianity the chief motivating power of the Western World for a thousand years to come—Constantine made one other major change of lasting importance in our history. He built Constantinople.

It was probably in the summer of 326 that Constantine paid an unhappy visit to Rome. Here he had already made ostentatious assertion of his Christianity by beginning to build a great basilica on the presumed site of the grave of the martyred Saint Peter. He is reputed personally to have joined in the work of construction, carrying a basket of earth in remembrance of each of the twelve apostles. With its lofty columns and arches, the church was an imposing structure and it stood for over a thousand years.[20] More acceptable to most of the inhabitants of Rome was the erection of Constantine's great (and conventional) triumphal arch. But now he ungraciously refused to participate in traditional Roman ceremonies. And the inhabitants of the city did not hesitate to show their hostility to him. They did not like the rule of a despot, nor the pomp of his court, nor his depriving their city of its ancient privileges. Constantine realized that he could never feel at home in the old capital; before the year was out, he had laid the foundations of a new capital.

The Emperor had reasons more cogent than mere dislike of Rome for founding Constantinople. Had you been Constantine, where would you have placed your capital? What should be the characteristics of the ideal site? A location near the center of the wide-spreading imperial territories? The possession of convenient facilities for travel and trade to distant markets? A moderate and healthful climate? Terrain that lent itself to defense?

All these natural assets Constantine found near the meeting place of the Hellespont and the Black Sea. Having chosen the site, he himself laid out the boundaries of the new city. He announced that he was inspired by the command of God: "I shall advance until he, the invisible God who marches before me, thinks proper to stop."[21]

New conditions, in a new kind of empire, cried out for this establishment of a new capital, unhampered by precedents or prejudices. As usual, Constantine demonstrated what has been called his unerring genius for understanding the needs of the times and the hopes of his subjects. Politically, Rome was the stronghold of the old-fashioned ideas which Constantine was overthrowing. His absolute government could best flourish in the uncritical atmosphere of a capital that owed its very existence to the new system. Strategically, Rome was inconvenient and virtually indefensible, whereas the impregnability of Constantinople, with its water defenses, was for centuries to testify to the military eye of its founder. Commercially, there could be no comparison between the two cities. In wealth and culture, the Empire was perhaps three quarters Greek and oriental rather than Roman. At the crossroads of trade, and with its safe and spacious harbor, Constantinople at once became a thriving business center. Above all, it was the religious revolution which was symbolized by the construction of the new capital. In Rome were the temples and priests of traditional paganism. But Constantine had decided for the new faith, and Constantinople was to be the first purely Christian city.

By his construction program Constantine set about creating what could become the cosmopolitan center of an empire of many, diverse peoples and cultures. He built the city of wood and marble, good supplies of which were readily available. There was, of course, a broad Forum, a Senate House, and a Great Palace. The impressive Library was to contain both pagan and Christian works; Constantine ordered copies of rare books made on rich and durable vellum.[22] The most famous of Constantine's buildings were the Church of Hagia Sophia and the Hippodrome, where a crowd of forty thousand could watch the chariot races. For the Hippodrome Constantine collected works of art from the world over, including the four bronze horses we can see today on the Cathedral of Saint Mark in Venice and the bronze pillar which memorialized the victory of the Greeks over Xerxes at Plataea.

Finally Constantine erected an enormous column as the repository for many venerable relics of the earliest days of Christianity. On its base was inscribed, "O Christ, Ruler and Master of the world, to Thee have I now consecrated this obedient city." The date of dedication was May 11, 330. In his new capital, Constantine "fused together the great political legacy of Rome, the equally great cultural legacy of the Hellenic world, and the explosive dynamism of the Christian faith."[23]

It was a gigantic enterprise to build Constantinople on the huge scale which the Emperor decreed. To meet the expense, heavy additional taxes had to be levied, with no prospect of any return from the unusual capital investment. To provide the decoration for the squares and public buildings, other cities were stripped of their ornaments and new schools of art set up. The palace, the Hippodrome, and the churches, were the wonderful achievements of their day. Despite all difficulties, the city soon prospered mightily. Perhaps it could not supply the population which flocked into it; then ship-convoys would bring in grain from Egypt. Perhaps the common people, as earlier in Rome, were corrupted by open-handed distribution of food. Perhaps much of the rapid building was poorly done. But, says Gibbon, "every wind wafted riches into the secure and capacious harbor."[24] And Constantinople was to be, until 1453, the center of the Empire and the guardian of culture and to remain, until today, one of the chief cities of the entire world.

8. *The accomplishment of Diocletian and Constantine seen in perspective*

Can we fail to be disappointed as we review the career of Constantine and see the valorous and forceful prince declining into the sinister and selfish despot? On the other hand, can we fail to wonder at and admire his magnificent achievement? Of course we must recognize that the praise should not be his alone. The successes of the Roman Empire in the early 4th century were the joint accomplishment of Diocletian and Constantine. Although apparently very different in character, both Emperors had ability, shrewdness, and courage. Neither one was a bold visionary; their idealism was tempered with practical common sense. They sought to find not the ideal solution to the problems of the Empire but the best possible solution, under the circumstances of the moment. A biographer describes Diocletian in words that seem equally applicable to Constantine: "Not very clever, nor perfectly good, nor altogether wise, he was a man of genius, a giant whose labors are immortal."[25] When Diocletian and Constantine settled upon the end of their actions, they pursued that end with persistence.

Their first aim was to substitute the reign of law for the chaos of the 3rd century, to ensure the survival of the Roman Empire. In 284 the collapse of the Roman state had looked inevitable, and the victory of barbarian men and principles imminent. The labors of Diocletian and Constantine halted the disintegration. The Empire as they revived and reorganized it was markedly different from the one that had existed before. Like Augustus, they have been credited with founding a new kind of state, but it may be seriously questioned if their new state was equal in quality to the earlier one. Its spirit was authoritarian, with reforms imposed from the top down, rather than cooperative, with initiative and vitality welling up from the mass of the people. Diocletian and Constantine had a genuine desire to do good, but they were not blessed with much human sympathy or creative imagination. It was easier for them to standardize administration by means of a bureaucracy—even though it be at times brutal, corrupt, and inefficient—than to attempt the reinvigoration of the system of municipal self-government which Augustus had devised. The incidental loss of democracy might be ignored. They preserved the Roman Empire, but they did not—and probably could not—reanimate it. The old enthusiasm and confidence had deserted the Roman people: they were submissive, not proud; passive, not active.

The Empire handed on by Constantine, with its hereditary ruler surrounded by a court of high officials and maintained by a mercenary army, bore litle resemblance to the Roman Senate and People of earlier, happier days. The interests and rights of the people were everywhere sacrificed. The essential nobility of the Roman spirit seemed to be dissipated even though the grandeur of the Roman state was preserved. The necessities of troubled and dangerous times apparently demanded that despotic decree replace individual initiative—that, as President Lincoln was to explain it, the government must do for people what they could not do for themselves. The new state lasted for 1,100 years, but its citizens were not prosperous or independent. Milman deplores the "profound prostration of the human mind and total extinction of the old sentiments of Roman liberty."[26] Life under Diocletian and Constantine might be secure for nearly all, but it was happy and productive for almost none. Rostovtzeff mentions the debasement of the quality of life, which he ascribes in part to the Emperors' willingness to standardize existing conditions even when they were bad. Security and uniformity are not always the most desirable goals. According to Rostovtzeff,

> The emperors of the 4th century grew up in an atmosphere of violence and compulsion. They never saw anything else, they never came across any other method. Their education was moderate and their training exclusively military. They took their duties seriously, and they were animated by the sincerest love of their country. Their aim was to save the Roman Empire, and they achieved it. To this end they used, with the best intentions, the means which were familiar to them, violence and compulsion. They never asked whether it was worthwhile to save the Roman Empire in order to make it a vast prison for scores of millions of men.[27]

It is not for unworthy ambitions that we can criticize Diocletian and Constantine, not for lack of skill or perseverance. Their limitation was narrowness of vision. Concerned with what was, they could not perceive clearly enough what might be. They did many important and valuable things; they failed to do, or did not even attempt to do, the really great things they could—perhaps—have done. They created an efficient machine of government and a unified state; they failed to create a Roman world abounding in vigor or in fresh talent. We admire them, justly, as great men; we may regret they were not even greater.

Diocletian and Constantine could not produce a new Golden Age. The Empire they established might last for a century, but the spirit of constructive enterprise had deserted it. Under their regime, the Roman people found themselves fatally tied down—

identified with a particular caste, forced to dwell in a particular place, restricted to a particular trade. Escape from these physical bonds being virtually impossible, the average man resigned himself to the inevitable. But his spirit was crushed, and the goal of life came to be making the best of his present lot rather than trying to improve it. In the face of the unrelenting pressure of his obligations to the state, he declined to run the risks involved in an effort to change his status. Indeed, opportunity as we know it—to make a fortune, to rise in society—was virtually non-existent. Fruitless to produce more than he needed to consume, if the government would only deprive him of the surplus or make him responsible for his out-distanced competitors. He was most secure if within his own family he could produce all the necessities of life.

A subsistence economy, with self-sufficiency the goal of every household, became the order of the day. People found all their horizons narrowing: political freedom disappeared, commerce contracted, artistic productivity declined. Only rarely did one leave the large estate, or villa, of one's landlord. The villa became the normal unit of political, economic, and social life. The world was too strong for the individual. The circumstances of his age and the dictates of his government conspired together against him. No one—from bishop to soldier, from imperial treasurer to day-laborer—was exempt from them. All were slaves, although in unequal degree.[28]

For convenience of administration Diocletian shared his authority, and Constantine moved his capital eastward and ultimately divided his realm. Unintentionally, no doubt, they were drawing the lines for a split of the Empire they had desired to unite—a physical split into two halves whose fates in history would diverge drastically, and a spiritual split as well.

In the East, the state absorbed the Church, as one of its departments. Constantinople stood until the beginning of modern times as the protector of Europe against Asia and the bulwark of Christianity against Mohammedanism. In the West, with the power of the state withdrawn to a distance, the Church remained to fill the vacuum. Christianity had received the imperial sanction. With the emperor himself removed from Rome, where he should have been, the head of the Church inherited the imperial prestige. "The mantle of the Caesars" began to settle on the shoulders of the Bishop of Rome. More and more the Church assumed the functions of the state. And Rome still felt like the capital of the world. As Milman indicates, people had for centuries grown accustomed to turning to Rome for ultimate authority and power. This habit was too deeply ingrained to be obliterated by merely moving the throne to Constantinople. If Rome could not be political capital of the world, then it could be religious capital. Even before the downfall of the Western Empire in the 5th century, the roots of the medieval power of the Bishop of Rome were beginning to take hold. So the political decisions of Diocletian and Constantine affected significantly the future development of Christianity.

In their momentous dealings with the Christians, Constantine far outshone Diocletian. For three centuries Christianity had been the object of scorn, suspicion, and persecution, and Diocletian's only contribution was to prove once again the futility of the old, stubborn policy. Constantine, equal in sagacity to Diocletian and more awake to realities, modeled a new policy to conform to the trend of the times. Burckhardt considers this Constantine's enduring claim to fame. He willingly granted Christians respectful recognition and imperial patronage and he initiated cooperation between State and Church. This new policy was a blessing, although not an unmixed one, to both institutions.

The unity of doctrine and possibly the very existence of the Church owe much to Constantine's interest, but there were other important effects of his policy. The gains for the Church were largely material. Constantine's action gave to the clergy "security, wealth, honors";[29] instead of being hounded to death, they were treated as privileged members of society. The Church as a whole enjoyed a new freedom—to meet in councils and to act publicly without fear. The political organization of the Empire was a useful model for the Church. Bishops' dioceses were grouped in provinces under metropolitans, and the provinces grouped in the patriarchates of Rome and Antioch and Alexandria. The metropolitans and patriarchs were treated with the greatest deference by the imperial officials, who were now required to carry out the decrees of the Church. Dissension from the Church was treason to the state, subject to the fiercest penalties.

But no matter how friendly its contact with the state, the Church was bound to suffer from it some spiritual loss. In return for his protection, the Emperor could reasonably expect to be given some control over the Church. The Church had thus lost some of its "apartness"—its utter separation from and unconcern with political measures. An emperor's actions now could not fail to influence church doctrine, appointments, and policy. State interference, whether favorable or not, was bound to make the Church more worldly. It became a large landowner; it administered law; its officials had responsibilities to Caesar as well as to God. There had to be some sacrifice of its original, purely spiritual quality. In the very material benefits which the Church received from Constantine lay the seeds of wealth and pride and corruption, which might one day cause disaster.

From the point of view of the state, Constantine's alliance with the Church may well have seemed indispensable. Christianity was not only the best force within the Empire; it was also the most energetic, the strongest, and the fastest growing. The state could not much longer ignore it, nor could the state safely continue to antagonize the Church. A revolutionary Church might well overthrow the state—as Constantine was astute enough to see. For the heartless state with its ever-stricter exactions was making enemies as rapidly as the Church with its promise of future happiness was making converts. Constantine reasoned that the state could not long survive without enlisting on its side the moral power and popular appeal of the Church.

A forced contract, or one made from weakness, usually holds pitfalls for the weaker side. For the state, although not for Constantine personally, his partnership with the Church was such a contract. In elevating the Church to a position of equality in regulating the lives of its citizens, Constantine exposed the state to unforeseen dangers. A minor one was soon apparent. Even under Constantine at Nicaea it was impossible permanently to unify the Church. When the Church was merged with the state, division within the Church became an additional source of dispute and rivalry within the state. For example, the conflict between two of Constantine's sons was embittered by the fact that Constans sided with the orthodox Christians and Constantius favored the contrary Arians.

A major danger developed more gradually. To recognize an equal power is always risky, but especially if that power should be morally superior to you. The state might prove to be either incapable or unworthy of maintaining any control over the Church. The new force enlisted now on the side of the state might one day come to oppose the state. For the principles behind the two institutions were antagonistic: the state was obedient to Caesar, the Church was obedient to God. For the Christian there could be no comparison between Caesar and God. Obedience to God implies the right to question and to criticize all earthly rulers and perhaps to disobey them. As Milman wrote: "The Christian alone, throughout this long period of human degradation, breathed an atmosphere of moral freedom which raised him above the general level of servile debasement."[30]

Suppose a bishop should defy an emperor. Then the same disciplined loyalty which had made the Church a potent ally of the emperor would make it a potent enemy of his absolutism. Constantine had enlisted the aid of the Church for the state. Soon the Church rivaled, and later overshadowed, the state. Finally, the Church attempted to dominate the state. The Edict of Milan can thus be pictured as the first step along the road by which the Church came to announce itself as the sole world-empire, commanding men to render unto it not only the things which are God's, but also the things which are Caesar's.

9. *The Roman Empire moves into the Middle Ages*

Reconstructed by Diocletian and Constantine, the Roman Empire gained another hundred years of life. These years included the wise reign of Theodosius and the productive labors of Saints Augustine and Jerome and Ambrose. During these years the barbarians entering the gates received enough education so that the contributions of classical civilization could never be wholly forgotten. The minds and hearts of coming generations, although they might not have experienced the political power of Rome, would yet be acquainted with Greek and Latin learning, with the principles of Roman law, with the basic writings of Christianity. Diocletian and Constantine had preserved the Empire long enough for it to serve, for centuries, as the model of the ideal political organization.

But their Empire was not the same old Empire which Augustus had originated. For the people as a whole were stagnating. Lethargy replaced enthusiasm and resignation replaced ambition; little new and exciting was done; artistic standards and living standards alike declined.[31] In the face of such conditions, Diocletian and Constantine were, to a great extent, powerless. The recurring criticism of them is that, skilled though they were as executives, they lacked imagination. Not creative or dynamic themselves, they had to struggle to conserve the good things already created. They seemed to be satisfied with "apparent splendor rather than real prosperity."[32] They were proud if the Roman Empire looked powerful and stable, even though the people within it were dissatisfied, barbarized, or bankrupt.

This criticism suggests that Diocletian and Constantine were important, almost in spite of themselves, because of the age in which they lived. It was an era of transition between ancient and medieval times. They stood "at the border of two world epochs," when the world was "reconciled to a new religion and newly organized in highly important aspects."[33] It was an era when cities were decaying and the old leaders of Senate and market place found their influence gone. In their places rose new men who owned huge estates or held high military rank. Life was again ruralized, the farmer not the merchant was the indispensable man, and the people spoke only through the mouth of the emperor. It was the fate of Diocletian and Constantine to rule during this turbulent era, and it was their genius which prevented a lapse into chaotic anarchy.

By the time of Constantine's death in 337 A.D., three elements were predominant in the life of the Roman Empire. These three elements were to be predominant throughout the next thousand years.

First, there was the Christian Church, strengthened and unified under Constantine. It proclaimed the central importance of religion in a man's life. The Church was the fountain of individual faith and, in addition, it was to be the buttress of order, the judge of morality, the moderator of manners, the guardian of learning. Second, there was the land. The economy was almost exclusively agricultural, and the productive unit was the villa. The land was the basis of social organization because the possession of it imparted power over people in addition to wealth. Hundreds of laborers farmed the estates, supporting the few great landlords, who might even grow strong enough to resist the government. From the 4th century on, security, such as it was, was chiefly provided by the ownership of land. Third, there was the monarch. He was almost a divine being, and the support of the Church gave to his decrees some of the authority of God. His absolute power depended, ultimately, on his command of the army, and the society of which he was the center adopted, perforce, a military flavor. Kings for centuries to come would attempt to assert despotic power; they modeled themselves on Diocletian and Constantine.

So history moves on, with change so gradual as to be almost imperceptible. The last days of the ancient world foreshadowed the medieval world. As our gaze sweeps over the Roman Empire in the 4th century, the landscape we survey merges across undefinable boundaries into the landscape of what will be called the Middle Ages. There may be a change or two in terminology, the development of an occasional new kind of relationship, a shift in emphasis or authority. But the organization of the life which is supported on that landscape will remain substantially constant.

The Empire Diocletian and Constantine constructed would last so long as the civil and military officialdom they established remained honest and loyal and effective. Then the Empire would crash, its strength undermined by selfish ambition and corruption, because the populace in general did not care if it survived. Looking back at the peace and health and prosperity of the population of the Empire even as early as the beginning of the 3rd century, Pope Gregory the Great is said to have remarked with keen perceptiveness, "While the world was flourishing in itself, in their hearts it had withered away."[34]

Finally, barbarians would flow into the Empire as conquerors, but the new ways of life would bear many of the imprints of the old, monuments to the durable achievements of Diocletian and Constantine. Molded inevitably by their era, they chose to support rather than to resist its tendencies. They could not re-invigorate classical civilization, as Augustus had known it. They did not have the supreme capacity to reshape their age; instead, as Carlyle puts it, their greatness lay in representing their time. They directed the forces they could not themselves create or overthrow. Even in favoring the spread of Christianity Constantine was only hastening a process that was probably inevitable. Following the current trends, but never allowing the state to escape from their control, they were building for the future as much as they were preserving the Roman Empire. They may have been unaware of the developments they were preparing, but their work was solid and its influence was lasting.

BIBLIOGRAPHY
AND NOTES

The author has attempted to provide for young scholars in manageable bulk a readable account of the salient features of Roman history. Intending no startling revisions of historical views, he has made use of the best available published sources in an effort to provide an accurate narrative of events, a searching analysis of causes, and a likely interpretation of motives.

Footnotes have been, in general, used sparingly. They do not attempt to cite each individual source, but rather to make important quotations and information accessible to the reader.

Many of the events mentioned in this book were, of course, first recounted by the classical historians and biographers—Polybius, Livy, Julius Caesar, Cicero, Sallust, Tacitus, Plutarch, Suetonius, Appian, Varro, and Lucan. Their works in entirety, or as much of them as has survived the past two thousand years, are printed in the original and in translation in the Loeb Classical Library. Excerpts from these primary sources are to be found in such useful collections as Robinson, *Selections from Greek and Roman Historians,* and Hadas, *A History of Rome as Told by Roman Historians.* Older collections of primary source material are Davis, *Readings in Ancient History,* Vol. II, and Munro, *Source Book of Roman History.*

In the study of Roman history from its beginnings through the 4th century A.D., many well-known accounts have proved generally reliable and useful. Among them are such "classics" as:

Gibbon, *Decline and Fall of the Roman Empire*
Ferrero, *Greatness and Decline of Rome*
Milman, *History of Christianity*
Mommsen, *A History of Rome*
Rostovtzeff, *Social and Economic History of the Roman Empire*

179

Other useful sources are:
Abbott, "Makers of History" series
Barrow, *The Romans*
Carcopino, *Daily Life in Ancient Rome*
Dudley, *The Civilization of Rome*
Fowler, *Rome*
Frank, *A History of Rome*
Gilman, *Rome*
Hadas, *Imperial Rome*
Hamilton, *The Roman Way*
Mattingly, *Roman Imperial Civilization*
Myers, *Rome, Its Rise and Fall*
Pelham, *Outlines of Roman History*
Rostovtzeff, *Rome*
Setonobos, *History of the Roman People*
Cambridge Ancient History, Vols. VII-XII
    More specialized works were the main sources of information for the separate chapters of this book. There is considerable variation in the profundity and authoritativeness of their scholarship. They are recommended for the student who wishes to study more thoroughly a particular topic or era. Some of the titles listed have been published only in very recent years.

For Chapter I—Hannibal
Baker, *Hannibal*
Cotrell, *Hannibal, Enemy of Rome*
de Beer, *Hannibal*
Lamb, *Hannibal, One Man against Rome*
Picard, *The Life and Death of Carthage*
Hart, "Hannibal and Rome" in *The Atlantic,* Vol. CXLII, pp. 532ff.

For Chapter II—The Gracchi
Boren, *The Gracchi* (Rulers and Statesmen of the World)
Glover, *The Ancient World*
Oman, *Seven Roman Statesmen*
Riddle, *Tiberius Gracchus, Destroyer or Reformer?* (Heath Problems of European Civilization)
Syme, *The Roman Revolution*

For Chapter III—Julius Caesar
Buchan, *Julius Caesar*
Dickinson, *Death of a Republic*
Duggan, *Julius Caesar*
Haskell, *This Was Cicero*

Oman, *Seven Roman Statesmen*
Pratt, *Hail Caesar*
Strachan-Davidson, *Cicero*
Taylor, *Party Politics in the Age of Caesar*
Walter, *Caesar*

For Chapter IV—Augustus
  Buchan, *Augustus*
  Earl, *The Age of Augustus*
  Haskell, *This Was Cicero*
  Mainzer, *Caesar's Mantle*
  Slaughter, *Roman Portraits*
  Weigal, *Life and Times of Mark Antony*

For Chapter V—Diocletian
  Burckhardt, *The Age of Constantine the Great*
  Dawley, *Chapters in Church History*
  Goodenough, *The Church in the Roman Empire*
  Grant, *From Augustus to Constantine*

For Chapter VI—Constantine
  Baker, *Constantine the Great and the Christian Revolution*
  Burckhardt, *The Age of Constantine the Great*
  Durant, *Age of Faith*
  Firth, *Constantine the Great*
  Jones, *Constantine and the Conversion of Europe*
  MacMullen, *Constantine*

It is pleasant to report that new magazines of the last decade or so, like *Horizon,* are attractive sources of knowledge about the Roman world. Given Plutarch and the famous Latin authors, there may be little new to learn about the history of events or the character of great men, but fresh discoveries by the archaeologists continue to give us more information about the fine arts and the daily life of the villa and the city. Examples are Grant's article on coinage portraiture and Temko's on the provincial city of Arles, both of which are among the magazine articles cited in the footnotes.

Notes for Chapter I, Hannibal

1. Lines 271-2 in Dryden's translation of Juvenal's Tenth Satire.
2. Livy, *The History of Rome,* is the author's chief ancient source for the narrative of Hannibal. Specific quotations are from the Everyman's Library Edition, translated by the Reverend Canon Roberts, volume 3, book XXI, 3.
3. *Id.,* book XXI, 1.
4. Livy gives a romantic account of the soldiers felling countless trees, lighting huge fires, and disintegrating the rock with boiling vinegar, in book XXI, 37. Modern authorities have deemed it doubtful that supplies of lumber or vinegar could have been collected adequate for this picturesque process.
5. *Id.,* book XXI, 44.
6. *Id.,* book XXII, 7.
7. Cotrell, *Hannibal, Enemy of Rome,* p. 145.
8. Mommsen, *The History of Rome,* translated by W. P. Dickson, book III, chapter 6.
9. Livy, *op. cit.,* book XXVI, 11.
10. Mommsen, *op. cit.,* book III, chapter 4.

Notes for Chapter II, The Gracchi

1. Plutarch, *The Lives of Noble Greeks and Romans* (Modern Library Edition), pp. 998, 1006; Oman, *Seven Roman Statesmen of the Later Republic,* p. 14.
2. Sallust, *The War with Jugurtha,* XLI, in Loeb Classical Library Edition, p. 223.
3. In *Hellenism,* pp. 176ff., Toynbee describes this period and calls it "The Age of Agony". See, also, the D. C. Somervell abridgement of *A Study of History,* pp. 258, 295, and *passim.*
4. Oman, *op. cit.,* p. 15.
5. Plutarch and Appian, *The Civil Wars,* are the ancient writers who deal at length with the Gracchi. Plutarch's biographical sketches of them are full of intimate glimpses of their manner and character, as though his information were derived from accounts of those who had "seen them in action". This speech and other quotations through p. 44 are to be found in Plutarch, *op. cit.,* pp. 999-1008, *passim,* and are paraphrased in Oman, *op. cit.,* p. 30-56, *passim.*
6. Mommsen, *The History of Rome,* book IV, chapter 3. Mommsen was thoroughly unfriendly to the Gracchi; he called Tiberius "a tolerably able, thoroughly well-meaning, conservative patriot, who simply did not know what he was doing." Book IV, chapter 2.
7. Oman, *op. cit.,* p. 65.
8. Sallust, *op. cit.,* XLII, in Loeb, p. 227.
9. Plutarch, *op. cit.,* p. 1021.
10. Mommsen, *op. cit.,* book IV, chapter 3.

Notes for Chapter III, Julius Caesar

1. This idea is expressed in different words in Suetonius, *The Lives of the Twelve Caesars* (Modern Library Edition), p. 49.
2. Cicero, "On the Consular Provinces", quoted in Haskell, *This Was Cicero,* p. 250. The many quotations from Cicero, in this chapter and the next, indicate his paramount importance as a first-hand source for the history of the collapse of the Republic. Quotations are often made from Haskell's biography which, although not a work of profound scholarship, is highly readable and quotes with accuracy.
3. Allen Temko, "Arles", in *Horizon,* July '59, pp. 90f.
4. Plutarch, "Caesar" in *Lives* (Modern Library Edition), p. 887.
5. See Mommsen, *History of Rome,* book V, chapter 11.
6. Sallust, "The Speech of C. Licinius Macer", in Loeb Classical Library Edition, pp. 421f.
7. Dio Cassius, quoted in Walter, *Caesar,* p. 39.
8. Plutarch, *op. cit.,* p. 861; Suetonius, *op. cit.,* p. 6.
9. Haskell, *op. cit.,* p. 140.
10. Cicero, "Pro P. Sestio", chap. 45, quoted in Dickinson, *Death of a Republic,* p. 282.
11. Haskell, *op. cit.,* p. 207.
12. *Id.,* p. 206.
13. Sallust, *The War with Catiline,* chap. 51, in Loeb, p. 89.
14. Plutarch, *op. cit.,* p. 860.
15. Plutarch, "Pompey" in *Lives,* p. 773 (for both quotations).
16. Plutarch, "Crassus" in *Lives,* p. 659.
17. Sallust, *op. cit.,* chap. 54, in Loeb, p. 113.
18. Plutarch, "Caesar" in *Lives,* p. 865.
19. *Id.,* p. 870.
20. Dio Cassius, quoted in Walter, *op. cit.,* p. 159.
21. Haskell, *op. cit.,* p. 157 (for both quotations).
22. Cicero, *2nd Phillippic,* XXXII, 79, in Loeb, p. 143.
23. Walter, *op. cit.,* p. 201.
24. Plutarch, *op. cit.,* p. 872.
25. Haskell, *op. cit.,* p. 250.
26. Dickinson, *op. cit.,* pp. 313f.
27. Plutarch, "Pompey" in *Lives,* p. 781.
28. Plutarch, "Cato the Younger" in *Lives,* p. 945.
29. Lucan, *The Civil War,* I, quoted in Spitz and Lyman, Eds., *Major Crises in Western Civilization,* Vol. I, p. 59.
30. Cicero, "To Atticus", quoted in Munro, *Source Book of Roman History,* p. 138.
31. Haskell, *op. cit.,* p. 280.
32. Lucan, quoted in Walter, *op. cit.,* p. 329.

33. Suetonius, *op. cit.*, p. 21.
34. The sketch of Caesar in this and the next two paragraphs is drawn from Suetonius, *op. cit.*, especially pp. 23, 27, 31, 42.
35. Haskell, *op. cit.*, p. 277.
36. "To Atticus", VIII, 7, 11, quoted in Dickinson, *op. cit.*, p. 196.
37. Plutarch, "Caesar" in *Lives*, p. 876.
38. Suetonius, *op. cit.*, p. 21.
39. Plutarch, *op. cit.*, p. 886.
40. Haskell, *op. cit.*, p. 309.
41. *Ibid.*
42. *Id.*, p. 227.
43. "To L. Papirius Paetus", quoted in Spitz and Lyman, *op. cit.*, p. 70.
44. Mainzer, *Caesar's Mantle*, p. 14.
45. Plutarch, "Brutus" in *Lives*, p. 1204.
46. Dickinson, *op. cit.*, p. 197.
47. Haskell, *op. cit.*, p. 282.
48. *Id.*, p. 293.
49. Quotations in this paragraph are from Dio's version of a speech by Caesar, in Walter, *op. cit.*, p. 479.
50. T. R. Glover in *The Ancient World*, p. 294, emphasizes the similarities in the programs of C. Gracchus and Caesar.
51. Plutarch, "Caesar", in *Lives*, p. 888.
52. Gibbon, *Decline and Fall of the Roman Empire* (Modern Library Edition), vol. I, p. 64.
53. Walter, *op. cit.*, p. 492.
54. Plutarch, "Caesar" in *Lives*, p. 891.
55. Walter, *op. cit.*, p. 511.
56. See Mommsen, *op. cit.*, book V, chap. 11, for his adulation of Caesar.
57. Appian, quoted in Walter, *op. cit.*, p. 525; see, also, Plutarch, "Brutus" in *Lives*, p. 1191.
58. Suetonius, *op. cit.*, p. 47.
59. *2nd Philippic*, XLV, 116, quoted in Munro, *op. cit.*, p. 137.
60. *Ibid.*
61. Pratt, *Hail Caesar!* p. 326.
62. Mainzer, *op. cit.*, p. 41.

Notes for Chapter IV, Augustus

1. Pelham, *Outlines of Roman History*, p. 357.
2. Appian, *The Civil Wars*, book II, 120, quoted in Munro, *Source Book*, p. 141.
3. Haskell, *This Was Cicero*, p. 323.
4. Suetonius, *The Lives of the Twelve Caesars* (Modern Library Edition), p. 56.
5. Cicero, "To Atticus", quoted in Buchan, *Augustus*, p. 35.
6. Cicero, *5th Philippic*, XVIII, 51, in Loeb Classical Library Edition, p. 307.
7. Haskell, *op. cit.*, p. 336.
8. Cicero, *5th Philippic*, XVIII, 50-51, in Loeb, pp. 307-9.
9. *Id.*, XVI, 43, in Loeb, p. 299-301.
10. Mainzer, *Caesar's Mantle*, p. 142.
11. *Id.*, p. 94.
12. Haskell, *op. cit.*, p. 338.
13. Suetonius, *op. cit.*, p. 68.
14. Haskell, *op. cit.*, p. 340.
15. Plutarch, "Cicero" in *Lives* (Modern Library Edition), p. 1069.
16. Suetonius, *op. cit.*, p. 68.
17. *Id.*, p. 106.
18. Augustus, *Res Gestae*, quoted in Munro, *op. cit.*, p. 144.
19. Suetonius, *op. cit.*, pp. 100-101.
20. Gibbon, *Decline and Fall of the Roman Empire* (Modern Library Edition), vol. I, p. 63. Read chapter 3 for Gibbon's fuller description of the "artful" and "crafty" Augustus.
21. Dio Cassius quoting Maecenas, as quoted in Buchan, *op. cit.*, p. 202.
22. Tacitus, *Annals*, book I, chap. 2, quoted in Munro, *op. cit.*, p. 143.
23. There were occasional, notable exceptions to Augustus' rule of clemency. He exiled Cassius for his vitriolic attacks on the members of the court. When he destroyed Labienus' history of the civil wars for treating Caesar as a traitor, the historian committed suicide. See Gilbert Highet in *Horizon*, Nov. '62, p. 88.
24. Suetonius, *op. cit.*, p. 86. The passages descriptive of Augustus are to be found in pp. 82-105, *passim*.
25. Bury, *History of the Roman Empire*, p. 138.
26. Mainzer, *op. cit.*, p. 337.
27. Munro, *op. cit.*, p. 144.
28. Bury, *op. cit.*, p. 32.
29. Epictetus, III, 13, 9, quoted in Buchan, *op. cit.*, p. 292.

30. Suetonius, *op. cit.*, p. 106.
31. Seneca quoted in Buchan, *op. cit.*, p. 351.
32. Buchan, *op. cit.*, p. 258.
33. Augustus to Tiberius, reported in Suetonius, *op. cit.*, p. 85.
34. Suetonius, *op. cit.*, p. 66.
35. Strabo, VI, 288, quoted in Buchan, *op. cit.*, p. 163.
36. Horace, *Odes,* IV, 5, in Loeb, p. 302.
37. Suetonius, *op. cit.*, p. 114.
38. *Id.*, p. 73.
39. *Id.*, p. 70.

Notes for Chapter V, Diocletian

1. Aelius Aristides quoted in *Rome, Life* Educational Reprint No. 6, p. 14.
2. Herodian, quoted in Rostovtzeff, *Social and Economic History of Rome,* p. 399.
3. Gibbon, *Decline and Fall of the Roman Empire* (Modern Library Edition) vol. I, p. 274. For the later Empire, scholars turn automatically to Gibbon as the best-known and most encyclopedic (even if not unchallenged) source. Gibbon made use of all the classical and Christian authors whose works were available to him. Certain materials, of course, have come to light since the mid-18th century: for instance, the text of the famous Edict of 301.
4. Rostovtzeff, *op. cit.,* pp. 453-4.
5. *Id.,* p. 394.
6. Baker, *Constantine the Great and the Christian Revolution,* p. 31fn.
7. Burckhardt, *The Age of Constantine the Great* (Anchor Edition A65), pp. 248-9.
8. *Id.,* p. 52.
9. For these and other comparable monetary estimates, see Frank, *History of Rome,* pp. 557-8.
10. It is a curious coincidence that stone tablets bearing large sections of this Edict were unearthed in Aphrodisias, Turkey, in the autumn of 1970, just as the Turkish premier Suleyman Demirell was announcing his plans to combat modern instances of inflation and profiteering.
11. Burckhardt, *op. cit.,* p. 234.
12. See Michael Grant, "Roman Coins", in *Horizon,* Sept. '63, pp. 33f.
13. Quoted in Burckhardt, *op. cit.,* p. 54.
14. Frank, *op. cit.,* p. 553.
15. Hadas, *A History of Rome* (Anchor Edition A78), pp. 175, 178.
16. This quotation from Lactantius and those in the next paragraph are from "On the Death of the Persecutors", chap. VII, *passim,* quoted in Munro, *Source Book of Roman History,* pp. 235-6.
17. Gibbon, *op. cit.,* vol. I, p. 328.
18. Quoted in Burckhardt, *op. cit.,* p. 55.

19. Baker, *op. cit.*, p. 188.
20. Burckhardt, *op. cit.*, p. 246.
21. Gibbon, *op. cit.*, vol. I, p. 341.
22. Myers, *Rise and Fall of Rome,* p. 390.
23. Gibbon, *op. cit.*, vol. I, p. 340.
24. *Id.,* p. 381.
25. *Id.,* p. 346.

Notes for Chapter VI, Constantine

1. Burckhardt, *The Age of Constantine the Great,* p. 325.
2. Gibbon, *Decline and Fall of the Roman Empire* (Modern Library Edition), vol. I, p. 540.
3. *Id.,* p. 562.
4. *Id.,* p. 654.
5. First Epistle to the Corinthians, I., 23.
6. Goodenough, *The Church in the Roman Empire,* p. 4.
7. Burckhardt, *op. cit.,* p. 114.
8. Epistle to the Galatians, III, 28.
9. From *Annals,* book 15, quoted in Edwin Fenton, *32 Problems in World History,* p. 43.
10. From *Letters of Young Pliny,* J. D. Lewis, ed., quoted in Fenton, *op. cit.,* pp. 44-5.
11. From Eusebius, *History of the Christian Church,* book IV, chap. 9, quoted in Fenton, *op. cit.,* p. 45.
12. From Eusebius, *op. cit.,* book VIII, chaps. 2 and 6, quoted in Munro, *Source Book of Roman History,* p. 174.
13. From Lactantius, "On the Death of the Persecutors", chaps. 34-5, quoted in Munro, *op. cit.,* p. 176.
14. This is the rendering by C. H. Firth in *Constantine the Great* of what all consider a difficult text of Lactantius. For a more complete version, see *Cambridge Ancient History,* vol. XII, pp. 689-90, or Hadas, *A History of Rome,* pp. 185-7.
15. From Eusebius, *Life of Constantine,* book I, chaps. 28-9, quoted in Munro, *op. cit.,* p. 175.
16. Thomas Hodgkin quoted in Myers, *Rome, Its Rise and Fall,* p. 403.
17. Constantine formally opened the meeting at Arles. This was the same Gallic city on the Rhone that Augustus had favored. Developed into a center of trade and communication, Constantine, as Caesar, had uséd it as his capital. Here he built magnificent baths, of brick faced with marble, with elaborate ribbed vaulting and an ingenious warm-air heating system. Here he married Fausta and discovered the conspiracy against him which his father-in-law Maximian was organizing. See Allen Temko, "Arles", in *Horizon,* July '59, pp. 130-1.
18. Gibbon, *op. cit.,* vol. I, p. 670.
19. Milman, *History of Christianity,* vol. II, p. 374.
20. Alfred Werner, "The Vatican", in *Horizon,* Jan. '62, pp. 22-26.
21. Durant, *Age of Faith,* p. 4.

22. Gilbert Highet, "The Wondrous Survival of Records", in *Horizon,* Nov. '62, p. 78.
23. Philip Sherrard, "Byzantium", in *Horizon,* Nov. '63, pp. 6f.
24. Gibbon, *op. cit.,* vol. I, p. 508.
25. Baker, *Constantine the Great and the Christian Revolution,* p. 189.
26. Milman, *op. cit.,* vol. II, p. 394.
27. Rostovtzeff, *Economic and Social History of the Roman Empire,* pp. 477-8.
28. See Rostovtzeff, *id.,* pp. 472f.
29. Gibbon, *op. cit.,* vol. I, p. 671.
30. Milman, *op. cit.,* vol. II, p. 395.
31. For instance, to decorate the Arch of Constantine in Rome, sculptured panels were stripped from the monuments of earlier reigns.
32. Gibbon, *op. cit.,* vol. I, p. 562.
33. Burckhardt, *op. cit.,* p. 325.
34. Dudley, *The Civilization of Rome* (Mentor edition), p. 242.

Exercises for Chapter I, Hannibal

I. Vocabulary:
    1. Look up the roots of the following words and be sure you understand the meaning of each word:

monopoly	dictator	attrition
exploit	plebeian	mandate
beneficiary	oligarchy	nadir
indemnity	aristocracy	hegemony

    2. Explain each of the following phrases and be prepared to give a modern example of it:

guerrilla warfare	status quo
caste system	vested interest

II. Projects:
    1. The classical authors particularly mentioned in this chapter are Juvenal, Polybius, and Livy. Look up the careers of these authors, read some of their works in translation, and describe their works.
    2. Tell the story of the life and accomplishment of Archimedes; of Publius Scipio.
    3. Trace the rise and fall of Syracuse.
    4. What was "Great Greece"? Why was it established? What happened to it?
    5. Rulers of minor states mentioned in this chapter are: Pyrrhus of Epirus; Antiochus of Syria; Philip of Macedon. Look up the life stories of these individual rulers. Assess the importance of these states in Ancient History.
    6. Like Zama, Salamis was a battle of world importance. Who fought at Salamis? What for? What resulted from the battle?

III. Topics for discussion:
    1. The Etruscans and their civilization.
    2. Macaulay's poem "Horatius at the Bridge". Is it a true story? What is its significance?
    3. Napoleon led the French army across the Alps in 1796. Why? What did he say to his soldiers? What was the effect of his Transalpine campaign?
    4. What interpretations are suggested in the text of Hannibal's failure to take Rome? Are there other valid interpretations? What is your personal explanation of his failure?
    5. If you had been the Carthaginian commander-in-chief, how would you have altered Hannibal's strategy?

6. If you had been Scipio, would you have been tempted to negotiate a peace? What arguments would have affected you?

IV. Map Work:

1. To illustrate the text, draw diagrams of Hannibal's famous battles.

2. On a map of the Mediterranean world, indicate the location of the following areas, places, and battles—outside of Italy—which are mentioned in this chapter:

Sicily	Carthage	Zama
Sardinia	Cadiz	Cynoscephalae
Crete	Tyre	Magnesia
Spain	Corinth	Alps Mts.
Epirus	Athens	Pyrenees Mts.
Macedonia	Syracuse	Taurus Mts.
Syria	Saguntum	Ebro R.
Bithynia		Rhone R.
Egypt		
Rhodes		

Exercises for Chapter II, The Gracchi

I. Vocabulary:
    1. What is the meaning of each of the following words?

republic	mortgage	patrician
empire	capital	yeoman
metropolis	speculation	radical
veto	subsidize	partisan
impeachment	nominal	sovereign
sacrilege		demagogue
mediation		tyrant
		proletariat
		faction

    2. Explain each of the following phrases:
          buyers' market
          public domain
          tax farming
          ipso facto
          coup d'etat

II. Projects:
    1. Look up the career and the work of the classical authors
        particularly mentioned in this chapter: Plutarch, Appian,
        and Sallust.
    2. What were the particular duties of the various officials
        of Republican Rome: quaestors, aediles, praetors, cen-
        sors?
    3. Look up the origins of the tribunate. What are your
        critical comments about the purpose, the usefulness, and
        the efficiency of this office?
    4. A number of interesting and important individuals are
        mentioned in this chapter: Cato, Marius, Sulla, Pom-
        pey, Crassus, Sertorius, Spartacus. Look up the life
        story of each of these individuals and explain his role
        and importance in Roman History.
    5. Stoics were believers in a particular philosophy, Stoicism.
        Look up the origin of their name, their leaders, their
        ideas, their history, and their effect on society.

III. Topics for discussion:
    1. Describe the differences of character between Tiberius
        and Caius Gracchus. Which do you consider the more
        effective political leader? Why? Which would you have
        preferred as a friend? Why? Were they cowards? If not,
        how do you account for the rather passive and humiliat-
        ing way in which they both met their deaths?

2. What is your opinion of the political role of the Gracchi? Were they conservatives or radicals? Were they reformers or destroyers of the Republic?

3. Dictatorship: Think of the dictatorships of the 1920's and the 1930's and of the dictatorships since World War II.
    a) Under what conditions do nations call on a dictator?
    b) What kind of people make effective dictators?
    c) What are the methods of a dictator? His base of support or power?
    d) Are dictatorships efficient in solving national problems? Is efficiency always an advantage?
    e) What are the weaknesses or vulnerability in dictatorial government?
    f) By what means are dictatorships usually terminated?

4. President Franklin D. Roosevelt had influence comparable to a dictator's in his first Hundred Days in 1933. What central problem did he face? Find out the various kinds of legislation that were enacted in the early months of his presidency.

5. What means of combatting widespread unemployment and the decline of agriculture have been devised in the 20th century? How do they compare with the policies of the Gracchi, in theory and in effectiveness?

6. Compare and contrast the motives, and the attitudes toward service as "agents of empire", of the Romans of the time of the Gracchi with those of Frenchmen and Englishmen in the 17th and 18th century and of Englishmen in the 19th century.

Exercises for Chapter III, Julius Caesar

I. Vocabulary:

  1. Look up the roots of the following words and be sure you understand the meaning of each word:

      anarchy   aristocracy
      monarchy   bureaucracy
      oligarchy   democracy

  2. What is the meaning of each of the following words? Suggest a modern usage of each.

      patron   despotism   purge
      connoisseur   junta   suffrage
      pontiff   legates   apathy
      emperor   tenure   treason
      arbitrary   prefect   sacrilege

  3. Define or explain each of the following:

      political party
      civil service
      preventive war
      noblesse oblige

II. Projects:

  1. Look up the career and the work of the classical authors particularly mentioned in this chapter: Cicero, Dio Cassius, Lucan, Plutarch.

  2. A great many leaders of importance are mentioned in this chapter: Pompey, Crassus, Cicero, the Younger Cato, Clodius, Brutus, Cassius, Cinna, Varro, Mark Antony, Cleopatra. Look up the life story of each of these individuals and explain his significant role in Roman History.

  3. Look up the details of the following battles: Pharsalus, Thapsus, Munda.

  4. Tell the story of the Social War: background, events, outcome.

  5. Tell the story of Catiline's conspiracy. What caused it? Why did it fail?

  6. Draw the plan of a Roman fortified camp.

  7. Who was Mithridates of Pontus? What happened to him? What is his story typical of?

  8. Find out all that you can about how the Romans treated the Jews.

III. Topics for discussion:

  1. Would you have joined the conspiracy against Caesar? Why?

  2. Do you believe that generals make poor politicians? Why? Give examples from American History.

3. Read Shakespeare's play *Julius Caesar*. Is it accurate as history? For what purpose might Shakespeare have distorted the story? What are his estimates of the various characters? Who is the hero? Was the murder a success?

4. Read George Bernard Shaw's play *Caesar and Cleopatra*. Compare this play with Shakespeare's and with history. What differences do you find between the two plays, and how do you account for them?

5. Read a couple of chapters of Caesar's *De Bello Gallico*. What are the characteristics of the author? Look up, especially, the careers of Ariovistus and Vercingetorix.

6. Account for the declining participation of the "average citizen" in the government in the years before Caesar.

IV. Map Work:

1. Looking up the details of the Gallic Wars, locate the sites of major battles and the homelands of various tribes. Include the campaign in Britain.

2. Trace the progress of Caesar's military campaigns after he crossed the Rubicon River in 49 B.C.

Exercises for Chapter IV, Augustus

I. Vocabulary:

   1. What is the meaning of each of the following words?

proscription	panacea	propagandist
hierarchy	sanction	expropriation
magistrate	pillage	bankruptcy
prerogatives	elite	cult
primacy	subversive	portent
premier	hereditary	
sovereignty	assimilation	
viceroy	alienation	
bourgeoisie	expediency	

II. Projects:

   1. Continue your accounts of the life and importance of Cicero and Mark Antony.

   2. Look up the careers of Lepidus and Tiberius.

   3. Look up the careers of Agrippa and Maecenas; what particular roles did these men play under the rule of Augustus?

   4. Tell the story of Brutus and Cassius at Philippi. How do you account for their actions?

   5. Look up the careers and work of the classical authors mentioned in this chapter: Virgil, Horace, Ovid, Livy, Suetonius, Tacitus, Strabo.

   6. Read Tacitus' account of the Germans. What chief points of difference do you find between the Germans and the Romans of the first century?

   7. Find pictures of Rome (and of the leading provincial cities) in the time of Augustus. What do you consider to be the chief characteristics of Roman architecture, especially as compared with Greek?

III. Topics for discussion:

   1. Read Shakespeare's play *Antony and Cleopatra* and compare it with *Julius Caesar* and *Caesar and Cleopatra*.

   2. How do you define "liberty"? What were the varying interpretations of liberty in the minds of Cicero, Brutus, Julius Caesar, Augustus?

   3. Contrast and compare the characters of Julius Caesar and Augustus. Which one do you feel was the more successful, admirable, personable?

   4. Thinking in terms of Augustus' time and your own, what would you say is the usefulness of government commissions? What kinds of commissions can be established? What kinds of reports or work do they accomplish?

5. Write a definition of "state socialism". Explain how and to what extent you think the Principate was an example of this type of government.
6. What are the dangers or risks of an hereditary monarchy? Of a monarchy which is not hereditary? (Consider Spain in 1971.)

IV. Map Work:
1. On the map of the Roman Empire, locate places and areas mentioned in this chapter, such as:
   rivers: Danube, Elbe, Rhine
   battles: Actium, Philippi
   cities: Massilia, Ravenna
   provinces: Illyria, Dalmatia, Roetia, Noricum, Pannonia, Palestine, Pontus; Parthia

Exercises for Chapter V, Diocletian

I. Vocabulary:
    1. What is the meaning of each of the following words?

        clique   abdication   inflation
        tyranny   heredity   depreciation
        appeasement   facade   middleman
        dynasty   opportunist   profits
        utopia   usurper

    2. Be sure you understand the meaning of each of the following phrases and are able to give a contemporary example of it:

        plenary power
        buffer state
        debasement of the currency
        coup d'etat
        fait accompli

II. Projects:
    1. Make a list, in chronological sequence, of the emperors from Augustus to Diocletian. Which of these emperors were murdered?
    2. Read the *Meditations* of Marcus Aurelius. What were the chief characteristics of this author-emperor?
    3. Who were the Druids? Reconstruct their history. Which of their monuments are to be found today? Where?
    4. Find out all that you can about the various opinions of the Roman Empire and its rulers that were expressed by early Christian authors such as Eusebius and Lactantius. Include in your investigation the authors of the New Testament and the early Church Fathers.
    5. Who was Aeneas? Recount his adventures.

III. Topics for discussion:
    1. Explain why inflation of prices is exactly the same thing as depreciation of money.
    2. Are creditors or debtors hurt most by inflation? Explain.
    3. Why is it unnecessary for the metallic content of American coins today to be actually worth the face value of the coins?
    4. What is the purpose and the machinery, these days, of price-fixing? Seek your evidence from the history of the New Deal, of the Kennedy and Johnson Administrations, of the Nixon Administration. What is meant by guidelines?
    5. Reach a critical judgment about Stoicism: What are its strengths? Its weaknesses or lacks? What evidences of it are to be found in today's society?

IV. Map Work:
1. Showing the extent of the Roman Empire under Trajan, and identifying such provinces as Armenia, Mesopotamia, and Dacia, explain Diocletian's attempt to "consolidate" the Empire.
2. Draw the boundaries of the new divisions of the Empire which Diocletian effected; explain the reasons for these divisions.

Exercises for Chapter VI, Constantine

I. Vocabulary:
    1. Define each of the following words:

        paganism   absolutism
        doctrine   prerogative
        sacrament   espionage
        schism   immunity
        synod   barbarians
        dogma   patronage
        orthodox   corporation
    2. Explain the meaning of the term, subsistence economy.
    3. Be sure you can explain the difference between the words
        in the following sets:

        production and productivity
        capital and income
        property tax and income tax and poll tax
        heretic and traitor
        migration and immigration and emigration

II. Projects:
    1. Find out what you can about the various mystery cults
        and oriental religions mentioned in this chapter.
    2. Investigate the Donatist heresy.
    3. Investigate the Arian heresy. In what ways did this repre-
        sent a conflict between reason and faith?
    4. Explain the Christian doctrine of the Trinity.
    5. With reference to "good works", investigate the Pelagian
        heresy.
    6. Tell the story of the conversion of St. Paul. Where do
        you find this story in the Bible?
    7. Recount the career of St. Paul; estimate the effects of
        his work.
    8. Look up the careers of: Emperor Theodosius; Saints
        Augustine, Jerome, Ambrose. What were the chief works
        of each of these great men?
    9. If Athanasius dared to resist Constantine's will, find out
        what Ambrose did to Emperor Theodosius and what
        Gregory VII did to Henry IV.

III. Topics for discussion:
    1. Is an income tax fair? A graduated income tax? When
        does such a tax begin to affect one's incentive to work?
    2. When in the 20th century have British or American
        taxes reached confiscatory levels (above 90%)? Why?
        With what effects? What are the highest tax rates now in
        effect?

3. What are the differences among: a citizens' army, a professional army, a mercenary army? Which army do you consider best?

4. Periodically throughout history we have witnessed sharp conflicts between Church and State, between morality and law. Are recent disputes over the draft law and the war in Vietnam of comparable nature?

5. Define faith; in what do people of the 20th century have faith?

6. How do you define religion? Describe the state of religion in the 20th century. Who are the "prophets" of today?

7. If you had been alive during the first three centuries, do you think you would have become a Christian?

8. Why were the Christians, in such large numbers, willing to undergo persecution for their faith?

9. Diocletian was seeking the "final solution" to a troublesome problem. What did Hitler propose as a "final solution"? Were the problems of the two rulers in any way comparable?

10. Rostovtzeff wrote: "The gradual absorption of the educated classes by the masses, and the consequent simplification of all functions of political, social, economic, and intellectual life, accelerated the process which we call the barbarization of the ancient world, debasing its standards and diluting its quality." Do you consider this process of absorption and barbarization inevitable?

IV. Map Work:

1. On the map of the Roman Empire, locate all the places that were of importance in the
    (a) early history of Christianity;
    (b) life of Constantine.

INDEX

Actium, 100-1, 103, 105, 107, 108

Adriatic Sea, 79, 100, 114, 143

Aegates, 8

Aeneid, 112

Africa, 5, 21, 48, 59, 80, 98, 99

Agathocles, 4

Agrarian Law, 37-41, 43, 46, 53, 69, 106

agriculture, 29, 34, 36, 44, 55, 98

Agrippa, 99, 102, 111, 112, 115, 116

Alesia, 77

Alexander the Great, 4, 5, 63, 85

Alexandria, 61, 80, 99-100, 103, 174

allies, 7, 11, 13-4, 15, 17, 20, 48

Alps Mts., 3, 11-2, 20, 59

Antiochus of Syria, 23-4, 30

Antony, Mark, 75-6, 79, 81, 83, 87, 91-2, 93-5, 96-101, 103, 143

Apennine Mts., 14

Apollonia, 18, 92

Aquae Sextiae, 55, 61

Archimedes, 18-20

Arian heresy, 166, 175

Ariovistus, 72

Aristides, 124

aristocracy, 6, 40, 54, 64, 70, 99, 106, 127, 137, 148

Arius, 166-8

Arles, 60, 166

Armenia, 128, 133

Arminius, 117

army, 3, 7, 8, 14, 16, 36, 46, 55, 61, 70-1, 84, 92, 94, 109, 117, 123-7, 128-9, 130, 134, 150, 177

Arrius Aper, 128

arts, 112, 143, 169-70

Asia Minor, 24, 30, 40, 46, 53, 60, 131

Assembly, 25, 31-2, 35-7, 40-1, 43, 45, 47-9, 51-3, 62, 64, 66, 75, 109

Athanasius 166-8

Atticus, 72, 76, 78, 83, 93

auguries, 49, 86, 164

Augustan Age, 112, 118

Augustus, 92-119, 143
  and Antony, 94, 96-101
  and Cicero, 93-5, 97
  appearance, 102
  character, 92-3, 95, 96, 102-3, 105
  conservatism, 104-6
  death, 119
  empire, 114-5
  family, 92
  patron, 112-4
  personal rule, 104, 106, 109-10, 115-6, 119
  political leader, 105-7
  princeps, 108-10
  reformer, 111-2

Augustus (references to, after his death), 123, 124, 127-8, 129-30, 136-7, 152, 154, 155, 171

Aurelian, 126-8

Aurelius Victor, 128, 137, 139

barbarians, 55, 61, 72, 84, 114, 117-8, 124, 126, 131, 143, 150, 176, 177

Baths of Diocletian, 139

Bibulus, 69, 77

biography, 77

Bishop of Rome, 173-4

bishops, 163, 165-6, 167-8, 174

Bithynia, 24, 61, 159

Black Sea, 169

Blossius, 29

Bohemia, 115, 117

bourgeois, 92, 104-6, 124, 125, 127, 129-30

Britain, 5, 10, 59, 114, 124, 140-1

Brundisium, 78

Brutus, 74, 82-3, 86, 91-5, 96, 97, 112

Brutus, Decimus, 86, 92, 95

bureaucracy, (see civil service)

204

Cadiz, 5, 63
Caesar, G. Julius, 59-88, 91, 99-100, 123
  a god, 87
  and Augustus, 103-4, 105-7, 114-5, 119
  assassination, 86, 91, 107, 115
  career in office, 62-3, 68, 69-70
  character, 61-3, 68, 71-2, 76-8, 81, 83-4, 85-6
  conflict with Pompey, 73, 75-6, 77-81
  dictator, 81-4, 87
  1st Triumvirate, 69-71
  funeral and will, 87, 91-2, 94
  general, 71-2, 79-80
  outlaw, 75
  politician, 69, 73, 77, 84
  reform program, 60-1, 83, 87
  would-be king, 85
  youth, 61
Caesarion, 101
Caligula, 124
Calpurnia, 86, 91
Cannae, 16-7, 20, 22
capital (money), 126, 149, 170
capitalists, 5, 9, 38-9, 52, 54
Capua, 17-8, 46
Caracalla, 125
Carausias, 133-4
Carinus, 129
Carrhae, 73
Carthage, 3, 4-6, 22, 24, 29, 30, 46, 48, 165
Carthaginian Empire, 5
Carthaginian government, 5-6, 11, 22-3, 24
Carus, 128
Cassius, 82, 86, 92-3, 97
caste system, 6, 136, 149-50, 160, 173
Catiline, 67
Catiline's conspiracy, 63, 67-8, 92
Cato the Elder, 34, 35, 137
Cato the Younger, 68-70, 74-5, 82
Celts, 13, 14, 55
censor, 81, 108
census, 43, 110, 135
character of the Roman people, 8, 31, 34, 40, 67-8, 74, 84, 86, 91, 103, 115-6, 129, 154, 171, 173, 176

Christianity, 153-4, 157-8, 158-61, 162, 166-8, 173, 174-5, 176, 178
Christians, 139, 149, 175
Church, 160, 161-3, 165-8, 173-4, 176-7
Church and State, 162-5, 166-8, 173-6
Cicero, 44, 59, 63-8, 69, 72-3, 74-6, 78-9, 81-3, 86, 87, 91-6, 97, 102, 119
citizenship, 7, 31, 48, 53, 66, 84, 105, 109, 110, 125, 158, 161
city-state, 4, 13, 47, 64
civil service (bureaucracy), 60, 82, 84, 110, 115, 134, 136, 148, 171
civil war, 54, 55, 75-6, 77-81, 103, 118, 124-5, 140, 141-3
class conflicts, 6-7, 31, 34-5, 41, 45, 51, 54, 55, 61, 66, 68, 87, 125, 129
Claudius, 124
Cleopatra, 80, 85-6, 98-101, 102
clergy, 149, 164, 174
Clodius, 68, 69, 73
coinage, 7, 136
colonies, 4, 7, 46, 48-9, 53, 60
commissions, 37, 111, 115, 165-6
Commodus, 125
conscription, 46
conservatives, 47, 75, 125
Constans, 175
Constantia, 142-3
Constantine, 140-4, 147-78
  accomplishment, 171-4, 176-8
  and Christianity, 153, 161-5, 174
  and Church, 164-5, 166-8, 174-6
  and Constantinople, 169-71
  and doctrine, 164, 166-8
  character, 147, 151-3, 163-4, 168, 171
  conversion, 163-5
  criticism of, 172, 176-8
  organization of Empire, 148-51, 153
  social legislation, 164
Constantinople, 169-71, 173
Constantius, 175
Constantius Chlorus, 131, 133, 140-1, 161, 163

constitution, 40-1, 47, 54, 56, 76, 81-4, 87, 96, 107-8, 125
consul (consulate), 6, 15-6, 21, 32, 43, 50, 55-6, 75, 82, 91, 95, 104, 108
Corinth, 24, 30
Corinthian Canal, 61
Cornelia, mother of Caesar, 62
Cornelia, mother of the Gracchi, 29
Cornelius, centurion, 95
Crassus, 56, 63, 67, 69-70, 73
Crete, 24
Crispus, 148, 151-3
Curio, 73
currency, 67, 127, 132-3
Cybele, 156-7
Cyprus, 153

Dacia, 143
Dalmatia, 117, 128, 131
Danube R., 114-5, 117, 124, 126, 130-1, 140, 143
debts, 34, 60, 67, 83, 106
decurions, 137-8, 149
demagoguery, 43, 51, 53, 67
democracy (democrats), 5, 44, 47, 49-50, 67, 118, 171
denarius, 127, 132
despotism, 55, 82-4, 87, 136-7, 177
dictator, 10, 15, 25, 43, 55-6, 75-6, 81, 148
dictatorship, 74, 82, 118, 124
Dio Cassius, 62, 72, 103
Diocletian, 128-44
    abdication, 139-40, 143
    absolutism, 136-8, 160
    accession, 128-9
    accomplishment, 133-5, 138, 171-2, 176-8
    and Christians, 160-2, 174
    board of emperors, 130-2, 138-40, 141-3
    character, 128, 129, 137, 171
    criticism of, 135-8
    economic program, 132-3, 137
    political reforms, 129-32, 134-5, 136-8
    references to, 148, 149, 151, 153, 163, 165
    retirement and death, 142-3
dole, 47-8, 51, 53, 60, 69, 74, 84, 111

domestic problems, 33-6, 52, 60, 69, 111
Donatist heresy, 164-5
Druids, 128
Drusus, son of Livia, 115-7
Drusus, tribune, 48-9
Dyarrichum, 79

East and West, 103, 173-4
Ebro R., 10-1
Ecnomus, 8
economy, national, 33-5, 52, 55, 173, 177
Egypt, 20, 24, 33, 59, 80, 98-9, 101, 104, 110, 133, 170
Elbe R., 114, 117
elephants, 12, 21-2
emperor, 81, 107, 123, 125-6, 129-30, 134, 135, 136-8, 140, 148, 155, 159, 172, 174
emperor-worship, 111, 155, 158, 167
empire, 5, 7, 31, 35, 47-8, 52, 59, 64, 70, 72, 84, 88, 101, 105-6, 108-9, 110, 114, 123
Etruria, 14, 29, 36
Etruscan, 4, 6, 155
Eusebius, 163-4
expansion, 7, 24-6, 30-3, 114-5, 117

Fabian Policy, 15, 20
Fabius, 15-6, 25
farm labor, 136, 150-1, 177
Fausta, 141, 152
Federalist Papers, 51, 54
Flaccus, 42, 50
Flaminius, 14
Forum, 14, 42, 63, 77, 170
Franks, 133, 141
free labor, 33, 35, 36, 60, 66
frontiers, 124, 126, 130-1, 133, 134
Fulvia, 98

Galerius, 131, 133, 138-43, 152, 161-2
Gallienus, 125
Gaul, 10, 59, 71-3, 74, 76-7, 92, 93, 111, 131, 133, 140-1
Germany, 60, 72, 117, 128, 133, 150
gladiatorial shows, 63, 151

gods, 87, 99, 143, 154-6, 161-2, 167
Good Emperors, 124
"good news", 154, 158
Goths, 143, 153
government, 6-7, 25, 35, 46, 64, 70, 74, 78, 87-8, 92, 96, 106, 115-6, 118, 123, 126, 130, 134-8, 148-9
Gracchus, Caius, 44-56, 84, 87, 91, 108
   character, 44-5, 47
   death, 50
   estimate of, 50-6
   prime minister, 47
   reform program, 45, 48
Gracchus, Tiberius, 29-30, 36-44, 50-6, 69, 87, 91, 108
   character, 36-7, 42
   death, 42
   estimate of, 42-3, 50-6
   land program, 37-41, 43, 46, 53
   politician, 39, 41, 42
grain, 33, 35, 51, 99, 111
Greece, 4, 23, 24, 30, 103, 143
Greek influence 4, 7, 9, 25, 35, 155, 170
Greek philosophies, 157
Gregory the Great, 177

Hadrian, 124, 159
Hagia Sophia, Church of, 170
Hamilcar Barca, 3, 8-10
Hannibal, 3, 9-26, 29, 64, 73, 114
   character, 10, 18, 25-6
   death, 24
   evaluation of, 24-6
   oath, 9
   politician, 23
   strategy, 13, 17
   tactics, 16, 22
Hannibal's army, 11, 12, 21-2
"harmony of the orders", 64, 68, 74
Hasdrubal, brother-in-law, 9-10, 11
Hasdrubal, brother, 16, 20
Hebrews, 154, 157
Hellespont, 131, 143, 169
Helvetii, 71-2
Heraclea, 142
Hiero, 17, 18

Hieronymus, 17
Himera, 4
Hippodrome, 170
history, 53-4, 81, 114, 151
Horace, 100, 101, 112-4, 118-9
Hundred, The, 6, 8, 9-10, 16, 23

Illyria, 18, 114, 129, 143
imperator, 82, 107
imperium, 56, 75, 107-8, 147
indemnity, 8, 22-3
inflation, 127, 132
Isis, 156-7
Italy, 3, 4, 6, 7, 11-3, 15, 29, 33, 39, 46, 48, 59, 76, 78-9, 89, 97-8, 114, 141-2, 147, 149

Jesus Christ, 154, 157-8, 166
John, St., 157
Jugurtha, 55
Julia, sister of Caesar, 92
Julia, daughter of Caesar, 73
Junonia, 48-9, 53
juries, 41, 45-6, 51

king, 42, 76, 82, 85-6, 106, 116, 177
knights, 38, 41, 45-6, 51, 53, 66, 67, 68, 69, 83, 96, 110

land commission, 37, 40, 46, 49
land grants, 68, 97-8, 150
landlords, 5, 25, 35, 60, 136, 150-1, 174, 177
land reform, 37, 60
land tax, 135-6, 150
Latin League, 6
law, 7, 64, 93, 111, 116, 176
legates, 74, 110
legions, 8, 21, 73, 75, 94, 97, 150
Lepidus, 91, 95-6, 98, 99
liberty (freedom), 68, 87, 95, 97, 101, 172-3
Licinius, 141-3, 152, 153, 161
Licinius, tribune, 62
literature, 112-4, 118
Livia, 99, 115, 116
Livy, 10, 11, 18, 114, 155
Lucca, 73
luxury law, 84-5

Macedonia, 30
Maecenas, 100, 102, 103, 112

magistrates, 32, 33, 36, 41, 47, 52, 81-2, 107-8, 127
Maharbal, 17
Majo, 16, 17
Mancinus, 36
Mantua, 98
Marcellus, 20
Marcellus, Augustus' son-in-law, 112, 116
Marcus Aurelius, 124, 160
Marius, 55-6, 61, 87
Massilia (Marseilles), 10, 60
Massinissa, 21
Maxentius, 140-2, 161, 163
Maximian, 130-1, 139-40, 141-2
Maximin Daia, 140, 142, 143, 161
Maximinus, 125
Mediterranean, 3-4, 23, 24, 30
merchant marine, 33, 35
Messina, 4, 6, 7, 99
Metaurus R., 20
Metellus, tribune, 79
Middle Ages, 177
middle class, (see bourgeois)
Milan, 131, 141, 142
Milan, Edict of, 161-2, 175-6
Milvian Bridge, 142, 163
Mithras, 156-7, 163
Mithridates of Pontus, 55-6
mob, 31, 34, 35, 47, 49, 51-3, 66, 74
monarchy, 43, 74, 82, 100, 139, 152, 177
monopoly, 5, 10, 22, 46
monotheism, 154, 157
morality, 8, 68, 74, 82-3, 85, 99
Munda, 81-2, 92, 107
Mutina, 95
Mylae, 8
mystery cults, 156-7

Nasica, 42
Naulochus, 99
navy, 8, 99, 114
Nero, 124, 159
New Carthage, 12, 20
Nicaea, Council of, 167-8, 175
Nicomedia, 131, 137, 138, 140, 143, 164
nobles, 32, 45, 67, 104, 125, 149
Nola, 119
Numerian, 128

Octavia, 98
Octavius, (see Augustus)
Octavius, M., tribune, 39-41, 43, 54
Odes (of Horace), 114, 118
officials, (see magistrates)
oligarchy, 5, 22, 24, 32, 87
omens, 18, 42
one-man rule, 53-6, 74-6, 81, 82, 109, 115-6, 139, 148
Opimius, 49-50
optimates, 66, 74
oracles, 155
Ostia, 33, 61
Ovid, 114

paganism, 163-4, 170
Palestine, 68, 154
Pantheon, 112
Parthia, 60, 73, 86, 98, 114
party leader, 67, 70, 73
party, political, 41, 54-5, 66-7, 70
patricians, 6, 29, 31, 34-5, 55, 92, 136
patriotism, 7, 38, 99
Paul the Apostle, 154, 157-8
Paulus, 15-6
peace, 59, 74, 103, 110, 118, 128, 147
peace settlements, 8, 21-2, 68
Pergamum, 40
persecution of Christians, 159-61, 162-3, 165
Persia (Persians), 4, 126, 128, 130-1, 133
Perugia, 98, 119
Peter, St., 169
Pharsalus, 80, 83, 103
Philip of Macedon, 17-8, 23, 30
Philippi, 97, 99, 103, 112
Phoenicians, 4
Picts and Scots, 140
pietas, 8, 40, 155
pirates, 24, 40, 56, 61-2, 99
plebeians, 6, 15, 30-1, 84
Pliny, 159
Plutarch, 42, 44, 52, 60, 63, 69, 70, 71, 76, 83, 85-6
Po R., 6, 12
poetry, 112-4
political murder, 42, 50, 54, 97, 126
Polybius, 3, 7, 22, 35, 118

Pompeia, wife of Caesar, 68
Pompey, 56, 59, 63, 68-70, 73-6, 78-81, 83, 86, 87, 99, 108
Pontus, 77
populares, 66, 87
praetorian guard, 109, 123, 125, 142, 148
price-fixing, 133
principate, 107-10, 111-2, 115-8, 123
proletariat, 43, 46, 54, 111, 127
propaganda, 99-100
proscription, 55, 62, 83, 96, 104, 125
provincial cities, 7, 60, 84, 106, 124-5, 129, 149, 171
provincial government, 30, 32-3, 45, 68, 72, 74, 82, 106, 108-9, 110-1, 125, 134, 149
public domain, 37-8
public enemy, 42, 50, 94
public welfare, 36, 50-1, 54, 66
public works, 46, 98, 125
Punic War, First, 3-4, 7-8
Punic War, Second, 11-22
Punic War, Third, 24, 29
Pyrenees Mts., 10, 11
Pyrrhus of Epirus, 4

Ravenna, 114
reason, 154, 156, 162, 166
reason vs faith, 166
reforms, 45-8, 52, 60-1, 98, 106, 111, 130
Regulus, 8
religion, state, 154-5, 158, 161-2, 167
Republic, 25, 31, 53, 55, 69-70, 76, 106, 115, 137
republican government, 25, 53, 64, 70, 74, 76, 81, 136
revolution, 45, 67-8, 76, 98
Rhine R., 59, 72, 114, 117-8, 124, 126, 130, 131, 141
Rhodes, 24
Rhone R., 11, 114
roads, 46, 111, 124, 158
Roman Empire, 101, 111, 119, 123-8, 129, 132-3, 134-5, 144, 148-9, 153, 158, 162, 165, 168, 170, 171-2, 176-8
Roman Peace, 124, 126

Rome (city), 3, 4, 13, 16-8, 34, 52, 55, 60, 66-8, 72-3, 74, 78-9, 92, 94, 99, 108, 111-2, 126, 131, 137, 138-9, 142, 148, 169, 173-4
Rome (state), 6-7, 20, 25-6, 30, 44, 47-8, 52, 54, 59-61, 95, 102-3, 106, 171-2, 175
Rubicon R., 76-7
ruling class, 6, 23-4, 32, 35, 87, 125, 148, 151

Saguntum, 11
Salamis, 4
Sallust, 34, 51, 71
Samnites, 4
Sardinia, 18, 21, 44
Satureius Publius, 42
savior of the state, 40-1, 43, 56, 104, 108, 135
Scaevola, 42
Scipio Aemilianus, 42
Scipio, Publius, Africanus, 20-2, 25, 29
Scribonia, 99
Senate, 6, 15, 16, 21, 31-2, 35-7, 39, 42-3, 45, 47, 50-1, 59, 61, 64, 67-8, 69, 74-6, 78, 81-2, 84-6, 91, 93-5, 96, 101, 106, 107-9, 111, 117, 123, 125, 130, 137, 142, 148-9
senators, 16, 38, 41, 45, 51-3, 66-8, 74, 76, 83, 86, 93, 96, 100, 109, 110, 125, 137, 148-9
Septimius Severus, 125
Sertorius, 56
service to the state, 7, 38, 44, 51, 135, 137-8, 154-5, 160
Severus, 140-1, 143
Sextus, 99
Sicily, 3-4, 7-8, 21, 22, 33, 36, 99
Sirmium, 131
slavery, 25, 33, 35, 66, 77, 112
Social War, 53, 66
sovereignty, 31, 54, 109, 118
Spain, 9-11, 18, 20-2, 25, 30, 59, 63, 70, 74, 79-80, 92
Spalato, 143
Spartacus, 56
Spoletium, 14
SPQR, 31, 172
squatters, 37-40
Stoics, 29, 115, 156-7

street-fighting, 39, 42, 54, 74
succession, 91, 116-7, 124-6, 130,
    132, 140-1, 148, 153
Suetonius, 63, 76, 86, 97, 101-2,
    112, 119
Sulla, 55-6, 61, 62, 78, 87
Syracuse, 3-5, 7, 17-20, 25
Syria, 24, 68, 126

Tacitus, 104, 159
Tarentum, 4, 20, 46
tariff, 35
Tarquin, 6, 42
taxation, 7, 18, 22, 33, 53, 60, 100,
    104, 110, 124-7, 135-7, 149, 170
tax-farming, 46, 53, 60, 83, 110
Teutoberg Forest, 117
Thapsus, 80
Theodosius, 176
Tiber R., 6, 13, 50, 61, 142
Tiberius, 115-7, 119, 123, 154
Tigris-Euphrates, 59
Titus, 124
toleration, 161-2, 167-8
trade, 4-6, 7, 30, 52, 99, 127, 169-
    70, 173
tradition, 93, 125, 169-70
Trajan, 124, 159
Trasimene, Lake, 14
treason, 39, 41, 68, 158-9, 174
Trebia R., 14
Treves, 131
tribes, 4, 6, 13, 17, 31, 48
tribunes, 7, 36, 39-41, 43, 45-6,
    54, 64, 81, 99, 108
tribute, 5, 33

triumph, 69, 77, 85, 100, 139
Triumvirate, 1st, 69-70, 73, 82
Triumvirate, 2nd, 96-8, 99, 107
tyrant (tyranny), 42, 43, 45, 50,
    68, 76, 78, 83, 86, 91-2, 101,
    110, 123, 133, 142
Tyre, 4-5

unemployment, 33-5, 46-7, 53,
    111, 127
urban law code, 60, 111
Utica, 21, 82

Valerian, 130
Varro, 15-6
Varus, 117
Velitrae, 92
Vercellae, 55
Vespasian, 124
Vestal Virgins, 68, 155
veto power, 36, 39, 43, 48, 54, 64,
    81
villa, 173, 177
Virgil, 98, 112-4
virtues, 114, 147

wages, 66, 133
will of the people, 40, 43

Xenobia, 126

yeomen, 34, 36, 44
York, 140

Zama, 21-2, 29